'Swiche was the morthere of Evesham; vor bataile non it was'
— Robert of Gloucester

1265

The Murder of Evesham

David Snowden

A 'Lion Roars' publication by

The Simon de Montfort Society

First published in Great Britain in 2020 by The Simon de Montfort Society

Text and maps © 2020 David Snowden
Additional graphics © 2020 Iris Pinkstone
Other copyright as acknowledged in the text

All rights reserved. Apart from any fair dealing for the purpose of private study, research, criticism or review, as permitted under the Copyright, Designs and Patents Act, 1988, no part of this publication may be reproduced, stored in a retrieval system, or transmitted in any form or by any means, electronic, electrical, chemical, mechanical, optical, photocopying, recording or otherwise, without the prior written permission of the copyright owner. Enquiries should be addressed to the publishers.

The right of David Snowden to be identified as the author of this work has been asserted in accordance with the Copyright, Designs and Patents Act of 1988.

Printed and bound by www.lulu.com

www.simondemontfort.org

For Iris, Sue, Margaret, Jennie, Jo and Clive

Contents

1. Magna Carta and Beyond 5

2. The Roots of the Quarrel 7

3. Lewes 18

4. After Lewes 23

3. The Protagonists 25

4. Sources for the Battle of Evesham 33

5. Mid-Thirteenth-Century Armies 50

6. The Armies 73

7. The Road to Worcester 77

8. Shock at Kenilworth 82

9. The Approach to Evesham 90

10. Mosham Meadow 93

11. Evesham and the Battlefield 96

12. The Armies Deploy 115

13. The Murder of Evesham 124

14. The Aftermath 141

15. Chivalry at the Battle of Evesham 145

16. Tony Spicer's Alternative View 149

17. The End of the Revolt 165

18. Evesham Today 167

19. Epilogue 179

Annex A. The Mind of a General 181

Annex B. Classic Interpretations 185

Annex C. English Heritage 191

Annex D. Received Wisdom 199

Annex E. 'My left foot ...' 215

Annex F. 'St George, he is for England' 221

Bibliography 222

Glossary 254

Index 261

The Simon de Montfort Society 271

The Battlefields Trust 272

List of figures

Figure	Description	Page
01	View westward across the Battlewell site, traditionally the climactic point of the battle	3
02	Henry III with his son and heir, Edward, on this York Minster choir screen	9
03	Simon looks out from his clock tower roost in Leicester	7
04	Plaque commemorating de Montfort's victory at Lewes	22
05	Sketch map of the final marches of the Evesham campaign	77
06	Aerial view of Kenilworth showing the extent of the priory's *demesne*	86
07	The location of Mosham Meadow	93
08	Two views of Mosham Meadow	94
09	Key points of the Battle of Evesham	99
10	The layout and extent of Evesham in 1265	103
11	No 31 Cowl Street, Evesham, originally built in AD 1210	104
12	The River Avon, in spate during the July 2007 floods	106
13	This bridge at Tilford, Farnham, Surrey was built in 1128	107
14	The Twyford bridge may have resembled the packhorse bridge at Rearsby, Leicestershire	109
15	'Evesham from Greenhill, Worcestershire', William Robert Earl, 1825	111
16	The Battlewell conservation area is outlined in white	113
17	Section through Greenhill	116
18	Tony Spicer of the Battlefields Trust leads a party of walkers up the lower slopes of Greenhill	117
19	Conjectural deployments at the start of the battle	121
20	'Snowden's view', two battles of infantry deployed forward as bait	123
21	The Simon de Montfort window in St Lawrence's church, Evesham	126
22	Detail from the Simon de Montfort window in St Lawrence's church	128

23	Looking through Abbot Ranulph's gateway from the churchyard to Evesham's market square	130
24	A bad omen! Guy de Baliol, Earl Simon's standard-bearer, breaks his banner	132
25	This near-contemporary illustration seems to depict the Battle of Evesham	135
26	A 'cuneus'	136
27	The crisis of the battle	137
28	Simon de Montfort's corpse is dismembered	140
29	The Almonry Museum and Heritage Centre, Abbey Gate, Evesham	168
30	Evesham High Street with the detached *campanile* of Evesham Abbey in the background	169
31	Customised pavement slabs on Evesham's High Street commemorate the Battle of Evesham	172
32	The original Simon de Montfort memorial in front of St Lawrence's church, Evesham	175
33	Abbey Manor stands on the western side of the ridge on which the battle developed	175
34	Lord Leicester's Tower built in 1842	176
35	Obelisk monument built in 1845 by Edward Rudge	177
36	Details from the obelisk monument in the grounds of Abbey Manor	178

Acknowledgements

I cannot express enough thanks to the committee and trustees of the Simon de Montfort Society for their continued support and encouragement and to our patrons, Dr David Cox and Professor David Carpenter, for providing the inspiration to write this little book and for pointing out the grosser errors. I offer my sincere appreciation for the learning opportunities they have afforded to me. I could not have completed this book without their support.

To the trustees of the Battlefields Trust – thank you for allowing me to use so much material from your website, particularly for the illustrations of the battlefield today, and for sanity-checking my copy. As always errors and omissions are all my own work.

I owe a special 'thank you' to Tony Spicer, a founder member of the Battlefields Trust, both for introducing me to the Evesham battlefield and for allowing me to reproduce his alternative view of the deployments and course of the battle that you will find in chapter 16.

I particularly want to thank my wife, Joya, not only for helping to make time for me to complete this book, especially when she had so many other demands on her time, but also for lending her knowledge of topography and geomorphology to the analysis of the Evesham battlefield.

There is also a myriad of others who have contributed to the knowledge and experience that has made this book possible. I cannot thank you all individually but if you recognise yourself from this description, thank you very much.

Preface

From time to time in your life you might be lucky enough to meet a remarkable person who, in some way, changes your life. I was lucky enough to know Mr Avery, history master at my school, from whom I caught his infectious enthusiasm for the subject. The twelfth son of a Durham miner, 'Spot' Avery had won a scholarship to Cambridge before the war, served in the R.A.F. during the war, and taken up a post at a traditional grammar school after the war. He set himself the daunting task of teaching history to the sons of miners on the South Yorkshire coalfield. In this task he had one or two advantages, particularly a charismatic personality and a contagious humorous cynicism.

We enjoyed our lessons and were soon absorbed in the Wars of the Roses and the Thirty Year's War, taking sides and reading ahead to find out what happened next. We were taught to analyse what history told us with a compact toolkit of questions and maxims, through which we learned to query the accepted wisdom of traditionally-taught history. The only sins were 'cribbing', naïve acceptance of orthodox views and taking verbatim notes.

Thinking about it, my interest in history is about as old as my interest in writing. 'Vince' Prooth (after Vincent Price, his forename was actually 'Victor') was 'Spot' Avery's counterpart in the English department. Vince believed that good writing followed on from good reading and we were expected to read a book a week in addition to our coursework and homework. It did not matter what the book was – science fiction, adventures, thrillers – so long as it was well-written.

I never saw either writing or history as a potential career, but history has been an obsession for as long as I can remember. I was the child who sought out castles, churches and museums; I am the husband who drags his wife into ancient buildings and darts off to investigate roadside markers and blue plaques on buildings. In some ways, this book is a tribute to a lifelong passion, and a 'thank you' to the two outstanding educators who started it all.

David Snowden, Evesham, 2020

Introduction

Despite the occasional outburst of liveliness during the annual River Festival or Mop Fair, Evesham is a quiet country town full of historic interest but better known for its plums and asparagus than for its place in the development of the nation. It is difficult to look at its weathered buildings and warren of old streets, to stand between its two town-centre medieval churches and view the few remaining scraps of its once rich and powerful monastery, and to imagine it all spattered with blood. Ordnance Survey maps identify only the battle of 1265, but Colonel Massey and his Gloucester garrison stormed Evesham in 1645 from the hill where Simon de Montfort had died four centuries earlier. In 1651 elements of Cromwell's army bivouacked on that hill on their way to the Battle of Worcester. A pattern of bullet pocks on the base of the town's trademark bell tower shows where a militiaman, who had molested a local girl, was shot to death after a drum-head court-martial ('zero toleration' really meaning something in those days). In the mid-twelfth-century civil war between King Stephen and his cousin, the Empress Matilda, on the other side of town, the abbot of Evesham's men had stormed the stronghold of the de Beauchamp family at Bengeworth and burnt it to the ground, possibly with the garrison still inside. In 1471 Lancastrian fugitives from the battle of Tewkesbury tried to cross the Avon by the old bridge. One hid his sword in a nearby ditch, but never returned to collect it. It now resides in the Almonry museum.

Although most British battlefields are marked, few are venerated in the same way as those of, say, the American Civil War, and few are exploited. The Battlefields Trust is working to remedy this but many of the public cannot understand why anyone would want to commemorate a site where thousands of men were killed, many of them not knowing where they were or for which cause they were dying. On the other hand, a battlefield is, in its way, an ancient monument and its preservation honours the memory of those who died.

Most battles were typical of their time, and a few were pivotal, with significant social or political consequences. Evesham was such a battle. If the outcome of the battle had been different, if Earl Simon had broken through and joined up with his son before turning at bay or if the younger Simon had pressed on down the Evesham road and arrived in time to attack Edward's army from the rear as his father engaged it from the front, then we may be living in a very different country today. This would be particularly so if Lord Edward had been left dead on the battlefield. Edward was the architect of Great Britain and the builder who laid its foundations. But for an accident of timing 750 years ago the United Kingdom might not exist today.

This book is an analysis of that battle, drawing heavily upon contemporary or near-contemporary sources. Such ancient voices, despite their (relative) immediacy, have obvious limitations. Their accounts can be brief and partisan, or they can be obscure, making it difficult to reconstruct even large and well-known battles. These vibrant echoes of the past are, nevertheless, indispensable and are supplemented in this volume by the work of later historians and of battlefield archaeologists, the study of many sources and a shrewd (I hope!) appraisal of the battlefield landscape, that survives largely intact.

Warfare that was about territorial adjustment, as most medieval wars were, was going to be limited and hardly worth putting to the test of battle. At the same time, an apparently unimportant squabble could escalate to the point where it destabilised kingdoms. The Battle of Evesham was a very different proposition. It was not about land or simply about status. It was the climax of a clash between fundamentally antagonistic interests with a kingdom as the prize on one side and survival on the other.

This analysis is written by a confessed Montfortian; nevertheless, the picture of Earl Simon that emerges is not that of a pristine hero meeting an end of Homeric drama and pathos. Instead it is that of a man riding a tiger. Not a good man, nor a bad one; just a man who had followed his destiny too far and so must ride it to its conclusion or be thrown off and destroyed.

Obviously, this is the book of a battle. It begins by providing a brief overview of the conflicts between Henry III and his barons that today we call 'The Second Baronial War' to set the context, then focuses on the events of 1264 when king and prince were captured, foreshadowing a realignment of allegiances that made a second battle inevitable. It is essential that the reader should understand the nature of the armies that met on Greenhill, so a long chapter looks at the recruitment, supply, arming and deployment of mid-thirteenth century armies and we go on to see what we can learn from the battlefield itself, its configuration and archaeology.

An assessment of the primary sources relating to the battle is essential to any book of this type. I have used thirteen key accounts (the full texts of some are available as *Lion Occasional Papers* from the Simon de Montfort Society) with notes on my assessment of the source's relevance and reliability. However, interpretation of the battle did not stop with the monastic chroniclers who wrote the contemporary and near-contemporary accounts, so I have also consulted interpretations of the facts by three venerable military historians, Ramsay, Oman and Burne and I am indebted to the work of Dr David Cox, Professor David Carpenter and Dr John Maddicott (see bibliography).

01 View westward across the Battlewell site, traditionally the climactic point of the battle (author's photograph)

I am delighted to have been able to include the full text of Tony Spicer's 'alternative' interpretation of the battle, the English Heritage battlefield report and the 'conventional wisdom' of the Battlefield Trust's interpretation. I cannot get away without at least a potted biography of the leading combatants.

The task of tracing the events that led up to the battle, how it transpired on the day and its consequences, immediate and long-term, involved sifting truths from historical accounts and distinguishing the bias and nature of sources written in Latin, old French or antique English. There was much collating of alliances, allegiances and vested interests that brought men to fight. There was a need for a thorough appreciation of the contest between designers and manufacturers of weapons and those of protection as well as knowledge of the strategy and tactics of the day, the military formations, command and control and the practice of offensive and defensive manoeuvres. Men had to eat, so there was also a need to appreciate logistics and supply, including animal husbandry. Most difficult of all was linking the standards and conditions of today to thirteenth-century values and beliefs fully to understand their influence on the behaviour of men in social groups, and in armies.

However, finally, I have no choice but to put up or shut up and to give my interpretation of the campaign and battle (or 'murther'). This covers Edward's spoiling attack at Kenilworth, the events at Mosham Meadow, how Edward deployed his army, the battle and its bloody aftermath. After the battle I step back to look at Evesham and its Vale today and to provide a little diversion in the appendices and two magisterial views of the battle, from English Heritage and The Battlefields Trust.

As an aid to readers unfamiliar with the military terminology of the thirteenth century I have included a glossary and there is a table of potted biographies of the main people you will meet in this book.

First, a brief reminder of the root cause of the conflict between the royal party and the barons.

1. Magna Carta and Beyond

Before he took up permanent residence in Worcester Cathedral, King John established a reputation not only as a tyrant but also as an incompetent and unsuccessful one. He antagonised every part of society, lay and ecclesiastical, but his biggest mistake was upsetting the barons, provoking what we now call The First Baronial War as he tried to repudiate the terms of Magna Carta, which had been extracted from him at Runnymede Meadow on June 15th 1215.

There was little in the charter for the common man; dictated by the barons, it defined the relationship between the king and the nobility. Its importance lay in being the first document imposed upon a king of England by a group of his subjects in an attempt to limit his powers by law and to protect their rights, the first step along the lengthy road that led to the rule of constitutional law in England and beyond. King John was forced to accept that his will was neither supreme nor arbitrary. Magna Carta was influenced by the AD 1100 Charter of Liberties, in which Henry I had specified particular areas where his powers would be limited.

Magna Carta was translated from Latin into vernacular Norman French in 1219 and regularly re-issued later in the thirteenth century and beyond in modified versions, the later versions softening the direct challenges to royal authority in the 1215 charter. The charter passed into law in 1225. The 1297 version, entitled (originally in Latin): *The Great Charter of the Liberties of England, and of the Liberties of the Forest*, remains on the statute books of England and Wales.

Magna Carta, rather than any other royal concessions, remains the sacred text of the British constitution. It is considered part of the 'unwritten' law. Lord Denning, Master of the Rolls, described it as 'the greatest constitutional document of all times – the foundation of the freedom of the individual against the arbitrary authority of the despot'. Lord Woolf, Lord of Appeal in Ordinary, described it as the 'first of a series of instruments that now are recognised as having a special constitutional status'. He named the others as: the Habeas Corpus Act (1679), the Petition of Right (1628), the Bill of Rights (1689) and the Act of Settlement (1701). By the time of the English Civil Wars in the seventeenth century it had become a symbol and rallying point for those who wished to show that the king was bound by the law. It influenced the United States Constitution as well as providing a model for many of the other former British colonies when they were developing their legal systems.

King John did not take kindly to having Magna Carta forced on him. Between 1215 and 1217 the kingdom of England was torn by a civil war between John and his supporters on one side and a group of rebellious barons on the other. The barons had offered the throne to the future Louis VIII of France.

John conducted his campaigns with surprising skill and determination; however, by October 1216 he faced a stalemate. Physically weak and ailing, he headed north. By the time he reached the royal castle at Newark he was unable to travel any further and King John died on the night of October 18th 1216. There were rumours at the time that he had been killed by poisoned ale, poisoned plums or a 'surfeit of peaches' (which is a kind of medieval code for 'we think he was poisoned but it might be unhealthy to say so'). His body was escorted south by a company of mercenaries and he was buried in Worcester Cathedral in front of the altar of St Wulfstan, being transferred to a new sarcophagus with an effigy, which we can see today, in 1232.

It is possible to argue that the Second Baronial Revolt, that climaxed in the Battle of Evesham, grew out of the tension between two contrasting men of power. This is not a re-run of the 'great man' theory of historical perception but a reflection of the fact that a revolt needs a cause and a focus. Henry III provided no shortage of causes whereas Earl Simon was nothing loathe to be the focus of revolt, particularly when his personal and familial interests were involved. Alternatively, one can also make a strong case for the 'irresistible historical trend' beloved of Marxist historians which would have Henry standing in the path of the decline of feudalism and the dilution of the monarchy, and being crushed as history rolled over him. Neither theory provides a wholly satisfactory explanation but both cast some light on the truth.

2. The Roots of the Quarrel

John's son and heir, Henry, shared his father's distaste for Magna Carta, although that was not apparent at first. Henry III became king only weeks after his ninth birthday. Because of his youth, William Marshal, Earl of Pembroke, was appointed regent to govern on his behalf. Marshal moved quickly to undermine the baronial opposition by swiftly issuing two revisions of Magna Carta in 1216 and 1217.

In 1225, Henry III issued a further revised version of Magna Carta in his own name. With only thirty-seven clauses, the 1225 issue of Magna Carta was considerably shorter than the 1215 original which had sixty-three clauses. Henry III's Magna Carta of 1225 is important because it was the text of this revised charter which was confirmed by Edward I in 1297 and was subsequently enshrined on the statute rolls.

Once Henry had the reins of power firmly in his hands he reverted to type. A weak king, he wanted to be strong and ended up being merely vicious. Overly impressionable, contemporaries said that he was a cushion: 'bearing the imprint of whoever last sat on him'. A lover of the arts he began ambitious projects such as the rebuilding of Westminster Abbey. The kindest judgement called Henry: 'A Simplex and God-fearing King'. 'Simplex' was a loaded word. It might mean 'uncomplicated, unsophisticated' or it might mean 'naïve, easily-led'. It might also mean 'simple-minded', which is apparently what Simon de Montfort, Henry's brother-in-law, had in mind when he told the king to his face that he should be locked up for his own protection.

In April 1258 frustration with Henry's rule boiled over and a group of barons, led by Roger Bigod, the Earl of Norfolk, marched to the royal palace at Westminster and forced the king to initiate a programme of reform. They demanded redress for a raft of financial, judicial and personal injustices, real and imagined, that had arisen during the king's personal rule. The king accepted and in May 1258 the reform movement set to work. The barons did not publish their reforms or grievances but, between April and June 1258, they drafted two documents that we have come to know as the *Petition of the Barons* and the *Provisions of Oxford*. These two documents dealt largely with three grievances, which have quite a modern sound to them and all three of which violated the word and the spirit of Magna Carta.

The first concerned 'foreigners' (although the word did not have the same meaning as today). The barons resented the amount of royal patronage being lavished on 'aliens' at court, and by their ownership of the kingdom's most strategic castles, particularly by the king's greedy and ruthless half-brothers, the Lusignans[1]. The second concern was judicial. The barons argued that justice was impossible to secure because the king was keeping the office of justiciar – the kingdom's chief legal officer - vacant and was undermining the office of chancellor by staffing it with incompetent clerks.

Royal favouritism and heavy-handed sheriffs extorting money to satisfy the king's ever-increasing demands for cash, were further nails in the coffin of justice.

The third concern was the king's inability to manage his financial resources. Over the previous twenty-four years the king had squandered his revenues, handed out swathes of the royal lands that he should have kept so that he could live on the income from them, burdened his subjects with an increasing number of taxes and was slow in paying his debts.

Between November 14th 1259 and April 21st 1260 Henry III was in France to ratify the controversial Treaty of Paris under which he and his heirs formally renounced their claims to Normandy, Anjou (south of Normandy, east of Brittany) and Poitou (coastal western France) in return for Gascony (in south-western France). The visit enabled Henry to stay out of the way of the reformers' sanctions. When he returned to England in the spring of 1260, many of the reformers were demoralised and public support was evaporating. Henry persuaded the pope to proclaim the reform movement to be unconstitutional; he and his family were released from the oath they had sworn, under duress, to honour the reforms. Henry replaced the sheriffs appointed by the reformers with his own men and took back control of the great seal. The reformers moved to make their peace with the king until, by the end of 1261, the majority had been welcomed back into the king's grace, even if, for some, it was an uncomfortable peace. Unable to stomach betrayal of the reforms, Simon de Montfort decamped to France.

Henry's resumption of royal authority suffered a major set-back in the early summer of 1263 when various members of the Lord Edward's (the future Edward I's) household intrigued with de Montfort and encouraged him to return to England.

---

[1] After King John's death in 1216 his widow, Isabella of Angouleme, married Hugh X of Lusignan. They had five children.

02 Henry III stands on the left of this York Minster choir screen with his son and heir, Edward, at his side (author's photograph)

Earl Simon arrived back in England in April 1263 and the slide into civil war began. De Montfort emerged as the leader and focus of the reformist cause. Silver-tongued, iron-willed, militarily experienced and well-connected across Europe, Earl Simon's diplomatic connections helped keep the baronial plan of reform afloat. His commitment to the programme of reform was deep, almost fanatical, motivated by personal piety as well as by political pragmatism.

When he returned to England, de Montfort rounded up his supporters and begin ravaging the estates of royal supporters. 'Ravaging' was a process of looting, pillage, rape, arson, cutting down fruit trees, burning crops, driving off animals, polluting wells and making the land into a desert. When the king's supporters retaliated in kind they became locked in a bitter game of pay-back.

The origins of Earl Simon's military reputation are obscure. Matthew Paris says that de Montfort was a *vir Martius*, 'a warrior famous and experienced in warfare', which view is echoed by William de Nangis: 'a man strenuous in arms and most skilled in the science of arms' but where did he obtain this reputation? Matthew Paris seemed to think that Earl Simon's military reputation was made, at least in part, on the Gascony campaign of 1242 at the Battle of Saintonge, a rear-guard action during Henry III's unsuccessful French campaign:

'The English, in their rage, attacked the French at the sword's point, and fought most desperately, so that, if they had equalled their enemies in number, they would have succeeded in gaining a glorious victory over the French, as the latter themselves bore evidence after the battle. In this battle, Simon de Montfort, earl of Leicester, the earls of Salisbury and Norfolk, Roger Bigod, John de Burg, Warren de Montchesnil, Hubert Fitz-Matthew, Ralph Fitz-Nicholas, and many other brave Englishmen, gained lasting renown, as even their rivals allowed.'

- Matthew Paris, Chronica Majora

It would help if we could be sure of Earl Simon's year of birth, which most historians put in the range 1200-1208. If his first taste of military action was in the Albigensian Crusade[2] it must have been before his older brother, Amaury, who had taken over leadership of the crusade on the death of their father, relinquished

---

[2] The Albigensian Crusade was a twenty-year-long series of campaigns initiated by Pope Innocent III to eliminate Catharism, a Christian dualist or Gnostic heresy, from the Languedoc in southern France. From 1209 the crusade was led by 'our' Simon's father, also called Simon de Montfort

leadership to the king of France in 1224, effectively ending the family's involvement. If young Simon did fight in the campaign it would probably have been in the later years, perhaps 1222 to 1224, after another older brother, Guy, had been killed. That assumes that Simon would have been old enough. Military careers did start quite early in the middle ages. The Black Prince (Edward of Woodstock, eldest son of Edward III of England) commanded the vanguard at the Battle of Crécy when he was just fifteen.

However, this is conjecture as the sources are inconsistent. With Henry III's Brittany expedition of 1230 we are on firmer ground, although no specific actions are recorded and there was little fighting throughout the entire campaign. Matthew Paris tells us that de Montfort saw action with the emperor on his journey to Rome in 1238, although again he is not credited with a leading role. He had taken the cross and served in the Holy Land in 1240-41, although he did little active campaigning and seems to have distinguished himself more as a politician than as a warrior. He accompanied Henry III on his 1245 expedition against the Welsh where, once again, there was little action. Even at Saintonge (above) he was one of eight named as distinguishing themselves, as far as was possible in that debacle.

None of this amounts to a reputation as a great military leader, so was he relying on the reflected glow of his father's reputation, bolstered by his presence on some (largely inglorious) campaigns? Or was there some aspect of his career about which we know anything? Did he serve as a free-lance under an assumed name in his early years? Was he accomplished on the tournament circuit? Strange that there is no record, no hint even, if he did.

Regardless of the validity of his military reputation, de Montfort was still a formidable obstacle to Henry securing the settlement that would satisfy him. Before returning to Germany in 1262 Richard of Cornwall, King Henry's younger brother, had counselled him to effect a reconciliation with de Montfort – whether he deserved it or not – as a piece of necessary *realpolitik*. He might as well have saved his breath; Henry was as petulant as a toddler and just as likely to throw a tantrum.

In truth, Henry began well by asking Louis of France to see if he could find a way to reconcile Earl Simon to his brother-in-law. Louis consulted Simon but had to report to Henry that de Montfort believed that Henry meant him well (most likely a negotiating device since Simon had few illusions about his relationship with Henry) but could not trust him not to act on the advice of 'evil advisors'.

Henry next tried issuing a series of 'constitutions' based on the *Provisions of Westminster* to show that he was right alongside the reformers. In reality, Henry promulgated only those items of reform that would damage the interests of the great magnates. Unfortunately, by this time nobody trusted the king, who regarded sacred oaths as something that happened to other people (Aside: an even less successful king of England – Charles I – had the same attitude but Henry got off lightly; Charles lost his head for it).

Meanwhile Lord Edward was keen to take up his career as nemesis of the Welsh. Llywelyn ap Gruffydd, whose links to Earl Simon the royal party thought particularly suspicious, had humiliated a major Marcher lord, Roger de Mortimer, and Roger was keen to have Edward join him in a revenge campaign. Snubbed by Edward, the other border magnates were content to sit back and let them get on with it. Reinforced by Edward and his company of mercenary knights, de Mortimer attacked the Welsh – and lost. Nevertheless, Edward retained his mercenaries and built a new retinue around himself, successfully alienating many of the lords who had recently reconciled themselves to the king. For two of them, the violent and possibly psychotic Roger Leybourne and the slippery Roger Clifford, this was the final straw. They asked Simon to return and promised him the necessary forces to support him.

If Leybourne and Clifford were typical of Simon's new supporters, then he must have thought twice about returning to England at their call; but he did return. He met his new supporters at Oxford. They swore or renewed sacred oaths to support the *Provisions,* but it was clear that Simon had surrounded himself with a crowd of vicious malcontents who each had an axe to grind, preparatory to hitting somebody with it. However, they were the best that were available.

Richard of Cornwall returned from Germany to see what he could salvage from the dog-fight that Henry had made of his policy. However, events had gathered a momentum of their own and were out of anybody's control. The *Provisions of Oxford* had assumed almost sacred status, with clergy across the country preaching in favour of the *Provisions*, and of the reformers. There *were* idealists in the movement; there were also younger sons keen to make their own way in life and older sons whose fathers were too long-lived for their liking, mixed up with those who had grudges, sometimes decades old, against the king and his supporters. It was an explosive mixture but it was Louis of France who eventually detonated it.

In the meantime the political manoeuvring continued as the disgruntled Marchers took the opportunity to dispose of the hated Savoyards[3], snatching back the cathedrals and castles that Henry had granted to them. The rebellion quickly spread beyond the Welsh border and soon Earl Simon was on his way to the Channel ports with a small army, to forestall the landing of any European reinforcements for Henry. First, however, he had to secure London, ensuring that the aldermen were still on his side and using them as a lever against Henry who was in London at the time. Simon's approach was conciliatory, but it foundered on the demand that the realm was to be governed by 'native-born men', to which Henry would never again agree. The Savoyards prepared to flee for France in the company of several of the reformers' other main targets.

At this point Lord Edward demonstrated his great skill for turning a crisis into a disaster by looting the coffers of the New Temple in London to pay his mercenaries. Nothing could have been better calculated to alienate the capital. The city erupted in riots and Henry was forced to put his hands up. The queen attempted to make her way by royal barge to the safety of Windsor castle but had to turn back as the Londoners who lined the bridges pelted her with rubbish and emptied their cess pots on her head. They were sure that the queen and her greedy free-loading relatives were the cause of all their miseries.

There is no record of any attempt to kill the queen or to do her serious harm – the mob were happy to humiliate her – but Edward would not forgive or forget, and would base another of his tragic miscalculations on his anger with the Londoners. Meanwhile, however, he took his mercenaries to Bristol where the townsfolk besieged him. He escaped by giving his oath to return to London to seal the peace agreement; instead he arrived at Windsor and started harrying the surrounding area. The Montfortians rapidly put an end to that, forcing the surrender of Windsor castle,

---

[3] In January 1236 Henry had married Eleanor of Provence, the daughter of Raymond-Berengar IV, and Beatrice of Savoy. The marriage opened the floodgates for Henry's new Savoyard in-laws from Savoy, Burgundy and Flanders. The favour Henry had shown his Lusignan half-brothers was repeated and he alienated his own barons by authorising high-powered positions for the new foreigners. The Savoyards gradually dug themselves in through grants of wealthy marriages and lucrative offices of state. Nevertheless, their presence was a constant irritation to the English baronage.

expelling the mercenaries from the country and letting Edward stomp off to suck his thumb in private.

The reformers imposed a new council on Henry, with Earl Simon as its leader, and drafted a peace agreement. Predictably the agreement stipulated not only that the country should be governed by natives but also called for foreigners to leave the country. There were thousands of foreigners, chiefly French and Italian, who had entered the country on the coat-tails of Henry's relatives and in-laws and it was now their turn to be on the receiving end of attacks from the lower orders of English society. Sadly, the anger and violence spread to engulf those with no connection to the Savoyards and Lusignans. It was no surprise that England's Jews were targeted, as the king's protection no longer seemed a threat to their assailants[4]. Of course, there was a get-out clause for those 'aliens', such as Simon de Montfort, who accepted reform. The agreement was aimed at the Savoyards and Lusignans.

Louis extricated Henry temporarily from the morass he had blundered into by summoning him to France. There, at Boulogne, Louis, Henry and his supporters met a delegation from the council, headed by Simon de Montfort. It was a trap for Simon but it misfired and by the end of the conference Louis had approved of the *Provisions* and agreed that England should be run by Englishmen.

If Henry returned to England looking like a beaten man, it was only a pose. He was returning to coordinate the royal resistance while the queen and their son Edmund remained on the continent to whip up support and raise mercenaries, ignoring their oaths to return to England.

The October 1263 parliament collapsed amid bickering over restitution and the right to appoint the king's servants. While the barons were distracted, Edward slipped away and occupied Windsor Castle. Henry joined him the following day and the barons were faced with a choice: Henry or Simon? Because of inherent ancestral loyalty to the notion of 'monarch', or because they did not want to risk destroying the system on which their own wealth and privilege depended, the majority opted for King Henry. Not all, though, and divided loyalties split families, 'son against

---

[4] By the middle of the thirteenth century the Jews of England, had become chattels of the king and were under his protection. Henry regularly milked them for funds, wisely leaving them enough capital to rebuild their wealth so that he could milk them again.

father, father against son, brother against brother'[5] as was said 2000 years ago. This was now going to be a true civil war with all the horrors that implied.

Most of the magnates joined Henry at Windsor. The dissident Marcher lords were pardoned and bribed to join the royal party. Others, while still supporting the *Provisions*, felt that they could not fight against their anointed king so defected from the Reformers but held aloof.

While Henry busied himself rebuilding the machinery of state he also decided to secure Dover to open a route for his continental mercenaries. However, Dover's Montfortian garrison declined to cooperate so Roger Leybourne, who had switched sides, was left to starve them out.

When news reached Earl Simon at his impregnable fortress of Kenilworth he assembled as many men as he could in the short time available and set off for London, camping south of the Thames at Southwark to avoid alienating the citizens.

A group of royalists in London closed the city's gates behind Simon, isolating him on the south bank of the Thames just as Henry's army was closing in. However, Henry's demand that de Montfort should surrender was met with a contemptuous reply and the people of London overpowered the royalist Fifth Column, opened the gates and escorted Earl Simon and his army into the safety of the city's walls.

It seemed that nobody wanted bloodshed on a grand scale at this point so, when a potential way out that would save sufficient face appeared, it was welcomed. King Louis offered arbitration. Both sides eagerly drafted their case, sealed letters of agreement to the arbitration and forwarded them to France. Earl Simon must have felt that it was a foregone conclusion. Under his persuasion and guidance Louis had already approved of the *Provisions* at Boulogne. Little had changed, beyond further evidence of Henry's and Edward's perfidy. What could go wrong? Well, Simon might fall off his horse in Catesby, fracture his femur and be forced to return to Kenilworth.

He was still there when news of the arbitration, which had taken place at Amiens, reached him. Louis had completely quashed the *Provisions of Oxford*. King Henry was free to rule as he pleased, appoint whomsoever he pleased as his officials and household, sheriffs and castellans, ignore any oaths and tear up any agreements. And if he wanted to flood England with aliens that was his business.

---

[5] Book of Matthew, Chapter 10, Verse 21

This was how Louis tried to put the clock back to 1258 and how he dropped a lighted match into a powder keg.

03 Simon looks out from his clock tower roost in Leicester (author's illustration)

3. Lewes

Louis' decision was condemned from Cardiff to Carlisle. The chroniclers worked themselves into a lather about the French king's bad faith, his dishonour, his complete turnaround on his words at Boulogne. To a twenty-first century mind the question is not 'why did Louis change his mind' but 'how could the reformers expect one anointed God-appointed king to agree to restrict the rights and privileges of another anointed God-appointed king?' Had he sided with the Reformers might not Louis' subjects feel that a dose of the same would be good for France? Reform had become radicalised into revolution since Boulogne and even the skills of the learned and persuasive Thomas de Cantilupe, leader of the Montfortian mission, could not persuade Louis to create a precedent that would have threatened his own position. Nevertheless, by dismissing the reformers' appeal outright, in its totality, and blaming the *Provisions* for all the kingdom's recent ills, Louis acted unwisely. If he believed that the barons would accept what today we call the *Mise of Amiens* without a murmur and it would end Henry's troubles then he was going to be disappointed because the conflict had built up too much momentum to be turned aside and would be fought with an internal logic of its own.

When Henry returned to England he found that the garrison of Dover castle was still determined to keep him out and London was no less hostile so he made his way to Oxford and summoned an army to fight against the Welsh. He fooled no-one; this was clearly his first move against the de Montforts. Earl Simon was still laid up in Kenilworth Castle but acted immediately to form an alliance with Llywelyn and sent a force to put de Mortimer – now a sworn enemy - out of the game. There was a history of implacable hostility between the two great magnates to which was now added an element of greed as Henry had promised de Mortimer a portion of the Montfortian lands.

So began a period of raids and counter raids. Mortimer evaded the Montfortians and joined up with Edward to ravage the de Bohun lands of the son of the Earl of Hereford. Edward managed to get himself trapped in Gloucester castle and escaped only through another violated oath.

Henry rejected peace overtures from the Reformers and continued assembling his army at Oxford, expelling the students to make room for his men and pillaging the surrounding area for supplies.

Earl Simon had commissioned a special carriage that carried him to London where the mob was getting down to some serious looting of royalist premises and lynching any Jews they could catch who would not convert and could not buy their lives. Other outsiders did not fare much better. The king ignored the opportunity to intervene and stormed Northampton instead, capturing Simon de Montfort the younger when local monks showed the royalists an exploitable weak point in the defences.

De Montfort was absent from London during the massacre, having set out to relieve Northampton. On his return he was horrified by the chaos he found and set about restoring order. He did pick up one ally on the way, Gilbert de Clare, Earl of Gloucester, and together they formed a plan to redirect the violence in the city towards Rochester, a royalist bastion on the way to Dover. The plan seems to have been to draw Henry and his army away from ravaging the Montfortian Midlands to rescue one of his key fortresses. The Montfortians failed to take the castle, pillaged the town and returned to London.

Henry seems to have believed that it was all over except for the mopping up. However, if he were to put an end to the revolt, he would have to take control of London, de Montfort's centre of power. A direct march on London was too risky. The Londoners would resist the royal army and the men of the south-east were likely to rise in the royal army's rear. The Cinque Ports needed to be reopened to clear the way for reinforcements paid for with the money raised in France by Queen Eleanor, and Henry wanted shipping from the ports to be used to blockade London.

Tonbridge Castle surrendered to Henry on May 1st 1264. From Tonbridge he went to Combwell, Battle Abbey and Winchelsea, arriving on May 4th 1264. His army was moving through hostile territory and had been harassed all the way by archers shooting from the cover of the woods. At Combwell an arrow killed Thomas, the king's cook. Henry summoned the local archers to attend him at Flimwell and, when 315 loyally trooped in, Henry watched while they were beheaded. A policy of 'Hearts & Minds' would have made no sense to a thirteenth-century monarch. Regardless of this example of the royal temper, when Henry arrived at Winchelsea his order for the wardens of the Cinque Ports to assemble a fleet was refused.

Henry's move south had given Earl Simon the space he needed to concentrate his forces in London, assembling some 5-6,000 men including 700 cavalry of various types. He had to move quickly before his army started to dribble away and he had to engage the king before Henry could receive reinforcements from France, so he marched off down the old Roman road via Croydon on May 6th 1264. News of de Montfort's approach soon reached the king.

I have based the account of the Battle of Lewes that follows on the narrative in the Battlefield Trust's Battlefield Resource Centre which is, in turn, based on the work of Professor David Carpenter.

Henry's army moved cautiously towards Lewes, intending to turn north and take the shortest route to London. In anticipation of encountering Earl Simon's army (and as protection against the Wealden archers) Henry's men travelled in full armour. They reached Lewes on May 11th 1264 and dispersed through the town to rest and refresh themselves.

The walled town of Lewes, with its castle held by John de Warenne, who had been defending Rochester for the king and was now in the king's party, sits on the west of the River Ouse in West Sussex. The river screened the east side of the town and marshland to the south of the town restricted movement from that side. The marshland has gone (the Ouse is no longer tidal this far inland) but Lewes's defensive strength in pre-gunpowder days is still clear.

There was adequate accommodation in and around the town, the castle and priory for an army of 9-10,000 men (as always, it is difficult to arrive at a satisfactory figure for the strength of a medieval army). There were supplies of food and drink for his hungry men to devour, and to replenish their supplies for the next stage of the march on London when the time came. Danger might come from the north or north-west so Henry had pickets posted on the high ground overlooking the town.

Earl Simon's army camped at Fletching, some eight miles from Lewes, on the night of May 11th 1264 then pressed on. Contemporary accounts say that Earl Simon had his soldiers sew white crosses, the mark of the armed pilgrims to the Holy Land, onto their tunics or surcoats, possibly for ease of identification in the mêlée, possibly to underline the sacred duty they felt that they were pursuing.

The Montfortians made one final attempt to secure a peaceful settlement, offering substantial concessions, but matters had progressed to far, too many vested interests wanted a battle. Their concessions rejected, they formally renounced allegiance to the king.

During the night of May 13th Earl Simon got his army on the move and occupied the heights to the north-west of the town, avoiding observation from the castle. His army reportedly found only one picket on the heights, and he was asleep. At dawn on May 14th, shriven, blessed and in battle array, Earl Simon's little army advanced on Lewes.

They were discovered by the royalist foragers who had set out to find breakfast on the hill. The king's army was probably largely asleep in Lewes: those under Lord Edward were at the castle and those with the king were camped at the priory, a little to the south of the town. When Edward heard that de Montfort had been sighted he mounted up and rushed from the town with his men without waiting for the rest of the royal troops to join him. By the time they moved, de Monfort had deployed his forces, which were out-numbered between two-to-one and three-to-two, depending on which source you believe, across the hill facing the town. With his father's command straggling onto the battlefield the ever-impatient Edward launched a ferocious cavalry attack on the left-hand battle of de Montfort's line, where inexperienced London recruits were stationed. Unsurprisingly, the raw Londoners quickly broke ranks and fled from the field with Edward and his cavalry in close pursuit.

Henry barely had time to deploy his forces before Edward charged from the field, forcing the king to attack in support of his son. The advantage of terrain was with de Montfort, with Henry's troops being obliged to attack uphill. Although the fighting was fierce all along the line de Montfort had kept a reserve, which he threw against the exposed flank of Henry's army. Assailed from the front and flank the royal troops began to give ground and the victorious Montfortians pushed them down the hill and right back into the town, where fighting continued in the streets. Henry took refuge behind the high walls of the priory. When Edward returned to the field after looting de Montfort's baggage he was inclined to continue fighting. His men were tired and their horses were blown but the castle still held out for the king. However, as the Montfortian army moved against him Edward was deserted by part of his noble cavalry, who fled to voluntary exile in France. No longer able to fight, Edward forced his way through to Lewes castle and made his way from there to the priory to join his father.

Although the royalists held both the castle and the priory they were trapped. Spasmodic fighting continued in the town until after nightfall as de Montfort's men mopped up any royalist survivors they could find. De Montfort now sued for peace, looking for a quick settlement, and he used all the leverage at his disposal. This included threatening to execute Richard of Cornwall (Henry's younger brother) who had been found hiding in a windmill on the Downs, a gift to the ballad-writers.

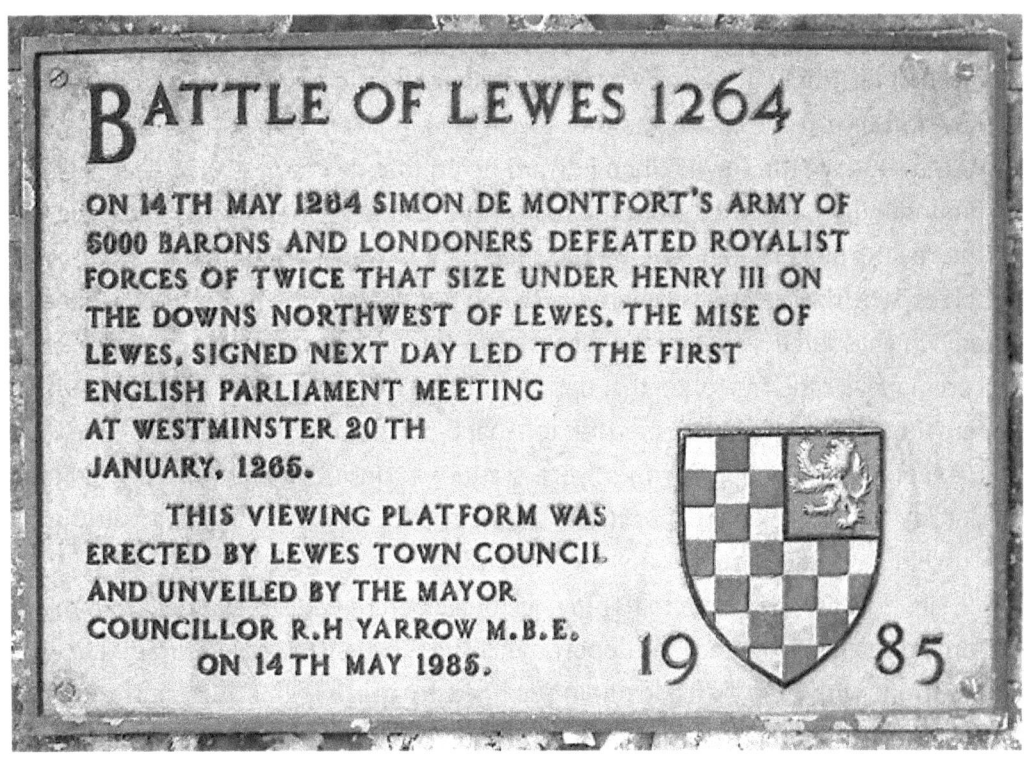

04 Plaque commemorating de Montfort's victory at Lewes (Source: Battlefields Trust)

Faced with such a threat, and uncertain of what support might come to his aid, Henry entered into negotiations on May 15th 1264. The royalists surrendered, and Henry agreed that the *Provisions of Oxford* should stand 'unbroken'.

4. After Lewes

The day after the battle the *Mise of Lewes* was signed. Among its more important provisions: Lord Edward and his cousin Henry of Almain were to become Earl Simon's hostages and, astonishingly, a permanent peace was to be secured through French arbitration. Simon must have been very confident of his influence over Louis.

The Earl of Leicester was now dancing in the light of his burning bridges. Simon claimed to be ruling in the king's name through a council of officials. In reality he was effectively the ruler of England with political control over the government. His first attempt to legitimise his position was at a parliament held in London in June 1264. He put forward a provisional scheme under which three electors: Simon himself, the Bishop of Chichester and Gilbert de Clare ('Gilbert the Red', Earl of Gloucester), would choose a council of nine to act as regent for the king. This scheme became known as 'The Councils of Three and Nine'.

The pope, Urban IV, received a request from Henry to intercede on his behalf and His Holiness decided to send a papal legate, Ottobuono de' Fieschi (later Pope Adrian V) who was tasked with mediating between the parties and preaching the crusade. He was not allowed to land in England.

Simon did not let the king out of his custody and took Henry with him wherever he went. Lord Edward was held captive at various places. He probably did not find spending Christmas at Kenilworth with Uncle Simon and Aunt Eleanor too onerous, but he was not going to bear his captivity for long.

The Montfortian Parliament

Simon de Montfort is famous (or notorious) for calling the first English parliament at which the 'commons' played a significant part. Simon forced Henry to convene a parliament at Westminster on January 30th 1265. Twenty-three barons – mainly the Montfortian supporters among the nobility – were joined by two knights from every shire, two burgesses from each borough and 120 churchmen.

The proceedings of this parliament are recorded in the *Liber Antiquis Legibus*. As a result of the parliament's deliberations it was announced on February 14th 1265 that:

'the lord King had bound himself on oath, by his charter, that neither he nor the Lord Edward in time to come would do no injury to, nor cause to be injured, the Earls of Leicester and Gloucester, nor the citizens of London or any of those who adhered to them, on account of anything done in the former time of disorder in the kingdom.'

Edward escapes

On March 11th Lord Edward was released from close captivity into the custody of the king, which meant that Earl Simon would not take his eye off them. Edward agreed to deliver three castles in the Welsh Marches into the hands of Montfortian sympathisers and Henry of Almain was to remain as a hostage for Edward's good behaviour until August 1st 1265. On May 28th Edward was out in the field near Hereford trying out horses, tilting at the quintain or simply exercising, when he mounted a fresh horse sent to him by Roger de Mortimer and fled, joining a troop of horsemen sent by de Mortimer who conveyed him to Wigmore Castle. This episode of Errol Flynn derring-do is likely to have taken place outside Hereford, which is conveniently close to Wigmore Castle.

Contrary to his agreement in parliament Edward began raising an army. His oath was meaningless; not only could he claim that an oath extracted under duress was invalid, but Edward's conduct regularly showed what little importance he put in oaths.

Before taking up the narrative again I am going to look more closely at the main actors in the forthcoming drama, the sources for the story and the fighting men of the mid-thirteenth century.

3. The Protagonists

I am flying in the face of English-language purists in the title of this chapter. The basic sense of 'protagonist' is 'the main character in a play' and can only be singular. Some traditionalists object to the looser use to refer to a number of characters in a play, film or event, although this usage is common and well established. Traditionalists also dislike the meaning 'a supporter of a cause', which is the sense that I am giving it because here are brief biographies of the main supporters of both the Montfortian cause and the royalist or Marcher cause.

Simon de Montfort

Simon de Montfort was a younger son of Simon de Montfort, 5th Earl of Leicester, a French nobleman and notorious leader of the Albigensian Crusade against the Cathar heretics, and Alix de Montmorency, daughter of Bouchard IV de Montmorency and Laurette, daughter of Baldwin IV, Count of Hainaut. His grandmother on his father's side was Amicia de Beaumont, the senior co-heiress to the earldom of Leicester.

As a younger son, Simon attracted little attention during his youth. We are not even certain of his date of birth. His first appearance in the record is a grant made to him in 1217. He may have been born shortly before his parents set out on his father's campaigns against the Cathars, or he may have been born while they were on campaign. He was certainly with his mother at the siege of Toulouse in 1218, where his father was killed. In addition to his eldest brother, Amaury, Simon had another older brother, Guy, who was killed at the siege of Castelnaudary in 1220.

The loss of most of the Angevin possessions in France had caused a dislocation for those families that held lands on both sides of the Channel. King John refused to allow the elder Simon, as a 'Frenchman', to succeed to the earldom of Leicester and instead passed it to Montfort senior's cousin Ranulf, the earl of Chester. The elder Simon had acquired vast domains during the Albigensian Crusade. When he was killed his eldest son, Amaury, was not allowed to retain them or to claim the English lands.

In 1229 Amaury and Simon came to an arrangement; Simon gave up his rights to the Montfortian possessions in France and Amaury gave up any claim to the earldom of Leicester. Freed from any allegiance to the king of France, Simon received a sympathetic hearing from Henry III, who was well-disposed towards 'aliens' from France. Henry permitted Simon to approach the aged, heirless, earl of Chester and Simon persuaded the earl to allow him the earldom. This was only a first step. He was unable to secure full possession of his lands for several years, and was not formally recognised as earl of Leicester until February 1239 (although he issued a charter as earl of Leicester in 1236 before he had been granted the title). Close in age and a possible ally, Simon became a favourite of Henry III.

Once confirmed as earl of Leicester, Simon expelled the small Jewish community from the city, banishing them: 'in my time or in the time of any of my heirs to the end of the world' for 'the good of my soul, and for the souls of my ancestors and successors'. It might have been a family obsession. Simon's mother had imprisoned the Jews of Toulouse and given them the choice of conversion or expulsion. It may also have been a strategy to enhance his popularity in his new domains by abolishing the practice of usury. However, the Jews of Leicester did not move very far, settling in the eastern suburbs, under the protection of de Montfort's great-aunt Margaret, Countess of Winchester.

In 1236 Simon tried to persuade Joan, Countess of Flanders to marry him. The idea of an alliance between the wealthy and strategically placed county of Flanders and a close associate of Henry III of England alarmed the French crown and the French queen dowager, Blanche of Castile, persuaded Joan to marry Thomas II of Savoy instead. In her place, in January 1238, de Montfort married Eleanor, daughter of King John and Isabella of Angoulême, sister of Henry III.

Even though the marriage took place with the king's connivance, the ceremony was performed secretly and without consulting the great barons, who were outraged. If the king's sister was on the marriage market, they should have had a chance at her! Scandalously, Eleanor had previously been married to William Marshal, 2nd Earl of Pembroke, and had been widowed at the age of sixteen. Subsequently she had sworn a vow of perpetual chastity, which she seemed to have forgotten. Eleanor's brother Richard, 1st Earl of Cornwall, revolted when he learned of the marriage and Henry had to buy him off with 6,000 marks, around £40,000,000 in 2020 values.

As Henry had hoped, relations between the brothers-in-law were cordial at first. However, the vow of chastity came back to haunt Simon and in 1238 he had to set out for Rome to secure papal blessing for his marriage. Henry aided and supported him. When Simon's and Eleanor's first son was born in November 1238 he was baptised Henry in honour of his uncle, Henry III, who stood godfather for him. Finally, in February 1239, de Montfort was formally invested with the earldom of Leicester. He also acted as the king's counsellor and was one of the nine godfathers of Henry's eldest son, Edward, who would inherit the throne and become Edward I.

Shortly after Edward's birth, however, Henry discovered that Simon owed a substantial debt to Queen Eleanor's uncle, Thomas II of Savoy, and had named Henry as surety for repayment without first obtaining the king's consent. Henry confronted de Montfort, called him an excommunicant, threatened to imprison him in the Tower of London and accused him of seducing the king's sister and forcing him to allow the marriage to avoid a scandal. Simon and Eleanor fled to France.

France may not have been far enough away from Henry, or Simon may have decided to expiate his sins by fulfilling the vow to go on crusade that he had made two years earlier. He raised the necessary funds and travelled to Outremer, the Holy Land. In autumn 1241, he left Outremer and Henry welcomed him back. The king needed Simon's experience, connections and reputation to help with his campaign against King Louis IX. The Poitou campaign that Henry led was a failure, ending at the Battle of Saintonge where only a ferocious rearguard action involving Simon de Montfort prevented a total defeat, and an exasperated de Montfort declared that Henry should be locked up like Charles the Simple, king of West Francia, who was deposed by rebel nobles.

Meanwhile a groundswell of anger and frustration was rising in England, although Henry either refused to see it or misunderstood its importance. There was a toxic cocktail of grievances from unrelieved famine caused by poor harvests to jealousy among the nobility as King Henry was too quick and too generous to dispense favour to his Poitevin relatives - the Lusignans - and Savoyard in-laws.

In 1248 Simon again took the cross with the idea of following Louis IX of France to Egypt, but Henry eventually persuaded him to give up this project and to act as viceroy in the turbulent Duchy of Gascony. Given *carte blanche* Simon suppressed the contending factions and humiliated the over-mighty *seigneurs*. They, in return, lodged bitter complaints with Henry who buckled and tried his lieutenant on the word of his enemies, instituting a formal inquiry into Simon's administration. Humiliatingly for Henry, Simon was acquitted by his peers on the charges of oppression, but Henry refused to reimburse Simon for his considerable expenses in Gascony, leading him to retire to France in 1252.

The French nobles offered him the regency of the kingdom, vacated by the death of Queen Blanche of Castile. However, de Montfort preferred to make his peace with Henry, which he did in 1253, influenced by Robert Grosseteste, Bishop of Lincoln. He helped the king to deal with disaffection in Gascony, but their reconciliation was hollow.

Over the next few years Simon's loyalties seemed to be ever changing. At the Parliament of 1254 he led the opposition in resisting a royal demand for a subsidy. However, in 1256–57, when the national discontent was coming to a head, he adhered to the royal cause, at least in appearance.

One of Henry's most spectacular pieces of self-delusion was his ambition to have his son Edmund crowned King of Sicily, which comprised both the island and much of southern Italy. Henry had given the pope his guarantee even though Conrad, the son of the late Emperor Frederick II, was currently in occupation. The pope had made no secret of the fact that a major military effort would have been needed for Edmund to take control of his kingdom.

By 1257 the pope was increasing the pressure on Henry, threatening excommunication if the king did not assemble an army and act soon. Working with his old enemy, Peter of Savoy, Earl Simon sweated to extricate Henry from the Sicilian morass. As a result, Henry's writs of this date mention de Montfort in friendly terms. However, at the 'Mad Parliament' of Oxford in 1258 Simon appeared, with the Earl of Gloucester, at the head of the baronial opposition. He was part of the 'Council of Fifteen' who were to exert control over the royal administration. The king, however, was successful in dividing the barons and, in 1261, Henry revoked his assent to the *Provisions of Oxford*. Earl Simon left the country in disgust.

The reforming barons were now convinced that there would never be a negotiated settlement with the king and were determined to raise a rebellion to restore the government of the *Provisions*. They invited Simon to return to England in 1263, as the leader of the revolt. Henry backed down quickly and allowed de Montfort to take control of the council. Lord Edward, however, began to undermine the opposition by winning over the less-committed with bribes and patronage. Their disruption of the October parliament led to a renewal of hostilities. The royalists almost trapped Simon outside London but he was rescued when sympathisers opened the gates and admitted him.

Eventually both sides agreed to submit their dispute to arbitration and accepted Louis IX of France as arbitrator. However, the reformers lost their leader when Simon broke his leg in a riding accident and was unable to appear in person before Louis. Civil war broke out in England almost as soon as Louis – predictably – found against the reformers and annulled the *Provisions* in his *Mise of Amiens* in January 1264.

Lord Edward

Born on June 17th 1239 at Westminster Palace, the first child of Henry III and Eleanor of Provence, Lord Edward ascended to the throne as Edward I on the death of his father in 1272. His father named his heir 'Edward' after his patron saint: Edward the Confessor. Although he was a delicate child, Edward grew to become a man of 1.88 metres (6 feet 3 inches), inheriting black hair from his mother and the fiery temper of the Plantagenets from his father. He also spoke with a pronounced lisp.

On November 1st 1254, Edward married his second cousin, the thirteen-year-old beauty Eleanor of Castile, to settle disputes about land in Gascony. Even though their marriage was a political alliance, Edward and Eleanor seemed to hit it off, producing sixteen children. Infant mortality struck all classes in society in the thirteenth century and their first two sons died in infancy, their heir, Alphonso, followed at the age of twelve. Their son Edward then became the heir. They married in Castile and Edward was appointed governor of Gascony.

Impatient with his father and eager to assume more power, he conspired with his uncle, Simon de Montfort, against his father, turning his coat when the reform movement seemed to pose a threat to his future kingship.

Edward commanded the main striking force of Henry's army at the Battle of Lewes, recklessly pursuing the Montfortians' left-hand battle beyond the battlefield and leaving his father to be defeated in his absence. Abandoned by his supporters, Edward was forced to surrender with his father and was taken into custody by Earl Simon.

Edward escaped from his rather ineffective captivity by a ruse and joined the Marcher lords who had been plotting against de Montfort either as their leader or, I believe, as a figurehead for de Mortimer.

Edward was impatient, ruthless, adept at circumventing oaths displaying considerable military prowess backed up by great savagery and vindictiveness.

Gilbert de Clare

Gilbert de Clare was the son of Richard, 8th Earl of Clare and Maud, daughter of John de Lacy, Earl of Lincoln. Born on September 2nd 1243, his bright red hair led to the inevitable nickname of 'Gilbert the Red'. When he was nine years old Gilbert married Alice of Angouleme, a niece of Henry III.

By 1246 Gilbert's father, Richard, controlled Glamorgan, and held the lordships of Llanbleddian, Talyfan, Rhuthin, Usk and Caerleon. On Richard's death in 1262 Gilbert inherited his father's estates and became the 9th Earl of Clare, the 7th Earl of Hertford and the 8th Earl of Gloucester. Initially Gilbert supported Simon de Montfort against the rule of Henry III and led the centre of the baronial army at Lewes.

With the king in Montfortian custody Simon and Gilbert called a new parliament. In addition to the barons and the leaders of the church, the reformers invited two representatives from each town, knights and burgesses, to attend parliament. The day-to-day running of the country was carried out by three men: Simon de Montfort, Gilbert the Red and the Bishop of Chichester.

Although unsettled by Earl Simon presuming to rule through the captive king, Gilbert nevertheless supported the parliamentary reforms; however, he disapproved of de Montfort's plan to ally himself with Llewellyn ap Gruffydd of Wales, with whom Gilbert had a dispute over lands that he owned in Glamorgan. Gilbert argued with Simon and left London.

In June 1265 Gilbert met Lord Edward in Ludlow after Edward's escape from Hereford. Joining de Mortimer at Ludlow the men raised an army and began their campaign.

Roger de Mortimer

Roger Mortimer, 1st Baron Mortimer of Wigmore in Herefordshire was born in 1231, possibly at his father's castle of Cwmaron. He was the son of Ralph de Mortimer and Princess Gwladys Ddu, daughter of Llywelyn ap Iorwerth and Joan Plantagenet, daughter of King John 'Lackland'. A minor at his father's death he received his inheritance on February 26th 1246 and was knighted by Henry III on Whitsunday 1253.

Henry used him in Gascony in 1253, and 1254; however, from 1255 to 1264 he was preoccupied with his duties on the March, trying to hold off his cousin Llewelyn ap Gruffydd, who was gradually uniting all the Welsh chieftains under his leadership. In 1256 Llywelyn invaded Roger's lordship of Gwrtheyrnion or Rhayader. He spent the whole of 1262 and 1263 fighting Llewelyn with varying success, in a conflict that would drag on until 1282 when both LLywelyn and de Mortimer were dead.

Roger's antipathy toward de Montfort may have stemmed from Simon's cordial relations with Llywelyn ap Gruffydd ('the friend of my enemy is my enemy') and from the friction between two powerful barons whose lands were geographically too close.

When war finally broke out in 1264 de Mortimer joined the king for the taking of Northampton, capturing a clutch of high-ranking prisoners. The tables were turned at the Battle of Lewes where the Montfortians won a famous victory, capturing the king, Lord Edward and several Marcher lords including Roger de Mortimer. With Llywelyn on the rampage while the Marchers were occupied in England, the Marcher lords, including Roger, were soon released. Lord Edward remained in custody until de Mortimer (or his wife) masterminded a plan to rescue him. Roger raised a force at Wigmore and joined Lord Edward at Ludlow.

One of the absorbing questions around the Battle of Evesham is 'who was really in command?'. In theory it was Lord Edward (the 'senior officer present'). However, would the Marcher lords respect his coolness, control and judgement after placing the blame for the calamity of Lewes squarely on his shoulders? Might they not prefer to be led by a more mature leader who had been hardened in years of border fighting? It is a moot point but there are hints that de Mortimer was behind the plan at Evesham with Edward acquiescing.

Whoever was the leader, de Mortimer's involvement in the Battle of Evesham was key and dramatic. While leading one of the battles of the Marcher army, the *New Account* places him in charge of a hit squad, and chronicles claim that he personally killed Simon de Montfort. He certainly sent Simon's severed head, and genitalia, to his home in Wigmore as a grizzly present for his wife, Maud de Braose, who had helped to rescue Lord Edward from Hereford. More of that later.

Humphrey V de Bohun

Born in Hereford in 1225 Humphrey V de Bohun was the son of Humphrey IV de Bohun, an Anglo-Norman aristocrat, and Maud de Lusignan. Humphrey married Eleanor de Braose, the youngest daughter of a powerful Marcher lord William de Braose, 10th Lord Abergavenny, and Eva Marshal, both of whom held estates in the Welsh Marches and Ireland.

Humphrey V died ten years before his father, so he never bore the title of earl. Humphrey and his father were on opposite sides during the baronial revolt. Humphrey IV had been part of the baronial opposition but had later defected to the royal side; Humphrey V on the other hand had remained loyal to the baronial cause and was captured at Evesham, dying in captivity at Beeston Castle from injuries he had suffered in the battle.

Henry de Montfort

Henry de Montfort was Earl Simon's eldest son. He sided with his father in the Second Barons' War and, in January 1264, he was one of the representatives sent to represent the baronial interest at the Mise of Amiens, the arbitration of Louis XI. When King Louis declared in favour of the royal cause, Henry commanded a body of troops despatched to secure the Welsh border. With his brother, Guy, he led the van at the Battle of Lewes. After the victory he was made constable of Dover Castle, Warden of the Cinque Ports, and treasurer of Sandwich. His forces sacked Worcester, and occupied Gloucester. However, on Edward's escape, he made a truce with him and retired to Kenilworth.

He was with his father at Evesham, being killed by the Marchers after the battle was over. The Almonry Museum in Evesham contains a skull that might have been Henry's, marked by catastrophic sword wounds.

4. Sources for the Battle of Evesham

There are two main types of written primary source for the Evesham campaign and battle. The first is the body of *writs* (letters) issued by the king and recorded on rolls kept by the chancellor. The place and dating clauses of these letters reveal the king's, and therefore the earl of Leicester's, itinerary over the days leading up to the battle. The second type is the surviving body of accounts by chroniclers. For the battle itself they provide almost the only written information. Other sources include physical evidence supplied by the battlefield itself and the traditions that have grown up around it.

If the writs issued in the days before Evesham were ever enrolled, then those rolls either vanished in the chaos following the battle or are lying in an archive waiting to be discovered. This throws a greater load on the accounts of the chroniclers. This book is based on analysis of thirteen main accounts of the scenes leading up to the death of Simon de Montfort, but none of them is fully trustworthy. Far and away the best is Robert of Gloucester even though the lengthy speeches he puts into the mouths of his characters are more an indication of what he thought should happen when a great man died, than of what took place.

Are the sources reliable?

Most of our accounts were written in Latin, the language of the literate classes in the thirteenth century. Although our writers use simile and metaphor expressed in an ancient vocabulary we cannot discard their work for this reason. There is a more damning problem: medieval (clerical) writers do not report on real individuals but idealised 'types', corresponding to a greater or lesser degree to recognised heroic stereotypes. They invented speeches for their characters, a rhetorical device copied from ancient Latin writers and used to convey aspects of character. Rather than recording what the character actually said they retailed the sort of things that he might have said or should have said.

Most of the chroniclers of the battle were writing an apology for the life of Earl Simon by describing the nobility of his leaving of it (that is those that were not using his fate as an object lesson against vaulting ambition). They were composing within a common literary model and made no pretence of writing objective history as we understand it today. There is no way definitively to cross-reference their testimony so it is impossible to prove them wrong.

The point I am labouring is that medieval chroniclers were not interested in accurate reporting. Even today several reporters can witness an event and give different or even conflicting views filtered through their experiences and preconceptions, and through the tastes of their readers. Look at any news-stand the morning a headline story breaks. What chance do we have with 750-year-old second- and third-hand reports? The written accounts are incomplete, flawed, damaged, compromised by the selectiveness of future generations of interpreters, and some are simply fraudulent.

On the other hand, there may have been cases where the writer knew the character well and may have been present when he spoke. Although the speech may have been edited for public consumption it may have retained a substantial part of the truth. My challenge has been to identify the accurate part. However, even when trying to record accurately the writer may not have coherent memories. Thoughts and memories have to be marshalled and interpreted in terms of the current need, to derive a structured and intelligible narrative. The narrative organises the fragments and can never present an unfiltered personal account. Worse, as far as we are aware, none of the chroniclers *was* close to Earl Simon.

At the risk of repeating myself, although this story of the Battle of Evesham is assembled as stringently as I can from contemporary or near-contemporary manuscript sources, it is always necessary to read them carefully and sceptically. The documents relating to 1265 are not windows on that time. Of themselves they do not illuminate anything, only what the document's author wanted to set down on parchment. They are not views of the events themselves but are stories told about those events. Often they were written years later. They were usually written for a specific audience. They are often confused (particularly when writing about battles), regularly formulaic and partisan. However, they do contain information.

Historians give greater credence to primary sources (letters, diaries, legal documents) than to secondary sources (commentaries, history books, articles in learned journals) with chronicles and journals lying somewhere in between. However, there is a danger that primary sources can adopt the character of sacred text, unchallengeable except by heretics. This conceals the fact that every primary text is the crystallisation of a great deal of interpretation that went before it. This evidence is a container into which someone has put information for a specific purpose, either to preserve it or to make it more widely known. Or both, of course. If we can prove that the information it contains is not founded in reality then we can discount it with some degree of confidence and enhance our confidence in what we cannot discount.

An important factor to bear in mind when examining these sources is the fact that, although they are interrelated, they do not appear to be derivative. They all incorporate accounts of the same basic events, but occasionally present some of them in a different sequence while omitting others altogether. The differences and similarities between these sources can sometimes be useful in attempting to interpret events.

What are the main issues?

We are looking at 1265 from a long distance through the wrong end of a telescope, focussing on a little scene here, a little scene there. The people of 1265 were not like us; their world was different from ours in ways that we can hardly imagine. All the same, human qualities are sufficiently constant for us to recognise them and to understand their motivation. If we are to interpret the contemporary or near-contemporary accounts, we must make an adjustment from our world to theirs.

Clerical Latin of the mid-thirteenth century was not well adapted to sober reportage, and monastic chroniclers could not interpret events in the way that a modern military historian can. Trained for rhetoric and discourse these scribes lacked the language to describe an army's deployment, the conduct of a battle and the appearance of a battlefield after the killing was over, not least because few of them had ever experienced anything like it. When groping for the right word they resorted to metaphor or simile or simply gave up and searched the classics for exemplars.

Historians find it difficult to reach consensus about the events of a particular battle, and small blame to them. Those who took part in the battle were usually too fully occupied with what was going on around them to be able to step back and take the long view, so eye-witness accounts are narrowly personal at best, misleading or contradictory at worst. And we have nothing that we can confidently call an eye-witness account of Evesham.

Non-eye-witness accounts are usually brief, tainted by hindsight or are adaptations of an idealised battle narrative with only the names changed. A writer who set out to use his subject to demonstrate the qualities of great men would choose his facts selectively because he wants to display his hero's virtues. These considerations apply even more to the chroniclers who may have belonged to institutions that benefited from Earl Simon's patronage so are likely to be even more biased in de Montfort's favour.

The accounts credit Earl Simon with several heroic statements during the lead up to the battle. It is difficult to believe that Earl Simon spoke these words, because they sound like what today we would call 'sound bites', owing more to literary convention than to sober reporting. Chroniclers reported words that their subject, in their view, should have said in that situation. For example, an 'eyewitness' to the death of Thomas á Beckett has the martyr vent himself of a lengthy speech of such moment and poignancy that it would have moved Shakespeare to tears of jealous rage, while his assassins stood around making conventional interjections. Very appropriate, but in reality all Beckett probably said was: 'What the!? Ow!' (in French).

How to approach the sources

Until recent years historical narrative was rooted in the rhetoric of historians, conclusions were bent around modern themes and preconceptions and evidence underwent a Procrustean transformation; any bits that did not fit were lopped off. This has not entirely died out among amateur historians like me. However, today's professional historians have become more sophisticated and employ methods similar to those that have existed in science for many years. Quantitative methods draw out general trends rather than drawing inferences from samples of data. Texts are analysed for their underlying meaning rather than being accepted as literally true.

Only in the area of political history is there a difficulty. Political acts are unique and do not adhere to recognisable trends; political intrigue rarely leaves a paper trail. However, that has not stopped historians trying to use cultural techniques and social theory to analyse events. However, often there is little option but to try to decide which sources are trustworthy and base conclusions on that evidence. This leaves an uneasy feeling that historians are again choosing the evidence they like and ignoring the rest (which some cynics might claim is also part of the 'scientific method'). However, in general modern historians of political history have exercised sound judgement and good faith.

I have tried to respect the sources and to give them their due weight and have, as far as I have been able, tried to allow the voices of the thirteenth century to sound through. You will find analysis and interpretation here but not, I hope, any invention. I have never felt any need to 'sex up' any account of the dramatic and tragic events, and Wagnerian denouement, of August 4th 1265.

Wherever necessary I have allowed my doubts to show through and have left the options open to the reader's judgement. However, an unrelenting diet of 'possibly', 'maybe', 'alternatively' would be indigestible so I have had to obtrude my opinions from time to time in an effort to keep the reader's interest. When reading the following chapters please remember that many of the narrated details are suspect, cannot be verified and were originally written to provide a pleasing or improving tale or to satisfy prurient interest. I have tried to provide a readable narrative by steering a middle course between the *Scylla* of credulity and the *Charybdis* of scepticism. If I had written down only what I was sure of, the covers of this book would have been a lot closer together.

To establish the background to the Battle of Evesham I am going to attempt to reconcile the various accounts. This involves establishing where they come together and where inconsistencies exist. They need to be reviewed to see which elements are consistent between them. I need to assess the likelihood of events that are described by, generally, pro-de Montfort writers. It is on the foundation of these different sources, of variable value, that we must attempt to reconstruct an account and an assessment of the Battle of Evesham and the events surrounding it.

This requires consideration and assessment of all of these sources against what we know of the contemporary scene. This will, I hope, help to avoid the influence of hindsight, the bane of historical writing, that weighs particularly heavily on the Battle of Evesham and Simon de Montfort. If I can establish an account that allows the main events of the accounts to be reconciled with archaeological and terrain evidence, then we are probably as close to the truth as we are likely to get at present.

Individuals do not always act rationally, being driven much more by emotion, instinct or conditioning than by careful weighing of the alternatives. Therefore, to understand the course of a battle we must try to understand the mental outlook of the leaders' class and age and estimate how far they were free to manoeuvre within or exceed these limits.

I hope that I have managed to make my point that we need to analyse the formative process that lies underneath our written evidence if we are to find the kernel of truth within a casing of propaganda and ignorance produced by the chroniclers listed in the following sections.

Robert of Gloucester

The *Metrical Chronicle of Robert of Gloucester*, is a chronicle of British, English and Norman history originally written in the mid- to late-thirteenth century. Partly derived from the *Waverley Annals* it nevertheless contains a wealth of original material. Some sixteen manuscripts of the *Chronicle* survive, although none are thirteenth-century originals, the extant copies ranging in date from the early fourteenth century to the mid-fifteenth century. Originally widely regarded and used by antiquarian scholars it drifted into obscurity after William Aldis Wright waspishly dismissed it as 'worthless as history' and 'verse without one spark of poetry'.

It is a manuscript volume containing a verse chronicle of the history of England from the legendary Brut[6] up to 1272. It has an extensive section on the second baronial rebellion. The chronicle is written in rhymed couplets in a south-west Midland dialect and it was copied in a good semi-cursive hand by two, or possibly three, scribes.

There are two known versions of the Chronicle; the longer version contains a reference to the darkness which enshrouded the countryside following the battle. References like this, and the author's apparent local knowledge of the area, has led to the traditional identification of 'Robert of Gloucester' as the author. On the verso of the second fly-leaf there is a 'Precepts in -ly' (moral or religious counsels) entitled *A spesiall glasse to loke in daily*, which is dated at *Holy Rode* on September 14th 1516. It may have been written by Richard Whitford (1476-1542), chaplain to William Blount, 4th Baron Mountjoy. It is possible that Whitford also copied the Robert of Gloucester chronicle. Folio 147 contains twenty-five lines of miscellaneous Latin, including a section relating to the prophecies of Merlin.

---

[6] Brut or Brutus of Troy, a legendary descendant of the Trojan hero Aeneas, believed in the middle ages to have been the founder and first king of Britain

The text is of interest primarily for its treatment of the Second Barons' War, to which the author of the *Chronicle*, or the author of a portion of the text incorporated in the *Chronicle*, might have been a witness. The portion reproduced in a *Lion Occasional Paper*[7] describes the death of Simon de Montfort at the Battle of Evesham and the aftermath of the battle. It is taken from British Library *Cotton MS Caligula A xi* and is in its original verse form.

William of Rishanger

Born at Rishangles, Suffolk, about 1250, William of Rishanger (nicknamed '*Chronigraphus*') became a Benedictine monk, and later annalist, at St. Alban's Abbey in 1271. There is some doubt over his year of birth which would seem to suggest that he was nine years old when he began continuing Matthew Paris!

His chief work was a continuation of Matthew Paris's *Chronicle*, entitled *Narratio de bellis apud Lewes et Evesham*, covering the baronial revolt from 1258 to 1267. He was still working on his account during 1312, the year of his death. He also wrote a brief chronicle about the deeds of Edward I entitled *Quaedam recapitulatio brevis de gestis domini Edwardi*.

The historical matter in the *Narratio* is derived from Matthew Paris and largely copied from the *Flores Historiarum* of St Albans, but it does have some original material. It is interesting for the evidence it affords of the extreme veneration in which Simon de Montfort was held at that time. The text raises a significant number of inconsistencies that tend to detract from Rishanger's trustworthiness, and this trustworthiness is further undermined by his very clear bias in favour of Earl Simon.

Nicholas Trivet

Born about 1257 (died 1328), Nicholas Trivet (or 'Trevet', as he wrote) was the son of Thomas Trevet (died 1283) a judge whose family came from Norfolk or Somerset. He was the author of a large number of theological and historical works and commentaries on the classics. However, he is chiefly remembered for his chronicle of the Angevin kings of England, *Annales sex regum Angliae qui a comitibus Andegavensibus originem traxerun*, an important source for the period 1136-1307.

---

[7] Robert of Gloucester: An Account of the Battle of Evesham, The Simon de Montfort Society, 2016

Print editions of *Annales* were published in Paris in 1668, in Oxford in 1719, and it was edited by Thomas Hog for the English Historical Society in 1845. Manuscripts are preserved at Oxford and in the British Museum. Trevet wrote other historical works as well as some theological and philological tracts. He died around 1334.

Nicholas Trivet experienced the reign of Edward I, if little of the reign of Henry III. He was the son of a judge and a lawyerly method underpins his writings. His Annals cover the period from the accession of King Stephen to the death of Edward I and he tells us that he tried to obtain the best evidence available from competent witnesses.

He was educated in London, possibly at a Dominican school, then at university in Oxford before completing his education in Paris. At some time, he joined the Dominican Order at Castle Baynard, Blackfriars, in London where there was a fine library and divided his time between there and teaching at Oxford.

His account includes interesting details of the reasons for the quarrel between Simon de Montfort and Gilbert de Clare, Earl of Gloucester. It contains an apparent error where the distance from Kenilworth to Worcester is described as three miles (Latin – *milliaribus tribus*). This is a mistake, either in the original manuscript or in the transcription, with thirty miles being intended, which is nearer the mark.

An intriguing puzzle is in the sentence '.... Edward moving himself from Worcester having crossed the river next to the town which is called Clive interposed himself with his army in the path of the Earl towards his son who was in Kenilworth Castle and of the son towards his father. ....' The Latin is *'Edwardus movens se de Wigornia transito fluvio juxta oppidum quod dicitur Clive, viam comiti versus filium, qui erat in castro de Kenilworthe, filiique ad patrem, cum suo exercitu interclusit'*. In the manuscript the name is 'Olive', generally regarded as a clerical error for 'Clive'. Some historians, albeit with reservations, have taken 'Clive' to mean Cleeve Prior and have interpreted the passage as implying that Edward's army, or part of it, crossed the Avon at Cleeve Prior and then re-crossed at Offenham. This theory has now been largely discounted although, before dismissing it entirely, a couple of points deserve consideration. Firstly, the Twyford-Offenham crossing was on the main Worcester to London road and one way or another, Edward needed to deny de Montfort access to it. Secondly, there is a local tradition that Edward saw Simon de Montfort's army at Evesham from a vantage point on Cleeve Hill. Having said that, the *Last Hours*[8] account gives compelling place-name evidence of Edward's and Clare's approach – via Mosham Meadow and Craycombe – which rules out any crossing of the Avon by them at Cleeve Prior. Dr David Cox explains that the sentence was intended to refer to de Montfort's earlier crossing of the Severn at Clevelode and Trivet's 'Clive' is in fact Clifton which is near Clevelode.

Trivet's description of the battlefield makes no mention of any hill. Instead he says that the armies met in a spacious field outside the town (La. *'in campo extra oppidum spatioso'*). *'Campo'* used on its own can simply mean the place where the battle was fought but the addition of *'spatioso'* implies a large flat plain and there is such a plain between Greenhill and the River Avon to the east. By walking out of Evesham along Common Road one can appreciate the extent of this plain. Trivet's account implies that in addition to the fighting on Greenhill this flat part of the battlefield saw significant activity, possibly a struggle to control the Twyford-Offenham crossing.

Trivet does not specifically say where de Mortimer was on the battlefield but he does say that Edward, de Clare and de Mortimer each approached Evesham from different directions and that Simon de Montfort would have been completely surrounded. This supports the view that de Mortimer's division was south of the Avon blocking the Bengeworth Bridge and preventing any retreat or escape in that direction.

Trivet's account has been published in a *Lion Occasional Paper*[9].

'Matthew of Westminster'

Matthew of Westminster was long regarded as the author of the *Flores Historiarum*, a remarkable achievement for a man who we now know never actually existed. Francis Turner Palgrave first discovered the error in 1826, calling Matthew 'a phantom who never existed'. Henry Richards Luard later proved this conclusion.[10]

---

[8] The Last Hours of Simon de Montfort, A Lion Occasional Paper, Evesham 2002

[9] Osney, Wykes, Trivet & The Evesham Chronicle: Four Accounts of the Battle of Evesham, The Simon de Montfort Society, 2015

[10] Luard was the son of Henry Luard. Originally education at Cheam, he graduated from Trinity College, Cambridge in 1847 and was elected to a Fellowship in 1849. He took holy orders and served

The misunderstanding originated in the title of a late manuscript of this history (Cotton, Claudius, E, 8). This erroneously describes the work as *liber qui Flores Historiarum intiulatur secundum Matthaeum monachum Westmonasteriensem*. The compilation was made between 1259 and 1265 at St. Albans. Between 1265 and 1325 there is textual evidence that some of the writers who contributed to it lived at Westminster. When Archbishop Parker printed the chronicle for the first time, in 1567, he attributed it to 'Matthew of Westminster'.

Luard re-edited it for the Rolls Series in 1890 with an introduction containing a detailed exposition of the origins and development of the chronicle. The error in identification of the author seems to lie with a copyist who connected the fact that the earlier part of the work was largely lifted from Matthew Paris's *Chronica majora*, while the latter part was written at Westminster Abbey. Putting two and two together, he concluded that Matthew was a monk of Westminster.

The *Flores Historiarum* covers the period from the Creation to 1326, although some of the manuscripts stop at 1306. The section from 1259, where Matthew Paris ends, to 1265 was of great interest while writing this book.

This account describes the rebellion of Simon de Montfort and his short-lived success in 1264. This chronicler is one of the few who were by no means sympathetic to the rebellion. The second baronial revolt is famous because Simon de Montfort summoned a parliament including the 'commons' which nineteenth-century historians commended as the first modern parliament. 'Matthew of Westminster' is not so easily impressed.

Walter of Guisborough

Walter of Guisborough (sometimes called Walter of Hemingburgh) was a canon regular of the Augustinian priory of Guisborough in North Yorkshire. Around 1300 he began writing his chronicle, which embraces the period of English history from the Conquest to the nineteenth year of the reign of Edward III, except for the years 1316-1326, and it ends with only the title of a chapter in which he was going to

---

as vicar of Great St. Mary's Church, Cambridge from 1860 to 1887. Luard was also a Fellow of King's College, London, and Registrar of the University of Cambridge. He worked on cataloguing the manuscripts in the Cambridge University Library and edited 17 volumes of medieval chronicles and other texts for the Rolls Series.

describe the battle of Crécy of 1346. The later portions are missing from some of the manuscripts and may have been added by a continuator.

In compiling the early part of the *Chronicle*, he seems to have relied heavily on earlier historians such as Roger of Hoveden, Henry of Huntingdon and William of Newburgh. However, his work on the reigns of the three Edwards is original, composed from personal observation and information provided by contemporary observers. For the years 1264-5 he seems to have had access to a contemporary narrative compiled by someone close to the events.

There are several extant manuscripts of the history. The copy presented to the College of Arms by the Earl of Arundel is regarded as the most useful as it contains copies of the great charters, *Magna Carta*. The first three books were published in 1687, appearing in Thomas Gale's *Historiae Anglicanae scriptores quinque;* the remainder were published by Thomas Hearne in 1731. The first portion was again published in 1848 by the English Historical Society, under the title *Chronicon Walteri de Hemingburgh, vulgo Hemingford nuncupati, de gestis regum Angliae*, edited by H. C. Hamilton.

Although Walter was interpreting an account written up to thirty years before he began writing, this is the most important chronicle source for the battles of Lewes and Evesham. The relevant portions have been published as a Lion Occasional Paper[11].

Evesham Chronicle

The original manuscript, written by a monk of Evesham who was probably among those who tended to the wounded or helped to bury the dead, is lost. However, there are five surviving copies or fragments that are catalogued as: A, B, C, D and E. Written some time after 1323, version A is the nearest in time to the original, but it is incomplete. Version B is the most complete, but it dates from the late fourteenth or early fifteenth centuries and it has addenda that seem to have been added over time. Version C, created in the late sixteenth century, is an abridged version of A. Version D and E both date from the sixteenth century and they contain little more than lists of casualties.

---

[11] Walter of Guisborough: An Account of the Battle of Evesham, The Simon de Montfort Society, 2015

The imperfect nature of the copies of the original manuscript, and some internal confusion over dates, reduces the usefulness of what should have been the most immediate and authoritative account of the battle. On the other hand, it is useful in helping to assess the number of men that the Montfortians had with them when they marched into Evesham. The Simon de Montfort Society has published the interesting part of the version A text[12].

Labordiere: New Account

This account had been written on the reverse of a document that had belonged to the College of Arms for more than three centuries. It is a vellum roll consisting of five membranes sewn together end-to-end giving a total length of around 3.35 metres (11 feet) and about 20 centimetres (eight inches) wide. On one side is written a genealogical history of England down to the time of Edward I. It is written in Norman French and probably belonged to a family of the gentry or lesser nobility.

Olivier de Laborderie of Paris, researching at the University of Nottingham, found, recognised and brought the account to light, realising its importance for the study of the Battle of Evesham. The account of the Evesham campaign and battle was added to the roll, apparently around 1330. The original author seems to have been an eye-witness of some of the events described, and may have spoken with other eye-witnesses; he may have been a monk at Evesham Abbey. The importance of this account lies in its description of the rendezvous at Mosham Meadow immediately before the battle and in introducing the idea of Edward forming a 'death squad' to kill his uncle.

The April 2000 issue of the *English Historical Review*[13] contains a detailed article about this narrative, its discovery and interpretation and the Simon de Montfort Society has published the translated text and commentary as: *The Last Hours of Simon de Montfort* (A Lion Occasional Paper, Evesham 2002).

---

[12] Osney, Wykes, Trivet & The Evesham Chronicle: Four Accounts of the Battle of Evesham, The Simon de Montfort Society, 2015

[13] O de Laborderie, JR Maddicott and DA Carpenter, Notes and documents. The last hours of Simon de Montfort: a new account, English Historical Review (2000) 115 (461): 378-412

William de Nangis

As with most of our other sources, little is known about William of Nangis. He was named after Nangis, or Nancy, in north-eastern France and is believed to have been a monk at the Abbey of St Denis, five miles north of the historic centre of Paris. He was active in 1275 and abbey archivist from 1289 to 1300 (both dates are approximate) and is believed to have died shortly after 1300. He was the author of three biographies of kings of France: Louis VIII, Louis IX and Phillip III. William's account of the Battle of Evesham appears in his biography of Louis IX.

This is an important account predating most of the other accounts identified in this chapter. He may have derived some of his information from ordinary government sources in France to which de Nangis, as an archivist, may have had access. However, the detail and drama of the Battle of Evesham itself suggest that the information came from an eyewitness or someone close to events on the Montfortian side, possibly a member of the de Montfort family itself, an idea put forward by Tony Spicer of the Battlefields Trust. Those of Simon de Montfort's family who survived the Battle of Evesham (his wife Eleanor, his sons Simon, Guy, Amaury and Richard, and his daughter Eleanor) all took refuge in France at some time.

This account describes the rift between Simon de Montfort and Gilbert de Clare, Earl of Gloucester, as violent, more so than the description in any other account that you will read about in this book. He says that Simon junior suffered a total defeat at Kenilworth (without naming the scene of his humiliation) rather than being seriously roughed up, as most other accounts agree. So ashamed was young Simon that he could not bring himself to tell his father who therefore committed himself to battle at Evesham believing that his son was on the way with reinforcements.

From what de Nangis says, messengers were able to pass between the Evesham Montfortians and the Kenilworth Montfortians. This does suggest a reason for Earl Simon's route; he was expecting his son's army to advance from Kenilworth toward Evesham and either combine forces or, if a royalist army intervened, one would attack from the front while the other attacked from the rear.

This is a second account (see Labordiere: *New Account*) that says that the Marchers organised a hit squad to make a dead set at Earl Simon and his sons Henry and Guy. However, de Nangis says that the squad was detailed to rescue the king and to capture Simon and his sons (a 'snatch squad' rather than a 'death squad') , not to kill them, a resolution supported by the rest of the nobility in the Marcher army. In the event Simon and Henry were killed, which may suggest that Edward was not in absolute command of the army and that de Clare and – particularly - de Mortimer felt free to follow their own policy. The main portions of the text have been published in a Simon de Montfort Society *Lion Occasional Paper*[14].

Osney Annals and the Chronicle of Thomas Wykes

These accounts of the Battle of Evesham were edited from the original Latin chronicles by H. R. Luard in *Annales Monastici (Rolls Series 1865) Volume IV* published by Longman, Green, Reader and Dyer in 1867. Both chronicles were written at Osney Abbey near Oxford and, because of that, and the similarities of the two chronicles, Luard had them published together although they were clearly written by different people. The Simon de Montfort Society has published translations of both accounts made by Rosemary Leamon and by Tony Spicer of the Battlefields Trust in *Osney, Wykes, Trivet & The Evesham Chronicle: Four Accounts of the Battle of Evesham, The Simon de Montfort Society, 2015*.

Osney Annals

The Osney Annals appear to have been written up each year, presumably by the relevant monk who was in charge of them at the time. We do not know who wrote the part relating to the campaign and Battle of Evesham. However, he was not only an admirer of Simon de Montfort, calling him 'this most steadfast of men' and 'this man of God' but was also sympathetic to his cause inferring that Simon fought to preserve the laws of the land. Also, it is in the Osney Annals that we find the reference to Simon's body being buried in a church in Evesham, presumably the Abbey, and then later, when this attracted hostility, its reburial in a secret grave.

There are suggestions that the Osney account of the Battle of Evesham was written very near to the time, perhaps within a year or two of the battle. This is not certain and all that can safely be said is that it was written before Wykes' chronicle. According to Osney, the main moving force behind the royalist cause was Gilbert de Clare, Earl of Gloucester with Edward only playing a minor role. Perhaps the author was reluctant to associate Edward with the death 'most foul and unheard of' of Simon de Montfort. Another significant point is that according to Osney it was near

---

[14] William de Nangis: An Account of the Battle of Evesham, Simon de Montfort Society, 2011

Worcester that Simon de Montfort heard of his son's defeat at Kenilworth. Although the dates are not entirely clear from the narrative, it appears consistent with Simon de Montfort hearing the news either on the evening of Sunday 2nd or the morning of Monday 3rd August when he was at Kempsey. The important point is that we have a near contemporary account saying that he knew about his son's defeat before departing for Evesham.

Thomas Wykes

Thomas Wykes lived from approximately 1222 to 1293. Originally rector of Caister, in Norfolk, he entered Osney Abbey as a canon regular in 1282. He is believed to have started writing his Chronicle in 1278, beginning at the Norman Conquest of 1066. If he wrote systematically, year after year, rather than episodically, it would have been some years before he wrote about the events of the Second Baronial war, possibly writing his account of the Battle of Evesham ten or twelve years after the event, probably between 1275 and 1282.

Although Wykes joined the Augustinian abbey of Osney in 1282, while composing his chronicle, he was still a secular clerk, possibly in the service of Richard of Cornwall, which would have given him a direct, if understandably biased, view of the events of 1264-65. His writing relied heavily on the language of the scriptures, drawing lessons on kingship and the nature of sin from the baronial revolt, as when he quotes Psalm 2:2 to say that the nobility of England 'had come together as one against the anointed lord [the king]'. It is safe to say that Wykes was not a fan of the Provisions of Oxford.

Melrose Chronicle

King David of Scotland founded Melrose Abbey in 1136, choosing a new site five miles from the ancient monastery where St Cuthbert lived in the seventh century. By the twelfth century Melrose had a community of Cistercian monks, the first Cistercian house in Scotland, invited from Riveaulx Abbey in Yorkshire.

The only surviving copy of the chronicle is a manuscript in the British Library, catalogued under *Cottonian Manuscript, Faustina B*. The authors remain anonymous but other evidence fixes Melrose Abbey as its place of creation. The manuscript is in two parts.

The first begins in the year 735 and ends in 1140 (around the time that Melrose Abbey was founded). This portion is derivative and was compiled from earlier histories including the Anglo-Saxon Chronicle and the works of Simeon of Durham and Roger of Hoveden. The second portion covers the period from 1140 until the chronicle comes to a sudden stop in 1270. This section is original; the handwriting changes over time as brother succeeded brother to add his contribution so that the handwriting of more than forty scribes is discernible. This suggests that folios were added as events were reported or discovered so the events recorded in this portion are considered by historians to be more credible than those in the first segment.

The section for 1260-1261 and 1263-1270 is currently covered in fourteen folios (at least one folio has been lost at the end) and was written by at least four scribes. Among other material it contains narratives of the Barons' War in England, a lengthy tract on Simon de Montfort and an extensive eulogy of Edward I. Positioned on a major route north from England the Abbey was well positioned to entertain travellers and to collect their stories, which may have become fodder for the chronicle.

Dunstable Chronicle

The Priory of St Peter - Dunstable Priory - was founded by Henry I in 1132 as a house of Augustinian Canons. The canons seem to have had a fairly rocky relationship with successive monarchs, the disputes being largely financial. At the time of the baronial revolt, and like most of the clergy and religious of the period, Dunstable was sympathetic to Simon de Montfort, who was widely regarded as a champion of the Church. Simon visited Dunstable in 1263 and was admitted to the fraternity of the house.

The chronicle, usually referred to as the 'Annals', covered the period from the Incarnation to 1297. The thirteenth-century portion is particularly valuable to historians as the annals are detailed and, from 1210, seem to have been written soon after the events they describe. The chronicle's support for the baronial cause between 1258 and 1265 is unstinting. Probably due to political idealism and veneration for Simon, it regards him as a martyr as well as a hero, and it attempts to analyse the causes, course and events of the war.

Waverley Chronicle

Waverley Abbey was founded near Farnham, Surrey, in November 1128 by Bishop William Giffard, who brought the first abbot and monks from L'Aumône Abbey in Normandy.

The chronicle covers the period from the Incarnation to 1291, although the ending is incomplete. Of all the chronicles and accounts mentioned in this book, the Waverley Chronicle supports the baronial side most intelligently. As with Melrose, Waverley's earlier section, up to 1156, is derived from well-known historical sources such as the Anglo-Saxon Chronicle (inevitably), Geoffrey of Monmouth, William of Malmesbury and Henry of Huntingdon. From 1157 it contains original material. The rule seems to have been that events were written up a year after they occurred

The political tone of the chronicle is anti-monarchist, identifying with Simon and his party, which may have been due to its close links with Simon's wife, Eleanor. It calls Simon and his supporters 'the saner party' and hails them as saviours of the country. It writes bitterly about the aliens who were ruining the country. The Waverley Chronicle summarises Simon in these words: 'Alas! A glorious martyr for the peace of the land, and for the redemption of the realm and of mother church'.[15]

---

[15] Annales Monastici. Volume 2, Annales Monasterii de Wintonia (AD 519-1277), Annales Monasterii de Waverleia (AD1-1291) / edited by Henry Richards Luard 1865

5. Mid-Thirteenth-Century Armies

Among a thousand other factors, the form taken by a medieval battle was conditioned by the types of soldier present, their morale and motivation, the weapons they used and the relative proportions of horse and foot. The following sections aim to give a reader not well-versed in the military of 1265 a clear mental picture of the soldiers who fought at Evesham. Even if you are familiar with the armour, weapons and organisation of thirteenth-century armies please read on. This chapter took a long time to write!

One of my main sources for this period is the *Maciejowski Bible,* valuable because it illustrates the first part of the Old Testament, from Genesis to David. The pictures were probably made in Paris around 1250. A facsimile was published in 1927; however, I used the reprinted version from either 1969 or 1975 (there is no date in the book itself). The 92 folios offer a wealth of visual detail about the thirteenth century. Details of the Bible, with selected illustrations, can be found at:

www.medievaltymes.com/courtyard/maciejowski_bible.htm

and a more up-to-date presentation, which calls it the Crusader Bible is at:

www.themorgan.org/collection/crusader-bible

Armour

The thirteenth century was a period of change in personal armour, particularly during the second half of the century, as plate was added to mail and gradually superseded it. That was true of those noblemen who could afford 'state of the art' armour. Obsolete and obsolescent armour remained in use among those who could not afford better, and had not picked it up from the battlefield, so that some fighting men in 1265 would have been quite at home on Senlac Ridge in 1066 while others were reaching forward to the wars of Edward III.

The Hauberk

Élite cavalry were protected by *hauberks*, knee-length coats, usually of mail, split to the crotch at the front and back to ease riding astride. The *hauberk* of interlocking rings of mail (contemporaries never called it 'chain mail') was known to the Romans (it is a common find in Roman archaeological sites) who credited the Gauls with its invention. They called it *lorica hamata*. Less affluent cavalry might wear obsolescent and hand-me-down *hauberks* with elbow-length or wrist-length sleeves; knights would have full-length sleeves terminating in mail mittens. A shorter form of mail shirt, the *haubergeon*, with sleeves only to the elbow or forearm, might still be seen occasionally.

A drawing in Matthew Paris (c. 1250) shows a cuffed gauntlet separate from the *hauberk* and the *Maciejowski Bible* (c. 1245) has an illustration of a *hauberk* with fingered gloves. With the ability by 1245 to produce tiny rings of mail this was feasible but would have been expensive. Separate leather gauntlets and gloves were rare. Mail mittens and gloves were tied in place by a thong at the wrist, generally threaded through the links, to reduce the drag of the heavy mail. They had a palm of leather or thick fabric to provide a secure grip, with a slit in the palm of the mittens to allow the hand to emerge and, in the latter half of the century, a more close-fitting hauberk sleeve became common.

Illustrations, starting with the Bayeux Tapestry, suggest that when fighting on foot the flaps of the *hauberk* could be tied around the legs like a cowboy's chaps. While mounted the flaps were allowed to hang loose like a split skirt, covering the thighs.

A full mail coat weighed roughly 13.6kg (30lb) depending on its length and the thickness of the rings. The waist-length version with three-quarter or elbow-length sleeves was correspondingly lighter, around 11kg (24lb).

Mail provided the wearer with a reasonable degree of protection while leaving him free to move. His waist belt would have helped to redistribute some of the weight of the *hauberk* to the waist and hips and have eased the pressure on his shoulders. The ability to use different sizes of ring — smaller rings across the vital areas of the chest with larger rings at the extremities — allowed armourers to condition the weight distribution of a *hauberk*. Mail was assembled from rings that may have been punched from a flat plate of thin metal but were commonly cut from wire and bent to shape, the open ends flattened and drilled to take a rivet. Each ring was interlocked with four others and riveted in place. Once assembled, the *hauberk* was annealed in a forge. It was a time-consuming, tedious and costly process. However, improvements to wire-drawing techniques in the thirteenth century and other advances in manufacturing brought mail within reach of the less well-off soldiers. It was also easy to repair, and captured or looted mail could easily be tailored to its new owner by adding or removing the requisite number of rings.

Armour was by no means proof against all weapons. Powerful shearing blows, especially those delivered with both hands with an axe or heavy sword, could cut through mail causing horrific injuries. However, it was effective against the weak or glancing blows that would have been common in a mêlée.

In his account of a fight between Richard the Lionhearted and William of Barres, the poet Guillaume le Breton refers to 'thrice woven' *hauberks* and there are other references to double and triple mail. Although in normal mail each ring interlocked with four others it was possible to assemble mail so that each ring interlocked with six others, which would have produced a denser armour providing greater protection for a little extra weight. There are modern re-creations of dense mail; however, I am not aware of any surviving authenticated original examples. It would have provided superior armour for a wealthy man. Alternatively, these may have been references to extra layers of mail worn over vital parts. Possibly the reference was to plates of metal being inserted between the *hauberk* and the *akheton* (see below). However, it is difficult to see how even 'triple woven' mail could withstand a square hit from the hardened tip of a lance head with the full weight of a charging knight and his mount behind it. Recent tests support this conclusion.

Scale Armour

Scale armour had not been completely superseded by mail in 1265. It had, however, become uncommon. In Europe it was constructed from small scales of iron, bronze or, occasionally, boiled hardened leather or whalebone, sewn to a textile backing with the scales overlapping downwards like those of a fish. It appears in contemporary illustrations, but usually worn by Saracens and other outlandish types to distinguish them from western knights.

The Coif

The neck of the *hauberk* was often extended up to form a mail hood or *coif*. These had enough mail to fit loosely around the throat or were made with a slit below the chin to allow the *hauberk* to slip easily over the wearer's head. Most commonly this slit would be laced shut to protect the throat or it might be extended on one side to form a flap that could be drawn up over the chin and mouth when going into action.

This was called a *ventail* and was probably lined or padded. It was usually secured either by a lace threaded through the rings at the opposite temple or buckled or attached to a hook. The *ventail* had been common since the twelfth century.

Some of the knights at Evesham may have worn the newly developed *coif-de-mailles,* a mail hood made separate from the *hauberk,* that spread out across the wearer's shoulders to provide extra protection from overhand blows, but most would have worn an integral *coif.*

Arming Caps

The *coif* was invariably worn over a padded or quilted arming cap, some of which incorporated a thick ring of material around the top to provide a snug fit and some support for the flat-topped great helm. An arming cap helped to absorb blows, reduced the friction of the *coif* against the head and kept the wearer's hair from being pulled out in tufts. It could be secured under the chin with tapes or laces.

Fabric Armour

Knights invariably wore their *hauberk* over a quilted or padded undergarment. This had three main functions: it prevented the *hauberk* from chafing; it cushioned the wearer against powerful blows that would otherwise drive broken links of mail into the underlying flesh or fracture bones; it caught pointed weapons that penetrated the rings of the mail and lodged in the garment. Tests have shown that mail can stop an arrow shot from normal combat ranges of up to 200 metres (220 yards) but it cannot prevent the arrow causing minor wounds. However, there are accounts from the Holy Land of armoured infantry wearing their mail shirts over a textile lining leaving the battlefield of Arsouf unharmed despite being feathered with arrows. The mail had slowed the arrows enough for the fabric armour to stop them.

The most common undergarment was a padded tunic known as an *akheton* (from the Arabic *al-qutun* – 'cotton') also known as *wambais, pourpoint* or (inaccurately) *gambeson*. The short-sleeved or sleeveless *akheton* was usually quilted vertically, consisting of two layers of cloth stuffed with wool, tow or similar material. Another type consisted instead of between 18 and 30 layers of linen, sewn into a diamond pattern. Some may have had a standing collar, perhaps of a rigid material such as boiled leather, whalebone or even metal. Some knights wore what appears to be a separate collar under or even over their mail. *Gambesons* were similar to *akhetons* but had long sleeves.

Some *akhetons* worn by infantry in the *Maciejowski Bible* seem to have inset sleeves but may represent a sleeveless *akheton* worn over a long-sleeved *gambeson* (an arrangement referred to in textual sources) for extra protection. There are references to *akhetons* and *gambesons*, probably made from silk or other rich materials, occasionally being worn over the mail and any reinforcements. *Akhetons* and *gambesons* that were intended to be worn without a covering of mail were thicker, higher in the collar and faced with leather or canvas. *Akhetons* and *gambesons* widely replaced other forms of armour for infantry in the thirteenth century. They were also widely adopted by non-élite cavalry as their main or only body armour.

Surcoats

A surcoat was a garment, usually of linen, worn over the *hauberk,* often close-fitting across the chest but falling more loosely from the waist down. The length varied from above the knees to ankle length with a straight hem or dagged or scalloped edges. They were usually (not always) sleeveless and were slit nearly to the waist front and back to facilitate riding astride. They appear to have been lined in a contrasting colour and secured by a cord or decorative belt at the waist, which may also have helped to support the weight of the *hauberk*. Surcoats appear to have been introduced in the second quarter of the twelfth century and they were increasingly popular by the early thirteenth century although, even towards mid-century, by no means all knights wore one. It is not clear why it was adopted, possibly to keep armour dry or to protect the knight from the sun. Or possibly western warriors were simply aping Saracen fashions. However, as surcoats were often left one colour or decorated in colours that bore no resemblance to the family's arms, it is unlikely that they were adopted primarily to display heraldry. A few surcoats may have had pockets to hold protective plates across the chest and they could be padded for extra protection.

Leg Armour

Élite cavalry and some others wore separate leg armour, primarily to protect them from increasingly effective infantry. Leg armour had been common since the middle of the twelfth century. Sometimes this was a broad strip of mail folded around the calf and thigh and laced at the back and probably attached at the top to a waist belt. More often it was a pair of complete mail stockings (Fr. *chausses*) fitted with leather soles for grip and braced up at the waist to a belt or girdle and worn over cloth stockings. Rather than attach them to the girdle of the knight's drawers (*braies*) he would have worn a separate leather belt. He may have laced the *chausses* to his knee to prevent sagging.

Early in the thirteenth century the *gamboised cuisse* appeared, designed to protect the thigh and knee. This was a quilted or padded tube probably tied to the same belt as the *chausses*.

The knees of mounted men were particularly vulnerable to foot soldiers so by mid-century small cup-shaped pieces called *poleyns* or *genouilliers* were occasionally worn over the knees either attached direct to the mail *chausses* or else over the *gamboised cuisses*. Very small at first, larger versions soon appeared, wrapping right around the knee. Some may have been made from *cuir bouilli* (made by boiling leather in wax, moulding the softened leather to fit and then leaving it to harden) and they may have been laced or stitched in place or riveted through to the mail. The *poleyns* may also have served to reduce the drag of the mail *chausses*. Occasionally a similar small cup-shaped piece was seen at the elbow. Shin-defences, called *schynbalds* or *greaves*, were simple gutter-shaped plates strapped around the lower leg over the mail.

Solid Body Armour

By 1265 the *hauberk* was being supplemented by solid body armour. Plate armour, in the form of small reinforcements fitted under the *hauberk*, began to appear at the end of the twelfth century. Illustrations cannot show the quality of armour and, since most supplementary armour (except for leg defences) was worn under the surcoat, they are not very good at showing the full extent of the armour a man is wearing. The apparent uniformity displayed by illustrations of mounted men probably concealed numerous variations of protection.

A description by Guillaume le Breton mentions a plate of beaten iron being worn under the *akheton*, presumably to protect the heart. There is no known illustration of such a defence. However, an effigy in Pershore Abbey church, Worcestershire, and another in the Temple Church, London, both dated to the mid-thirteenth century, show some form of breastplate and backplate buckled over the mail but under the surcoat. The sculptor may have meant to depict metal or *cuir bouilli*; it is impossible to tell which, but an educated guess suggests from the moulding that it is *cuir bouilli*. Several thirteenth-century manuscripts show infantrymen wearing a leather body armour, the *cuirie*, with or without metal reinforcements, laced down one side. Is this what the Pershore and Temple figures are wearing under their surcoats?

Around the middle of the thirteenth century a new item of protection appeared. The 'coat of plates' was worn like a Second World War flak jacket, pulled over the head with side panels that wrapped over the back flap where they were tied or buckled in place. The front and sides (and back? I have no conclusive evidence either way) were lined with large rectangular plates, presumably of iron, steel, lateen (a type of brass) *cuir bouilli*, horn or whalebone, riveted to the fabric (the rivet heads are visible on contemporary illustrations). By the end of the century English documents refer to the coat of plates, or just 'plates', being worn over the mail but under the surcoat.

By the end of the thirteenth century what we would recognise as proper plate armour had become available so we can assume that at least the wealthier knights and lords at Evesham would have been wearing mail skilfully reinforced with plate.

Neck Defences

By the end of the thirteenth century the French, and possibly others, had developed an early form of *gorget* or *bevor* to protect the throat and chin. Illustrations from earlier in the century show that they might be worn over the mail or beneath it and were probably covered in cloth, but it is not clear what they were made from: metal, *cuir bouilli* or even whalebone. Nor is it clear whether they were removable or attached to the *akheton* (as appears to be the case with some infantry armour). They may either have fastened at both sides of the neck or have hinged at the left and fastened at the right.

Padded Shoulders

It is also possible that the shoulders of fighting men could be padded as extra protection against blows from above if unhorsed. Some knights in the *Maciejowski Bible* show upwardly curved shoulders under their surcoats. Could this be extra leather armour? Or some other form of padding? Textual sources of 1224 mention an *espaulier* of *cendal* silk. Possibly this was a padded shoulder defence. There are a few examples of illustrations showing a long flowing garment issuing under the lower edge of the *hauberk*. This flows too freely to be padded. Was this the *espaulier*?

The constant effort to improve protection ended with the knight swathed in combinations of mail (perhaps dense or reinforced) padded *ahketon*, *gambeson* or both, steel plates, leather breastplate, padded surcoat, armoured surcoat and coat of plates. The total weight carried into battle by a thirteenth-century knight was 40-42kg (88-92.4lb) and possibly more if all possible reinforcements were won. The combination of armour and shield protected the knight from all but direct hits, if the knight was not killed or wounded in the initial clash of lances, in the mêlée.

Shields

A shield was essential for a fighting man to parry direct thrusts from lance, sword or spear, to catch arrows and quarrels and to turn aside direct blows. Shields were made of wooden planks laid side by side and were often bound with metal to reinforce the edges. Such reinforcement would have been invisible under a canvas or leather facing covering the shield of the richer fighting man. They were probably also lined with leather or canvas, although I do not know of any English shield that has survived from the period. There are surviving examples from the continent, but these are usually special votive items and so probably not representative of battle shields. Many have raised mouldings on the face of the shield; no man-at-arms would relish going into battle with a shield that would trap a point rather than deflecting it.

Although some obsolete designs would still have been in use in 1265, shields had gradually diminished in size during the century from the cumbersome 'kite' shields to the smaller and thicker 'heater' shield, named in Victorian times for its resemblance to the sole of an old-fashioned smoothing iron. The reduction was made possible by improvements in body armour.

As was true for body armour, funerary effigies are a rich source of contemporary information on arms and shields, the sculptor usually modelling the figure with commendable clarity and accuracy. There are several that show the arrangement of straps on the back of the shield, confirming manuscript descriptions. There were usually three carrying straps (*brases* or *enarmes*) riveted through to the front. They sometimes had buckles to adjust their fit. To avoid bruising, or even a fractured forearm, there was usually a pad nailed between the straps. A mounted man would have had a *guige strap* to hang the shield from his neck when he needed both hands, to prevent him from dropping the shield in battle and to strap it to his back for extra protection. Crossbowmen also did this to protect themselves as they turned their backs on the enemy to reload. It could also be used to hang the shield up when not in use.

A small circular wooden parrying shield with a central metal boss riveted or nailed over a single central hand grip, which would later come to be known as a *buckler*, was known but is not commonly seen in illustrations. However, as these pay little heed to the infantry this might have been a common defence amongst foot soldiers. Shields of leather stretched across a wicker skeleton persisted in some Celtic regions. Earl Simon's borrowed Welsh spearmen may have carried them.

Helmets

In 1265 several varieties of helmet were in use, some of them archaic types. Conical helmets with nasal bars, similar to those depicted on the Bayeux Tapestry, occasionally appear in contemporary illustrations but, as with scale armour, they are frequently used to distinguish the 'baddies' from the 'goodies'. By the start of the century round-topped and cylindrical variations of these types were common, usually with a nasal but sometimes with a face mask. A few had neck-guards. If contemporary illustrations are to be trusted, helmets of these types would still have been met with occasionally on the heads of cavalry and it seems likely that some of the foot soldiers would have sported them as hand-me-down kit.

Great Helm

By around 1220 a fully enclosed helmet, the 'great helm' that protected the back and sides of the head as well as the face, had begun to appear and became increasingly popular with the cavalry as the century progressed. Some had a single vision slit across the front of the helmet; on others the slit was divided down the middle as reinforcing bars were added around the slits and down the nose. Assembled from plates, the front plates overlapped the plates at the rear to provide a glancing surface. The flat top was bent around the upper edges to provide a flange through which it was riveted to the body of the helmet. By 1265 some of the better-equipped men-at-arms might have been wearing great helms with an upwards taper, although the top would have remained flat.

Close helms were not particularly heavy but soon grew stiflingly hot. They muffled hearing and limited vision, which probably explains the number of contemporary illustrations of men-at-arms wearing a variety of other types of helmet or even open-faced, protected only by the mail coif and arming cap.

Cervellière

By the middle of the thirteenth century the *cervellière* had become popular. This was a small brimless close-fitting skull of iron that covered the ears but left the face free. It increasingly replaced the conical and round-topped helmets. It could be worn over the mail *coif*, but illustrations show that it could also be worn over the arming cap but under the mail *coif*. This would explain the many illustrations of men-at-arms going into battle apparently without a helmet but wearing a bulbous *coif*. Some might have had a small mail curtain called a *tippet* riveted inside them to remove the need for a *coif* and some had a nasal bar attached to the rim.

Chapel-de-fer

The *chapel-de-fer*, a shallow broad-brimmed helmet, often called a 'kettle hat', was popular among the better-off infantry, sergeants, squires and non-noble cavalry. They also seem to have been favoured by knights who wanted better ventilation and greater visibility, although the broad brim was also useful in siege work for deflecting missiles shot or dropped from above. The first illustrations in the mid-thirteenth century show a deep bowl that sat low on the head and a broad brim sheltering the head and shoulders. A variant with a flat top and sloping brim mimicked a civilian straw hat. They provided adequate protection and were cheap and easy to produce, being assembled from metal sections riveted together. The design was resurrected during the First World War in a diminished form as the 'battle bowler' to protect the heads of 'tommies' (and later 'doughboys') in the trenches.

Padding and Lining

All helmets were fitted with a padded lining, like modern military helmets, although it is very difficult to find a contemporary illustration of the inside of a helmet. However, the nature of the lining can be reconstructed from preserved examples of helmets; the linings of fabric or leather have decayed but the fittings and staple holes remain. Padding of wool or tow could be glued to the inner surface of the helmet or stitched to a line of small holes along the brim or to a canvas or leather band riveted inside the helmet. The lining of great helms was probably cut into scallops that could be adjusted with a drawstring to ensure a good fit and to line up the vision slits with the wearer's eyes. All types of helmet were usually laced or buckled under the chin. Manuscript illustrations and textual references show that helmets could be painted.

Combinations of Helmet

Written sources often refer to soldiers wearing more than one helmet. This is supported by pictorial and monumental evidence. For example: a large kettle helmet could be worn over a close-fitting helmet, over a mail *coif*, or over a *cervellière,* which could even be worn under a great helm as extra protection. Conversely, if contemporary illustrations are accurate, then many knights scorned the constriction and restricted field of vision of a close helm and preferred to fight with only the protection of their *coif* laced to their head. The illustrations do not always make it possible to see which of them might be wearing a *cervellière* under their *coif*.

Infantry Equipment

The equipment of each fighting man was appropriate to his role, but the differences were more than just functional. Every man brought his own equipment. The equipment of an élite cavalryman would not only have been more extensive than that of an infantryman but of much better quality. Even when fighting on foot, knights carried superior equipment. Contemporary illustrations impose a suspect uniformity on what was probably a diverse reality. Weapons and armour evolved only slowly so enjoyed a long life. The better off would have bought the most up-to-date arms and armour; their prestige demanded no less. The rest would have had to content themselves with cheaper versions to suit their purse, or with hand-me-downs, altered, patched and updated as far as possible.

Contemporary illustrations of lightly-armed men fighting on foot appear to show fabric armour, a simple iron helmet and a shield as the equipment of an infantryman of the middling sort. In the *Maciejowski Bible*, among other sources, there are illustrations of infantry protected by quilted and padded *akhetons* or *gambesons* and steel caps or helmets. Assizes of arms confirm that this was the kind of equipment that citizens were expected to provide for themselves. The better-equipped infantry would have worn full *hauberks* with *coifs* and long or short sleeves (maybe looted or obsolescent) or lighter mail shirts, quilted *akhetons* or *gambesons* either with mail or on their own. They would have worn brimmed kettle-hats, close-fitting helmets, pot-helmets of various sorts and padded arming caps. Infantry of this period rarely wore armour on their legs or additional armour on their arms. Chief among this class of infantry were the crossbowmen. They were the élite among the infantry and the contrast between the poor archer and the professional crossbowman is clear from the *Maciejowski Bible*.

Manuscripts show well-armed infantry wearing *hauberks* and *coifs*, and other types of armour with *coifs,* but these may have been dismounted knights or may represent mercenaries. The *gambeson* or *akheton* is evident on some of the infantry in the *Maciejowski Bible*: padded knee-length tunics with high standing collars and iron caps. However, there is a spearman protected by only a simple helmet and a slinger protected only by a small round shield, more representative of the run-of-the-mill infantryman.

Weapons

If the thirteenth century was a period of change in personal armour, there was little corresponding development of the weapons used.

Swords

By the thirteenth century swords were no longer exclusive to the knightly classes (if they ever had been) although they were still inescapably bound up with the cult of knighthood. The sword was common for a wide range of classes in society and they could always be picked up from the battlefield. The prized weapon of the century was the broadsword, of which Oakeshott[16] identified five major types. The most common type was a flat cut-and-thrust weapon with a light-blade that, until

---

[16] Ewart Oakeshott (May 25th 1916 – September 30th 2002) was a British illustrator, collector and historian, a *Fellow of the Society of Antiquaries*, a founder member of the *Arms and Armour Society* and the Founder of the *Oakeshott Institute*. His classification of the medieval sword, the Oakeshott typology, is a standard system used to categorise medieval weaponry

the latter part of the century, tapered to a relatively acute point with a fuller (a groove to lighten the blade without weakening it) on each side running at least three-quarters of the way down the blade. The standard single-handed broadsword weighed around 1.4kg (3lb) and was well-balanced with a hefty pommel at the end of the hilt acting as a counterweight to the blade, bringing the point of balance nearer to the hilt, to avoid tiring the sword arm. However, broadswords were made in various lengths and by 1265 some were large enough to wield with both hands, another approach to defeating improved armour. These were the 'great' or 'bastard' swords-of-war. Pommels varied and could be decorative. Cross-guards were usually simple, usually straight, but some curved down towards the blade. Swords were carried in scabbards of wood, lined with leather or sheep's fleece, with a metal *chape* or cap at the closed end of the scabbard and a metal rim to protect the mouth of the scabbard.

The *falchion* was another expedient for defeating armour. It was a heavy-bladed single-edged weapon of appalling power that widened toward the point like a large machete. Shorter than a broadsword, a falchion contained the same amount of metal and its main weight fell on a curved cutting edge close to its point, giving it a fearsome cleaving power. Falchions were used by both infantry and cavalry, although they afforded a shorter reach on the back of a horse than a knightly broadsword.

Lances

Lances remained the characteristic cavalry weapon although illustrations and written accounts suggest that by 1265 cavalry were starting to favour close combat weapons: swords, maces and axes, in the charge. The design of lances remained much the same from the eighth century until the end of the thirteenth century when tapering tilting lances with defined hand grips were developed and came into widespread military use. In 1265 a lance was likely to have a cylindrical shaft of a suitable wood (ash is often mentioned) around 4 metres (12 feet) long with the lance head socketed onto the end of the shaft. The butt of the lance would also have been protected by a plate to prevent splintering. According to several modern authors the lance was first used 'couched' (with the full weight of the knight behind it) in the twelfth century, enabled by changes to saddles that afforded the rider a more secure seat. However, the Bayeux Tapestry shows the lance being used underarm and other manuscript illustrations take the couched lance back to the eighth century. The light lance was used in much the same way that lancers used it in the Napoleonic wars, wedged under the arm during the charge, wielded at arm's length in a mêlée or swung overarm to reach an enemy lying on the ground. Barons and some knights carried rectangular banners attached to their lances, the longer side attached to the shaft. These were embroidered or painted or the designs were stitched on as panels of a different colour. The banner was stiffened for clarity of display.

Axes

The axe was a popular weapon at all levels in society, from the huge Danish axe carried by infantrymen to a long-handled single-handed axe favoured by horsemen. By the thirteenth century a single-handed axe was in use by knights and a long-handled version was used by the infantry. A new weapon emerged during the century: the horseman's poll-axe. With a hammer-head on one side and a sharp beak or spike on the other, like a modern climber's ice axe, it had greater penetrative force than a broad-bladed axe.

Clubs and Maces

Clubs and maces varied from heavy wooden clubs studded with large nails to professionally-made steel maces. Maces are not often referred to in contemporary accounts although they are frequently illustrated in, for example, the *Maciejowski Bible*. The flanged type of mace became the most common in the west, probably coming from the Islamic east and most of the maces used at Evesham would have been of the flanged type with short thick wooden or iron shafts, although there are likely to have been some of the earlier studded wooden variety in use.

Knives and Daggers

Fighting men carried knives and daggers, although they were little regarded by the élite cavalry who thought of them as nasty treacherous Saracen weapons. Daggers had a double-edged tapering blade; knives were single-edged. Welsh stabbing dirks could have blades up to 60 centimetres (2 feet) long, almost a short sword. For most fighting men the knife or dagger was a multi-purpose tool, cutting a throat one day and preparing breakfast the next.

Infantry Weapons

By the time of the Battle of Evesham, illustrations show a fearsome variety of weapons in the hands of infantry: spears, clubs, maces, axes, daggers, *falchions*, broadswords and odd weapons that appear to be all edges and that so far have defied identification. Identifying the weapons carried by infantry is tricky with each weapon enjoying several regional names, the same name being applied to different weapons and unnamed weapons appearing in pictorial sources.

Spears

We are on safer ground with the archetypal infantry weapon, the spear, one of the earliest types of weapon. Spearheads were either narrow penetrative types or had wider, leaf-shaped, blades. In theory, the narrower type of spearhead would have been used on cavalry lances while the broader blades were better adapted for infantry hack and stab tactics. But only in theory. The *Maciejowski Bible* and other sources depict cavalrymen armed with broad-bladed spears, and infantrymen expecting to face mailed cavalry may have favoured narrow spearheads. There seems to be no simple classification between infantry spears and cavalry spears, with wide local variations. However, we can tentatively classify spears under five broad headings:

1. **Javelin.** This was a light spear intended for throwing. A modern male Olympic athlete using an official 800gm (1.76lb) javelin would expect to make a throw of around 90 metres (98.4 yards). A medieval javelinman, on foot, would be content with a throw of 23 metres (25 yards). He would be likely to carry three or four javelins. Javelins were occasionally still employed by cavalry, as late thirteenth-century textual sources and illustrations testify. Edward I was aware that lances were of little use in the close terrain of north Wales and ordered his mounted men to carry javelins instead.

2. **Short spear.** This was the most common type of spear. It was light enough to be thrown at close range but was essentially a hand-to-hand weapon used for stabbing and, if the head was suitable, for slashing.

3. **Long thrusting spear.** These were purely hand-to-hand weapons for use by the infantry, although similar in design to the cavalryman's lance. It was an excellent weapon for repelling cavalry, developing into the pike.

4. **Heavy spears.** Some long thrusting spears had weighted heads to improve the force of a thrust.
5. **Boar spears.** Derived from hunting weapons, a boar spear had a short thick shaft with two 'lugs' or 'wings' jutting out from the spearhead's socket behind the blade, which originally acted as a stop to prevent an impaled boar charging down the length of the spear and goring the holder. In battle the lugs could be used to hook a shield out of the way as well as to prevent a spear thrust from going too far into a charging horse, making it easier to withdraw and the spearhead less likely to break off.

Other Polearms and Slings

English infantry used a variety of other polearms including bill, *gaesa*, *godendac*, *croc*, *faus*, *faussa*, *pilote*, *guisarme* and *voulge*. The *guisarme*, which was basically a scythe blade mounted on a long-shaft and swung like an axe, seems to have been particularly popular. Agricultural tools made serviceable weapons and slings were not uncommon. An illustration of around 1250 in Matthew Paris shows a staff sling in use during a siege.

Bows

The word 'longbow' was not used in English in the thirteenth century and there was no corresponding word in French or Latin. It is a modern trend to use 'longbow' to describe the ordinary stave bow, as distinct from the crossbow. Let us call it a 'bow', a single wooden stave, frequently of yew (especially Spanish yew) but occasionally of ash, witch hazel or witch elm. Composite bows fabricated from wood, horn and sinew were known in the west (Gerald of Wales noted them in the twelfth century) but never proved popular because the glue dissolved in damp conditions.

Bows were of various lengths. However, it is impossible to be dogmatic about the length of bows in the thirteenth century because there is no objective evidence to match the staves of sixteenth-century bows recovered from the wreck of the *Mary Rose,* and the pictorial and manuscript evidence is contradictory and inconclusive. Contemporary manuscript illustrations, such as those in Matthew Paris and the *Maciejowski Bible*, provide a general impression but, before the fifteenth century, illustrations are too impressionistic to provide more than a broad representation of the length of the stave. However, if we measure the bow against the figure holding it then the bow in use at Evesham might be anything from 1.73 metres (5 feet 8 inches) upwards and I believe that there is no reason to subscribe to the idea, once prevalent, that bows did not develop to their full length before the fourteenth century.

There *is* some evidence that bows could have been up to 1.83 metres (6 feet) long. Their range and power depended on the length of the stave and the strength needed to bend it so normal battle range could be anything from 200 metres (220 yards) to 350 metres (385 yards). A yew bow found in a *crannog* at Ballinderry, West Meath, in 1928 had a stave 1.85 metres (6 feet) long. It was dated to the ninth or tenth century by a fine broadsword found with it. Made of yew it had a 'D'-shaped cross-section, the flat back of the bow toward the enemy and the curved belly toward the archer. When strung this stave would have formed a smooth arc of a circle. Although a Viking weapon it is almost identical to the medieval English longbow and 'D' section bows of yew are known in England from as early as 2700 BC.

Henry III attempted to restrict the possession of bows, with little success. This was a dilemma for those in authority: there was a need to foster military archery while avoiding arming a popular insurrection. As evidence that bows were around in plenty consider the profusion of related surnames at the time, such as: Archer, Bowman, Bowyer, Stringer, Bowknocker, Arrowsmith and Fletcher.

Crossbows

Crossbows were common in our period, although they were less favoured by English infantry than they were on the continent. The crossbow was especially associated with trained mercenaries such as the Gascons employed by Edward I and crossbowmen enjoyed a high status as professionals.

A crossbow comprised a short stave bow set on a grooved stock and equipped with a trigger. It took time and strength to bend the short rigid bow but it shot a short bolt or *quarrel* on a flat trajectory and with formidable penetration up to 200 metres (220 yards) and at that range a narrow-headed quarrel could penetrate three inches of oak. By the beginning of the thirteenth century a normal-size military crossbow had a draw of about 85 centimetres (34 inches). During the century the bow strengthened, the arms shrank, and the draw shortened permitting the use of shorter, aerodynamically superior quarrels with a greater punch. Bows were sometimes of composite construction for greater power.

The Church was not keen on crossbows, for political reasons. A crossbow enabled any peasant hiding in ambush to bring down the best and bravest knight. The church's prohibition against the crossbow was intended to take a formidable weapon out of the hands of the lower orders. It was anathematised by the second Lateran Council in 1139 as *artem mortiferam et deo odibilem* ('an instrument deadly and hateful to God') with the usual exemption allowing its use against heretics.

The crossbow's other name, 'arbalest', is derived from the Latin *arcubalista* giving rise to the surname Arbalaster.

Horses

The mounted knight or man-at-arms is associated with the charger, of which there were two classes. The larger and heavier warhorse was the *destrier* (from the Latin *dexter* for 'right-hand-side'). *Destriers* were valuable animals and some knights refused to risk them on campaign, reserving them for use in tournaments. The cost of a *destrier* rose steadily throughout the thirteenth century. At the start of the century an average war-horse could cost up to £50 (£500,000 in today's values – *calculated with the aid of Professor David Carpenter's 'Patent Currency Converter'*) - and be well over £60 (£600,000) by the end of the century.

Warhorses were bred on royal studs or imported from Spain, Italy and France. They were bred for deep chests, capacious lungs and powerful muscular necks. They were agile, could turn quickly in their own length and had impressive speed and acceleration over a short distance. They were always entire stallions and their natural aggression was enhanced by training, sometimes to the point where the horse itself became a weapon. However, this developed aggression could be a drawback; warhorses were inclined to attack other horses on their own side and might provide their owner with a dangerously bumpy ride.

Despite their strength and power over a short distance, warhorses lacked the stamina for a long gallop. Men-at-arms returning from a mounted pursuit would have been riding exhausted mounts, as Lord Edward found at Lewes in 1264.

By the end of the thirteenth century the term 'great horse' had come into use, possibly because increases in the weight and completeness of armour for both man and horse required a heavier horse. Warhorses were invariably large animals but not the hairy-footed carthorses of popular fiction. The total weight carried into battle by a mid-thirteenth-century warhorse was the body weight of the knight plus 40-42kg (88-92lb) of arms and armour, possibly more if all possible reinforcements were worn. By comparison, First World War troop horses carried a total weight of up to 130kg (290lb) on campaign, including the rider.

It is possible to estimate the size of thirteenth-century warhorses. The dimensions of the stalls on the ships that transported horses to the Crusades suggest an animal similar to a heavy hunter of fifteen to sixteen hands not unlike the typical troop horse of the First World War. Surviving horse armours seem to have been made for animals of this size.

In battle many men-at-arms rode the second class of warhorse. A *courser* was an expensive horse but not as expensive as a *destrier*, which would have been beyond the resources of a mounted sergeant or poorer knight. A wealthy knight or lord might have taken one or more spare war-horses on campaigns, with a squire detailed to lead forward a fresh mount as his master returned from a charge on a blown horse.

For travelling, the man-at-arms would have ridden a *palfrey*, a good-quality mount for long distance use and he may have had two or three spare travelling horses. Valets, butlers and squires would have ridden *rounceys* or *ronsons*, travelling horses appropriate for superior servants. The *hackney* or *hack* was a cheaper mount for other servants and thought suitable for mounted infantry. The master would also have provided pack animals, either *sumpters* (pack ponies) or mules, and possibly draught animals if wagons were used. A knight would have brought on campaign as many spare horses as he could afford.

The war saddle had a high cantle (back support) that curved slightly around the rider's body while the bow (front support) usually curved slightly forward, snugly enfolding the rider's body. Along with the long stirrups this produced a military riding posture that guaranteed a secure seat but prevented the knight from standing in his stirrups to deliver a downward blow. The horse was controlled by a snaffle bit or curb bit, and reins were usually of leather although they could be fashioned from, or reinforced with, chain to prevent them from being cut. Harness could be highly decorated.

Lords and wealthier knights often covered their warhorses with a cloth trapper or *caparison*. This was a cover or housing that came down to the horse's hocks and sometimes covered the tail, sometimes made in one piece but more often divided at the saddle. They were usually extended forward to form a head covering with either holes for the animal's ears or shaped ear coverings. The entire trapper may have been dyed a plain colour, often not related to the colours of the owner's arms. However, by the end of the century trappers frequently bore the owner's arms, reflected on his shield but not always on the surcoat, which could still be left plain. Horse trappers appear to have had linings, possibly to absorb the horse's sweat. From illustrations these linings seem to have been integral with the trapper.

The first armour for horses seems to have been a solid *shaffron* or *champron* for the horse's head. There is textual evidence that they were in use during the mid-twelfth century and there are illustrations of them in use on the continent. There are few representations in English illustrations; however, this might be because it was customary for horses to wear their *shaffron* under their head covering or housing. A *shaffron* could be fitted with a crest.

There is evidence for horses wearing iron armour as early as 1187 and there are illustrations of horses protected with mail from the next century. Other horses wore quilted trappers, textile armour similar to that worn by the horses of *picadores* in the modern *corrida*, forming an equine equivalent to the *akheton*. Cloth caparisons covering horses in thirteenth-century illustrations make it difficult to see what armour is worn underneath. However, by mid-century some illustrations show trappers of mail which must have overlain a quilted trapper or a lining of several layers of linen. Such trappers covered the entire horse except for the ears.

Horses were an expensive option for logistical use. Donkeys could be used as pack animals and mules were commonly used as pack animals, to draw wagons and occasionally for riding. Mules were calmer and hardier than horses so they were favoured for strenuous tasks such as carrying or hauling supplies over difficult terrain. The size of a mule, and the work it was capable of doing, depended largely on the breed of mare that bore the mule. They could be lightweight, medium weight or even, when produced from draught horse mares, of moderately heavy weight.

Raising and Discipline

Thirteenth-century armies lacked the logistical sophistication of later armies and still depended heavily on foraging for supplies, rapidly depleting the area around them. The largest armies that could be put into the field were limited in size by the difficulties of supplying them and rarely numbered more than a few thousand.

Thirteenth-century armies were not a disorganised rabble. Their camps and quarters we selected and laid out by specialists. Discipline and respect for authority were demanded by the commanders and enforced by marshals, provosts and constables.

Vegetius, a late Roman writer on military matters whose writings were popular in the middle ages, wrote that the strength of an army was in its training, discipline and cohesion. The problem shared by most western armies was that knights, while well-trained in the individual exercise of arms, were highly independent. Because of the ad hoc nature of armies any group of soldiers, cavalry or infantry, were likely to lack cohesion and would be of uneven quality. Commanders exerted some control, although this control was usually limited and separate groups within their armies had considerable autonomy.

Transport and Logistics

Food for men invariably meant bread. However, once baked, the bread did not last for long. Grain was more durable but grain also meant carrying the means to mill it into flour and ovens to bake it into bread. Carrying flour, ready milled, saved weight and the trouble of milling but flour spoiled easily. In 1265 Simon de Montfort's troops were unable to get their normal food in Wales and suffered from having to live off the land.

It is possible to estimate the size of a medieval supply train. Take, as our basic building block, 1kg (2.2lb) of bread or its calorific equivalent, enough to feed one man leading an active life for one day. A packhorse could carry up to 150kg (330lb) of food, enough for 150 men for one day. So, a force of 3,000 men would need 20 packhorses to carry their food for one day. One horse occupies roughly 2.5 metres (2.75 yards) of road so these 20 horses would take up 50 metres (55 yards) in single file.

There would also need to be fodder for horses as there was unlikely to be sufficient grazing along the way and each mounted man could have had several horses. The pack or draught animals could have been allowed to graze as their condition was less critical than that of warhorses but there may have had to be fodder for them, too. A horse would have consumed around 11kg (24.2lb) of grain and fodder a day.

Pack animals had several disadvantages. They could not carry large or ungainly loads, their loads had to be carefully balanced and they had to be unloaded at night and during any lengthy halts. Their great advantage was that they could go anywhere a man on foot could go.

Carts and wagons could carry proportionately more than pack animals. Ladder-sided carts drawn by two horses are shown in the *Maciejowski Bible* and other illustrations. These carts may have been able to carry 450kg (990lb) enough to feed 450 men for one day.

By the thirteenth century the padded horse-collar and harness had made the horse the preferred beast for pulling wagons. By 1265 wagons usually had a pair of shafts rather than the single draft pole (still found on carts); the whippletree, a traverse bar pivoted in the middle and positioned in front of the wagon made driving easier; the front axle was pivoted, providing a tighter turning circle and greater manoeuvrability. Horseshoes fixed by nails, common by the eleventh century, were universal by 1265. Allied to this, cargoes were carried in tight-fitting and durable kegs and barrels.

These improvements in horseshoes and harness meant that a single horse could draw a load of up to 900kg (1,980lb) although not for a sustained period. The better harness and linkages meant that horses could be linked to wagons in teams and, by 1265, four-wheeled wagons with swivelling front axles were replacing two-wheeled carts.

If carts or wagons were available the armour of the senior ranks would be carried in them, the pieces perhaps carefully wrapped and padded and locked into chests or barrels. Other soldiers, mounted and on foot, had to carry their armour, along with any spares, blankets and rations for one day. Food was essential, together with casks of wine and ale. There also had to be room for crossbow quarrels and arrows along with spare shafts and heads. Mobile forges and anvils were needed by the smiths and armourers and farriers. The wealthier men would have had bedding and tents, folding chairs, beds, sideboards, chests of various sizes, all carried as part of the army's impedimenta.

Despite the improvements in vehicle design and cargo packaging, commanders continued to have transport problems. Good carts and wagons were not always available. Horses were not always available. Often oxen (usually bullocks but any bovine creature could be pressed into service) had to be harnessed to wagons, which reduced their endurance. Even the best-made wagon was hindered by the unmade roads of the thirteenth century, especially when rain turned the surface to mud and filled the potholes with water. Nevertheless, under the right conditions, wagons made a tremendous difference to an army's logistics.

The speed of movement of an army was limited by the number travelling on foot and by the width and state of the roads, such as they were, the time it took to pack up and get on the road in the morning and to pitch camp and eat in the evening. We cannot say with any confidence how much road construction and maintenance took place in the thirteenth century, although in England royal roads were supposed to be regularly maintained. They were to be wide enough for two carts or wagons to pass or for 16 horsemen to ride abreast.

For a fully-manned army, with its supply train, daily distances would have been around 25 kilometres (15.5 miles) and there would have been an occasional day of rest and repairs. Allow 150 kilometres (93 miles) a week, which is similar to the distances covered in the European portion of journeys to the Holy Land during the Crusades. See also chapter 7.

Too elaborate a supply train could hinder a military operation, if speed and mobility were paramount. A raiding force, for example, would expect to subsist on forage and pillage. Supply was always a constraint on the size and mobility of armies and the effort to maintain a large army on a campaign over time was enormous. The risk of taking an army into the presence of the enemy was also enormous so Edward wanted to ensure that he had the odds on his side and that his men were well-supplied with food and drink.

6. The Armies

At this point I have to face the challenge of assessing the strength and composition of the two armies at Evesham. As a wargamer of old I am aware that I am taking the lid off a can of worms and whatever figures I posit here will be challenged often and vigorously (I hope!).

Edward and the Marchers

It is possible to set an upper estimate for the size of the 'Marcher' army at Evesham. In 1277 Edward I committed 15,500 men in Wales and he raised around 20,000 men for the war of 1282-3. He fought the rebellion of 1287 with 17,000 men and the 1294-5 rebellion with 31,000 men. All of these were total figures for the campaign; not all were raised at the same time, contingents were disbanded when no longer needed and others were raised as needed.

Edward raised 7,800 men for the Flemish Campaign of 1297 and 26,000 for the Falkirk Campaign of 1298, although the numbers were soon reduced by desertion. These were large armies, raised over time with funds provided by parliament and other sources. The army at Evesham, largely raised from the retinues and followers of the Marcher lords, is likely to have been no larger than the lower end of these numbers.

Looking at the composition of armies during the thirteenth century and taking into account Edward's speed of movement during the campaign, I am going to guess that he led an agile force of no more than 8,000 effectives including around 1,000 mounted men. Most of these would have been knights and sergeants. However, in the Welsh Marches, there were free but non-knightly 'riding men' who may have been light horse or mounted foot soldiers. Taking representative ratios from thirteenth-century armies, I am going to suggest that the Marchers' army consisted of 350 lords and knights, 700 sergeants and riding men and 7000 foot-soldiers.

From whence came the Marcher army? I call Edward's army 'Marcher' because the Marcher lords were the main source of its strength. A great lord could levy as many men as he could afford from his lands and these formed the core of Edward's army. Some of the lords' vassals owed him service for their lands but there was no fixed norm or quota. The Marcher barons frequently responded to Edward's summonses with more knights than they owed. Ruling their little kingdoms on the hostile frontier they maintained forces to match the threat they routinely faced and de Mortimer and de Clare had two factors to encourage them: service freely given in a time of crisis was a guarantee of future political influence and each had a profound grudge, personal or political, against Earl Simon. Honour had to be satisfied by deploying all but a skeleton force left behind to hold the border castles.

Assembling such an army depended on the length of time available, the urgency and the size of the army to be mustered. If the various contingents of the army had to be summoned from widely-separated locations it could take a couple of weeks to gather the available men to a central location, counting the time taken to send out a summons by messenger, to prepare the contingents and to march them back to the appointed rendezvous. The Marcher lords would have despatched groups of riders who spread out to round up the available men.

In more normal times the heart of the royal forces would have been the royal household, the *familia regis*, a small but professional permanent fighting force that served at court. Other household troops garrisoned royal castles and important cities. With the king in de Montfort's custody the household men were likely to have taken themselves home to avoid serving de Montfort or might have deserted their king to serve his son.

Service in the king's army was increasingly being replaced by the payment of *scutage* or 'shield money', which allowed the monarch to hire better trained and more effective professional soldiers while the feudal aristocracy continued to provide a small military elite as well as constituting the military leadership. However, this transition was by no means complete, particularly on the Marches, where a raiding force or even an invasion might appear at any time and the Marcher Lords were expected to maintain sufficient forces to see the enemy off and to defend their castles.

Edward would have had access to knights, mounted sergeants and men-at-arms, lighter horsemen for scouting, escorting, pursuit, foraging and raiding, sergeants on foot, spearmen, archers and crossbowmen and men armed with cutting weapons (sundry variations on the theme of 'axe').

Earl Simon and the Montfortians

The bulk of Earl Simon's army seems to have been borrowed from his Welsh ally (see chapter 7). The armies of the Welsh princes, although small, reflected Anglo-Norman practice. Llewelyn had an elite force of household horse and foot – the *teula* – some of whom were itinerate adventurers and all of whom owed their loyalty directly to him as their prince. Their commander, the *pentuela*, was normally one of the prince's sons or other younger close relatives. The elite of the *tuela* wore armour and some may have ridden armoured horses. By 1265 the most prosperous Welsh aristocracy, as well as the *tuela*, were armed and accoutred in much the same manner as their English foes, although perhaps in styles a generation or two old.

Earl Simon would have been hoping to recruit some of Llewelyn's armoured horsemen. Instead he drew men from the general levy of foot from among freeborn landowners. Men were summoned from the age of fourteen and were expected to serve for forty days. Unfree men could volunteer, and they may have been paid.

During the twelfth and thirteenth centuries the Welsh had resisted the Anglo-Norman encroachments by mounting prolonged campaigns of guerrilla warfare. They would exploit the difficult terrain of the wooded, marshy or mountainous Welsh countryside and rarely faced their enemies in open battle. Earl Simon must have wondered how his borrowed infantry would fare against a well-armed Marcher army away from their native terrain. It would have made sense to him to place them ahead of his horsemen where they could be prodded forward by the lances of their temporary allies, absorb the impact of Edward's charge and be ridden down if necessary. His anger when he found them lagging behind the horsemen as they marched out of Evesham is understandable.

The Montfortian mounted men would have been drawn from the retinues of the lords and their attendant knights. If the enrolled accounts of the royal household for the days leading up to the battle were available then we could estimate the number of horses in de Montfort's force from, among other things, the quantities of fodder bought. Without those accounts I am going to leave myself open by making an informed guess.

As mentioned in chapter 4, the Evesham Chronicle is the only source I am aware of that attempts to give a figure for Earl Simon's infantry at Evesham: 6,000 men, mostly Welsh. Had Earl Simon deployed 6,000 infantry he would have been outnumbered only 7:10. With a force of that size he could have stood his ground in

Evesham, where the river that trapped him also protected his flanks, and waited for young Simon to turn up in the rear of the Marcher army. Other chronicles accept that the Montfortians were greatly outnumbered and Melrose is specific: the Marchers had six or seven men to every two of the Montfortians. If we fix the strength of the Marcher army at 8,000 effectives then Earl Simon can have had no more than 3,000 men of whom maybe 400 would have been mounted, counting earls, knights, sergeants and light horse. It seems likely that Llewelyn was able to raise only 1,000-1,500 men to supplement the 1,000-1,500 foot soldiers with Earl Simon, although he may have been assembling reinforcements to follow on. So, again sticking my neck out, I am going to suggest that the Montfortians had no more than 130 lords and knights, 260 sergeants and lighter horsemen and 2,500 infantry.

7. The Road to Worcester

The narrative of the manoeuvrings and machinations that happened between Edward escaping from Hereford on May 28th 1265 and arriving at Worcester with his army on August 1st 1265 is complicated. I find it difficult to follow the manoeuvrings in a campaign without a roadmap so I am going to try to describe the events of these decisive days with the help of a map and a timeline. Numbers and letters in square brackets in the text refer to movements on the map.

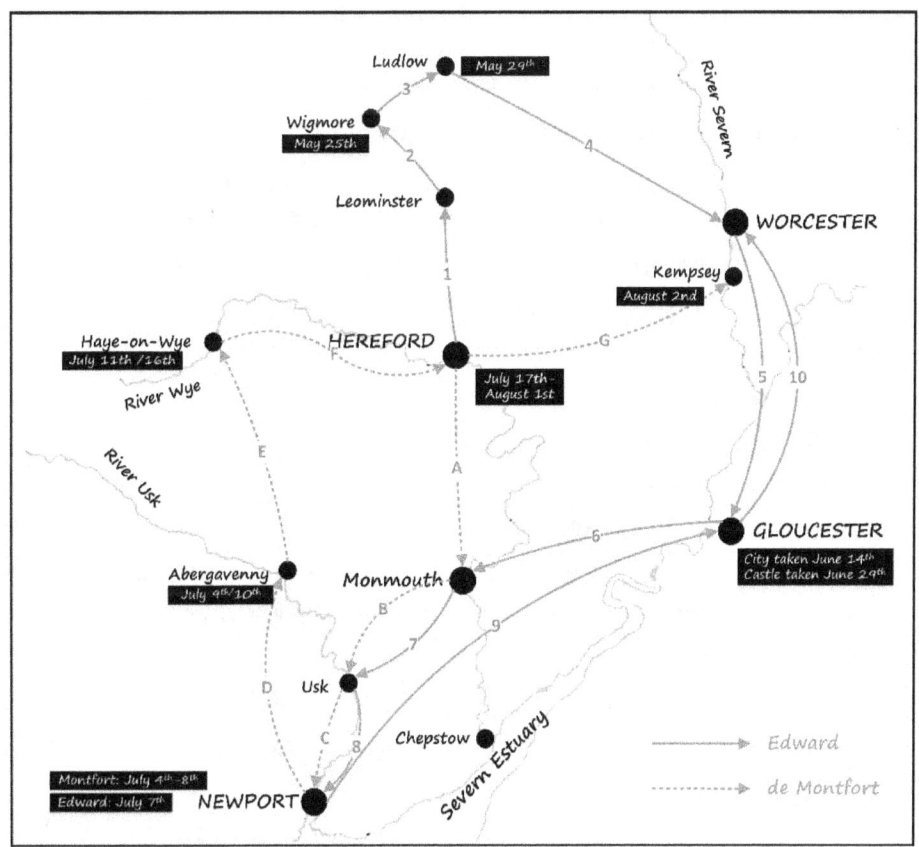

05 Sketch map of the final marches of the Evesham campaign (Source: author)

The two armies covered a lot of ground during the campaign and one question I have been asked on occasion is how fast a medieval army could move. At its simplest the rate at which an army could travel largely depended on the proportion of mounted men in its ranks. Mounted men obviously travelled faster than those on foot. However, the difference might not be as great as one might imagine. Marching on good roads with his arms, armour, equipment and supplies carried on carts, wagons or pack horses, an infantryman could make good time.

Stenton[17] concluded that marching over adequate roads in open terrain a mounted traveller could cover 32 kilometres (20 miles) a day on a sustained march and 48 kilometres to 65 kilometres (30 to 40 miles) a day at a push. Foot travellers and driven herds might cover 13 kilometres to 24 kilometres (8 miles to 15 miles) a day while wheeled traffic might make 8 kilometres to 16 kilometres (5 miles to 10 miles) a day depending on the condition of the road. These figures have generally been accepted ever since Frank Stenton published them.

Having analysed a number of campaigns from this period I am going to hazard the following estimates: a mixed force would be able to march 16 kilometres to 24 kilometres (10 miles to 15 miles) a day over long distances with occasional bursts of 32 kilometres to 40 kilometres (20 miles to 25 miles). Coincidentally that is much the same as for infantry forces up to the days of mechanised transport. Smaller, all mounted, forces could travel a lot faster, as Edward showed before and after his raid on Kenilworth. Such a force could comfortably have covered 48 kilometres to 65 kilometres (30 miles to 40 miles) a day.

For Edward's campaign against his uncle, Simon de Montfort, average rates of march are less important than the forced marches made to counter the earl's movements. Both sides seem to have made maximum use of the best roads available. Roads would have helped them to move long distances quickly but they were a double-edged sword, restricting movement along known routes and making it easier to predict an enemy's movements.

May 28th. Having slipped the leash Edward rode to Leominster **[1]** where he was met by a mounted force, sent by de Mortimer, which escorted him to Wigmore castle **[2]**.

May 29th. Losing no time, Edward met de Clare at Ludlow **[3]** on the following day, reached an accommodation with him and agreed to raise an army. John de Warenne and William de Valence, who had landed at Pembroke, putting an end to their self-imposed exile in France, arrived and joined the alliance.

---

[17] Stenton, Frank, *The Road System of Medieval England*, English Historical Review 7 (1936)

May 30th. In response to these threats Earl Simon summoned an army to muster at Worcester.

June 7th. Matters started to go awry for Earl Simon. Edward captured Worcester **[4]** and broke its bridges across the Severn. With his little force trapped on the wrong side of the river Earl Simon transferred the rendezvous for his army to Gloucester.

June 12th. Short of manpower and cut off from his recruiting grounds Earl Simon opened negotiations with Llewelyn, Prince of North Wales, at Pipton near Glasbury. These negotiations would last until **June 19th** and, although they resulted in Earl Simon being able to add a force of foot soldiers to his little army, the distraction of the negotiations allowed Edward a free hand.

June 14th. The Marchers took Gloucester **[5]** and closed the city's bridge over the Severn. They did not take Gloucester castle, on the eastern bank of the Severn, but invested it to keep the Montfortian garrison from escaping.

June 24th. With his reinforced army Earl Simon moved to Monmouth **[A]**, with the king in tow, intending to reach Newport where he expected to be able to find ships that would ferry his force across the Severn estuary to Bristol. However, he was not able to move on immediately as John Giffard, an ally of de Montfort at the Battle of Lewes who had subsequently swapped sides, had orders to delay de Montfort's army at Monmouth.

June 29th. Gloucester castle surrendered on terms to the Marchers. Edward enhanced his reputation for integrity and fair play by violating the terms of surrender and executing some of the garrison.

July 2nd. Having dealt with Giffard the Montfortians were able to press on and arrived at Usk **[B]** where de Clare's castle fell to the Montfortians almost as soon as they had arrived. Meanwhile the Marchers, in hot pursuit, had arrived at Monmouth **[6]**.

July 4th. Two days later the Montfortians arrived at Newport **[C]** leaving Edward and de Clare to recover Usk **[7]**.

Edward's intelligence network was working well. He soon became aware of the Montfortians' reason for visiting Newport. To counter it the Marchers assembled a makeshift fleet that intercepted the flotilla coming from Bristol to ferry the Montfortians across the Severn, destroying many of the vessels and scattering the rest.

July 7th. Having closed the Montfortians' escape route Edward and his army appeared outside Newport on the east bank of the Usk **[8]**. Earl Simon immediately had the bridge across the river burned and prepared to withdraw from Newport under cover of darkness.

July 8th. In the early hours of the morning the Montfortians left Newport unmolested and took the road for Abergavenny. Balked of his prey Edward took the Marcher army back to Gloucester **[9]**.

July 9th. The Montfortians marched via Pontypool to avoid the Marcher garrison at Usk and arrived in Abergavenny **[D]**.

July 11th. Earl Simon led his men out on the road to Hay-on-Wye **[E]**. It is not clear whether they crossed the Black Mountains or went around them but, either way, it was a remarkable feat of endurance.

July 16th. The Montfortian forces set out from Haye-on-Wye, marched to Hereford and as far beyond as Leominster, but were unable to find the Marcher army because the strategic situation had begun to swing in Earl Simon's favour. On **July 18th** Simon and the king arrived in Hereford **[F]** and took up temporary residence, not leaving until it was time to seek out the younger Simon **[G]**.

The younger Simon de Montfort had meanwhile been assembling an army in London, a city that was favourably disposed toward the baronial cause. From London he headed west in anticipation of joining up with his father once Earl Simon had crossed the Severn. He arrived in Winchester on **July 16th**, while his father's troops were marching on Hereford. His army sacked Winchester and stayed there for two days while young Simon tried to ascertain his father's intentions and discovered that the elder de Montfort was still on the western bank of the Severn. He moved his army to Oxford and stayed for three days while his *scurriers* (scouts) felt out Gloucester's defences to see if he could force a crossing over the Severn to join his father. Thwarted by the strength of Gloucester's defences he swung his army up through Northampton and headed for the family's stronghold at Kenilworth, arriving after sunset on **Friday, July 31st**.

Although he had not been able to join up with his father the younger Simon's probe at Gloucester had caused Edward to pull his forces back to Worcester **[10]** where they were now standing between the two Montfortian armies. This was dangerous for Edward. If the two Simons could have coordinated their actions they might have trapped him between them and destroyed the Marcher army. As it was, the elder Simon could now return to Hereford and look for ways to unite the two armies.

It is not clear whether Simon junior chose Kenilworth for himself or was obeying his father's instructions when he marched his army there. Either way it was a sensible objective, a powerful stronghold (it proved its strength during the siege of 1266) in the heart of England. It was 58 kilometres (34 miles) from Worcester and 98 kilometres (61 miles) from Hereford so they were close enough for messengers to pass between the two armies.

To summarise: by July 31st 1265 Lord Edward and the Marcher lords were at Worcester, Simon de Montfort was at Hereford with one Montfortian army (including his contingent of Llywelyn's spearmen) and his son was at Kenilworth with a rather larger army than the one accompanying his father.

8. Shock at Kenilworth

Lord Edward was now presented with an interesting strategic situation. He was faced with two Montfortian armies separated by 48 to 64 kilometres (30 to 40 miles) and, by virtue of his position at Worcester, he had the advantage of what the military men call 'interior lines'. In other words, although he was in danger of being the filling in a Montfortian sandwich, Lord Edward had an opportunity: if he moved fast enough and decisively enough he might defeat each of the two armies in turn rather than having to face a united Montfortian army.

So why did Edward choose to attack the younger Simon and his army at Kenilworth rather than trying conclusions with Earl Simon? The Kenilworth army was believed to be numerically stronger than the elder de Montfort's army but it was led by an inexperienced young man rather than by the old fox himself. Tindal[18] states, based on Knighton[19], that young Simon had gathered a force to the strength of 'twenty bannerets, and a great number of the commonality'. A banneret usually led a troop of 10-12 knights bachelor, occasionally up to 20. So if we allow each troop 12 men, including the banneret, we might have 240 lords and knights, 480 lesser mounted men and 4800 foot soldiers, a respectable force.

There was also the question of the River Severn. The Kenilworth army was on the same bank of the Severn as Edward's army. To attack Earl Simon Edward was likely to have to cross the river and operate on Earl Simon's bank. Edward's strategy then is clear: attack the larger but less well-led force first and then return to try to crack the tougher nut on his own terms.

Vegetius[20] had written: *courage is worth more than numbers, and speed is worth more than courage.* Edward may have picked this up during discussion or he may have read it for himself. Either way he understood the value of surprise and, to achieve it, he had examples before him of commanders, such as Julius Caesar, who

---

[18] The History and Antiquities of the Abbey and Borough of Evesham, William Tindal, London, 1794

[19] Henry Knighton, Augustinian canon at the abbey of St Mary of the Meadows, Leicester, wrote a four-volume chronicle, first published in 1652, giving the history of England from 959 to 1366

[20] A late Latin writer, Publius Flavius Vegetius Renatus composed *De re militari* (La. 'Concerning Military Matters'), a treatise about Roman warfare and military principles that was widely admired as a 'how to do it' book in the Middle Ages, even though the extant text dates to the fifth century

had marched at night and split their forces. Heeding the lessons taught by those commanders of old he would have insisted on discipline and his scouts would have been joined by local guides and informers to keep the raiding force to its route and to prevent surprise. Everything would have been done to take the enemy off guard.

If a force had to stay in one place for any length of time it would try to move into a nearby castle (Kenilworth castle in this case). Otherwise the force had to occupy temporary quarters, a combination of billeting and camping. Camping was probably the more important and more common. At Kenilworth, the younger Simon's army would have camped behind the walls of the priory or in the surrounding fields with the luckier men billeted on the townspeople.

Jan Cooper, chair of the Kenilworth History and Archaeology Society argues persuasively that, at most, only a small part of the Montfortian army – possibly only the leaders - could have been lodged inside the grounds of the priory. She writes: 'although [the priory] was a twenty-acre site there were a lot of buildings on it which are no longer there, Priory Pool was much larger and there were also orchards and vineyards. It seems unlikely that the prior would be comfortable in allowing a lot of, probably, drunken soldiers (with their female camp followers) to camp within his priory. They were probably scattered around the town area, with some near the Mere. Edward's spies obviously knew what was happening and it would certainly be easier to surprise and overpower smaller clusters.' I cannot refute Jan's logic; nevertheless, I believe that at least the elite of the army would have been entertained by the prior inside the walls of the priory.

Looking at the timetable of the operation from 750 years in the future it scarcely seems possible that a medieval army could perform such a feat. Edward's force covered the 55 kilometres (34 miles) from Worcester to Kenilworth in six to seven hours, an average of 8-9 kilometres (5-6 miles) an hour. They travelled to Kenilworth, carried out the raid and were back at Worcester by the early hours of August 3rd.

Mounted troops of this period were expected to be able to cover around 40 kilometres (25 miles) a day. The comparable rate for infantry was 24 kilometres (15 miles) a day. So is it possible that Edward marched some or all of his infantry to Kenilworth? Not if this timetable is accurate, and the *Evesham Chronicle*[21] seems to

---

[21] Osney, Wykes, Trivet & The Evesham Chronicle: Four Accounts of the Battle of Evesham, The Simon de Montfort Society, 2015

support this view. According to the *Chronicle* Edward's entire army marched out of Worcester as if heading for Shrewsbury. However, this was a deception; when they reached the road to Kenilworth Edward had his wagons and foot soldiers continue some distance on the road toward Shrewsbury while he led a cavalry raid using his knights, mounted sergeants, light horse and, possibly, some foot soldiers double-mounted behind the lighter horsemen or riding spare horses. It is known from indentures that knights, sergeants and men-at-arms were expected to attend for military service with extra mounts if they could afford them. It would not have been beyond Edward's wit to mount some of his infantry (who, coming from a predominantly agricultural society, would have been familiar with horses) to add weight to the blow that he was aiming at the younger Simon. The raiding force was at Kenilworth by 0445 hrs on the morning of August 2nd, just as dawn broke.

The Domesday survey of 1086 lists two 'Kenilworths'. *Optone* (Up Town, comprising the current Little Virginia, High Street and New Street) appears as: *'Albert the clerk holds four hides of the king, in alms. There are two priests, with two ploughs, ten among the villeins, and the bordars have four ploughs. Wood half-a-mile* (805m) *long and three furlongs* (603m) *broad.'* The older part of town, *Chinewrde*, along both sides of the present Warwick Road, south of the clock tower, appears as: *'In Chinewrde, Richard the Forester holds three virgates* (36 hectares or 90 acres) *of land of the king. There are ten villeins, and seven bordars have three ploughs. Wood half-a-mile* (805m) *long and four furlongs broad* (804m) *broad. These two members lie in the king's manor of Stoneley.'* Two small but thriving settlements that would soon be further separated by the establishment of the Priory of St Mary. Redevelopment has completely erased the older part of Kenilworth but in Optone it is still possible, with a little imagination, to see where the bones of medieval Kenilworth show through.

Figure 07 provides an idea of the layout of Kenilworth in 1265. The two anchor points of the town were the castle to the west and St Mary's Priory (later elevated to the dignity of an abbey) to the east. Optone contained homes and other premises and would have included a malt-house, a pound for stray animals, a village oven, inns, alehouses and other places of resort for thirsty soldiers.

The castle was founded in the early 1120s by Geoffrey de Clinton, Lord Chamberlain to Henry I, probably with a motte and bailey layout but benefitting from a stone tower. Contemporaries considered it to be well defended. The castle passed into the possession of the crown and King John spent £1,115 (over £11,000,000 in today's value) on the castle between 1210 and 1216, adding a stone outer bailey wall, creating Mortimer's and Lunn's Towers and strengthening other features.

John was also responsible for improving the castle's elaborate water defences, originally created by damming the Finham and Inchford Brooks to create the Great Mere. He left Kenilworth one of the largest English castles, with one of the largest artificial lake defences of the time. So powerful was the castle that John was forced to cede possession of it to the baronial opposition as part of the provisions to guarantee the Magna Carta. It reverted to royal control early in the reign of his son, Henry III, and Henry granted it to his sister, Eleanor, and thereby to Simon de Montfort, in 1244. The Great Mere covered the western side of the castle and curved around to defend the southern front. A moat protected the northern and eastern sides and the eastern side was further protected by the castle pool and the lake belonging to the priory, of which only a fragment remains today. This was not intended to be a defence but a source of fish for the monastic diet. Nevertheless, it acted as an obstacle to approach from that side.

The raiding force took cover in a ravine (to date unidentified) outside Kenilworth and Edward sent scouts to report on the disposition of de Montfort's forces. When they returned, their news delighted him: instead of entering the castle and camping in the great bailey young Simon's army was camped in the grounds of the priory or in the surrounding fields, or had dispersed through the town taking whatever shelter they could find. No doubt many of the men would have gone in search of ale, food and other comforts.

Young Simon has been criticised for not accommodating his army in the security of the castle. However, before judging him too harshly, we need to be aware of a couple of facts. First, recent archaeological investigation has revealed that the whole of the priory's 28 hectare (70 acre) *demesne* appears to have been surrounded by a defensive wall. Where fragments of the wall survive, an examination of the foundations suggests that the wall stood 4 metres (12 feet) high, entered by a single gateway. It was not a castle but it was a secure camping ground and provided more space for at least his senior followers to camp in than the castle's more restricted *enceinte*.

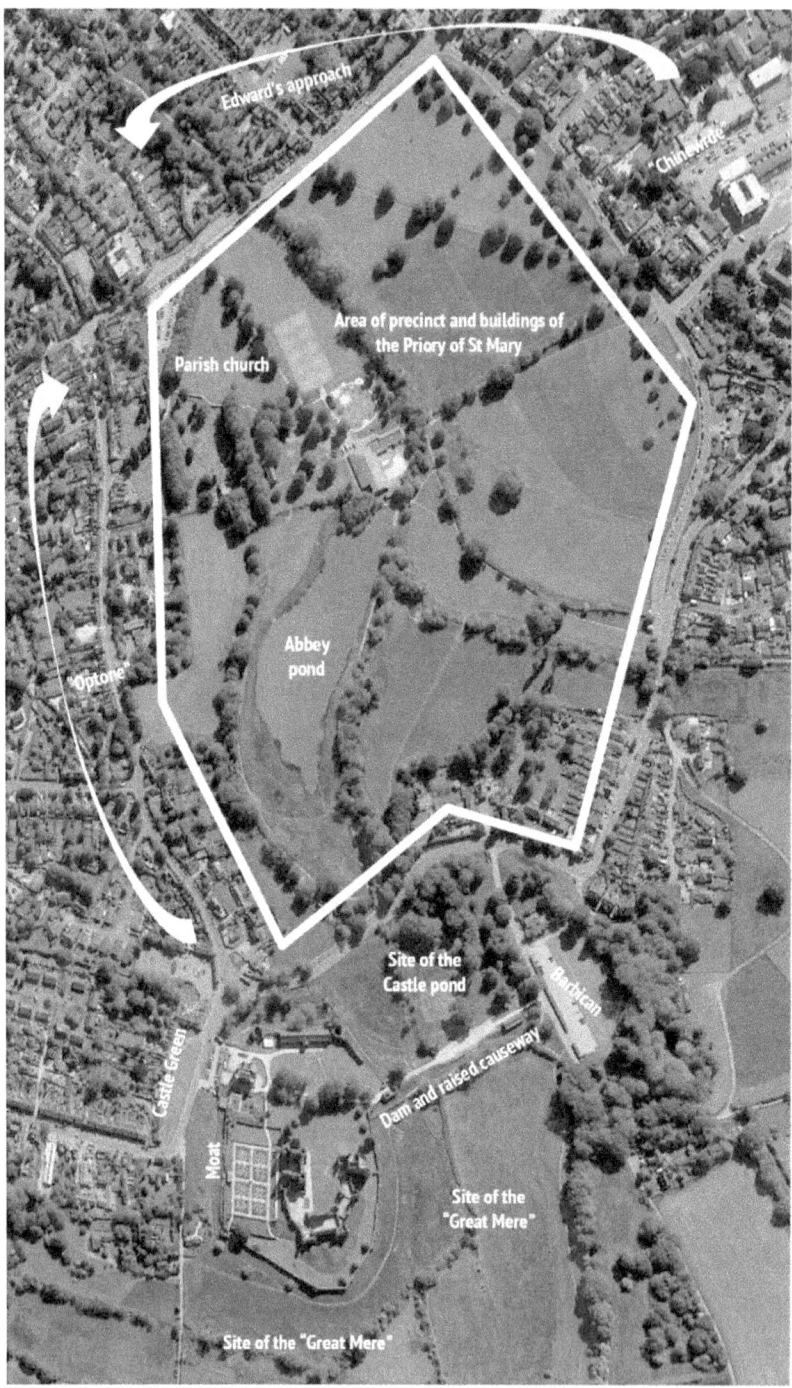

06 Aerial view of Kenilworth showing the extent of the priory's *demesne*, the position of the castle, location of the medieval town and conjectural route of Lord Edward's approach on August 2nd 1265 (source: Google Earth)

There was another reason for camping in the town and priory rather than in the castle. An army, even a friendly army, devastated the area where it bivouacked. It would have taken the castle months, maybe years, to recover from their visit. As the castle would have been fully garrisoned at that time the constable may have resisted having an army billeted on him. Better to let the town and the priory bear the cost and inconvenience of accommodating the army (and of entertaining young Simon and his senior men in the priory's guest lodgings) than to burden his father's estate.

Again quoting Knighton, Tindal tells us that Edward maintained a female spy called Margoth who was probably the lover of Ralph de Arderne, a young man in the service of young Simon, and a skilled intelligencer. Tindal tells us that Edward: 'departed from Worcester by night, with such force as he deemed sufficient, and halted in a deep valley near Kenilworth, which his spy had pointed out to him as a proper place to prepare for the attack.' This remarkable woman may have been in Worcester when Edward was planning his raid and taken along as a guide.

Reliable reconnaissance, scouts and pickets were used and valued by every professional commander. However, if young Simon had put out sentries and pickets Edward's men either avoided them or silenced them so the surprise was complete.

Tindal has a confusing detail. He tells us that Edward had a scare:

'During this preparation a great clamour, which seemed to proceed from the enemy's camp, gave a sudden alarm to his little troop. Concluding that young Montfort had been apprised of the ambuscade, and was hastening to frustrate his intentions, in great haste and trepidation they drew up, in the best order they were able, and advanced to meet him.'

It proved to be a false alarm:

'The alarm soon ceased, when they perceived the long baggage-wagons of young Montfort's army, coming forth in quest of provisions. These they immediately attacked; and taking the escort prisoners, appropriated the horses, which they wanted, to their own use.'[22]

If the noise of this skirmish did not alert the men in Kenilworth, then Edward must have stationed his force a good way from the town. Having taken part in

---

[22] 'The History and Antiquities of the Abbey and Borough of Evesham,' Evesham, 1794, 4to.

nighttime patrols in days long gone by I know how sound travels at night and this incident is not credible. Certainly, Edward might have wanted horses. If his mounted troops had carried foot soldiers double mounted behind them, then they would have welcomed the chance to get rid of them. However, there is another interpretation. The convoy was most likely to have taken the road through Chinewrde toward Warwick, passing Edward's hiding place. Edward had his men saddle up and headed into Optone toward the gateway of the priory, with the noise and disruption of the departing convoy masking his approach. Another view, which I find attractive although I have no evidence for it, is that Edward waited for the convoy to return to the priory and tagged along behind, gaining access to the priory when the gate was opened to admit the carts and wagons. Referring to the supply convoy Burne suggests that the defenders may have been distracted by its arrival at Kenilworth at around the same time Edward's army turned up.

A future generation of warriors would call what happened next 'beating up the enemy's quarters'. The attacker would not expect to inflict a decisive defeat on the enemy, not even to inflict a large number of casualties, although every opportunity would be taken to do so, but he would aim to obtain a moral ascendancy over the enemy's men by panicking them, scattering them and showing that the attacker could strike at them whenever and wherever he chose.

Robert of Gloucester describes the raid in these words:

'Prince Edward's troops fell upon Simon's army, giving them a rude awakening, finding them in their beds as they entered the town. With no warning, they slew many before they could dress, and others were captured.'[23]

Simon's men fled as Edward's mass of horsemen erupted out of the dark, abandoning weapons, armour, clothes, even their standards. The good folk of Kenilworth barred their doors and hid under their beds and in their cellars. Some of de Montfort's men would have sought refuge in the priory church or the parish church; others would have tried to make it to the castle. The majority would have fled into the surrounding countryside and found whatever cover they could. Young Simon escaped to the shelter of the castle's walls and left Edward's horsemen to

---

[23] Wright, William Aldis ed., The Metrical Chronicle of Robert of Gloucester. 2 vols. Rolls Series 86 (London, 1887)

rampage through the town and the priory demesne. Tindal says that Edward took fifteen standards as trophies and 'a prodigious booty'.

A number of leading Montfortians were captured, including Richard de Grey, Adam of Newmarket and Baldwin Wake. One of the few who we know died was Stephen de Holwell, de Montfort's clerk. He was dragged out of either the abbey church or the parish church of St Nicholas and beheaded on de Clare's orders, possibly because he had been previously engaged by de Montfort to help resolve his territorial disputes with de Clare (in de Montfort's favour)[24].

Although it was a well-planned and brilliantly executed operation, it is possible to over-estimate the effects of Edward's raid. Young Simon's men suffered few casualties, he was able to rally a substantial portion of his army quickly and continue his march south, and Edward's men had had little time to burn supplies or destroy materiel. However, as Edward's cavalry cantered away from Kenilworth, taking young Simon's abandoned standards as trophies, they could take satisfaction in having achieved three objectives. Young Simon's army had been badly shaken, it had been weakened (not all of the refugees would return) and, most importantly in Edward's eyes, they had gained a window of opportunity to defeat Earl Simon before they had to deal permanently with his son.

---

[24] CPR, 1258-66, page 479; Ann. Lond., page 68. Chron. Melrose, into A.O. and M.O. Anderson, page 130; Chron. Mailros, e4d. Stevenson, pages 198-9

9. The Approach to Evesham

Lord Edward had called in his cavalry patrols on the banks of the Severn to strengthen the mounted force that he sent to Kenilworth. When Earl Simon moved out from Hereford in the early hours of August 2nd, intending to join up with his son, he might have expected the far banks of the river to be patrolled or defended. Instead he found that the enemy had gone and he was able to cross at Kempsey, four miles south of Worcester, unmolested. The sources say that he crossed by boat which must have taken most of the day even for his small force. However, after making two forced marches and fighting a battle Edward's force would have been in no condition to mount an immediate operation against Earl Simon.

All the signs are that Earl Simon was leading his army to join the larger Montfortian force which he appears to have known was stationed at Kenilworth. The most direct route to Kenilworth would have been through Alcester but the direct route to Alcester would have taken Earl Simon's army within 4.8 kilometres (3 miles) of the enemy. There is no evidence from the contemporary sources that Earl Simon contacted his son at Kenilworth and asked him to move south. It is possible that the attack at Kenilworth galvanised young Simon into action and, having rallied as much of his force as he could within a short space of time, he hurried south to meet his father without waiting for him to reach Kenilworth. At the same time Earl Simon might have sent messengers to his son asking him to join but leaving the choice of route to the younger Simon.

In Charles Oman's reconstruction[25] the Marcher army set out from Worcester in three columns and Edward led his force through Flyford Flavell and Dunnington before turning south to Evesham. De Clare approached Evesham from the north-west by way of Wyre and Fladbury. De Mortimer approached Evesham by Pershore, following the outside of the south end of the Avon, arriving at what is now Bengeworth bridge.

The point of blocking the roads to the north of Evesham was to prevent the junction of the two Montfortian armies. However, there was another consideration:

---

[25] A History of the Art of War in the Middle Ages, Vol. I: A.D. 378–1278 (1898; 2nd ed. 1924)

Earl Simon could head back toward Wales or hurry toward London. Sending Mortimer along the lower road behind de Montfort would enable him to block the Bengeworth bridge and seal off both the road to London and the way to Wales. Edward would still cross the Avon at Offenham with his own and de Clare's contingents and ascend Greenhill.

David Cox has examined a reference by the Evesham Chronicler to: 'a place called Sineldestone' and identified it as Siflaed's stone, an ancient boundary marker 210 metres (230 yards) west of the Avon at the top of a road, the surviving portion of which is now Blayney's Lane, that ran up from the crossing at Offenham to Greenhill. If Edward crossed the Avon at Offenham this was his most direct route up Greenhill.

It is not clear who Siflaed was. There is a record of an Anglo-Saxon woman called Siflaed who lived in Norfolk in the late tenth/early eleventh centuries. Having left her property to Bury St Edmunds Abbey she went overseas on pilgrimage. Did she visit Evesham on her return? Beyond the fact that Bury St Edmunds and Evesham Abbeys had Benedictine communities there is nothing to link Siflaed to Evesham. However, the Siflaed of 'stone' fame seems to have been a woman of substance, possibly the owner of the land around Siveldeston and possibly down to the River Avon.

Guisborough[26] states that when the royal army was first spotted, they were approaching from three different sides which would suggest that Edward had not yet crossed the Avon.

Given the lack of radio communications in 1265 it would not even have occurred to Edward that he could split his army into three divisions, march them across country by different routes and expect them to assemble at Evesham at the same time. The royal army approaching Evesham from three sides does not necessarily mean that they travelled by three night marches. It is likely that Edward kept his army together until he was sure of de Montfort's intentions.

In spite of Wyke's assertion about Margoth, Edward's cross-dressing female spy, he cannot have had an exact knowledge of de Montfort's movements or intentions. Throughout the night of August 3rd/4th the two armies were close. The Montfortians advanced along the present B4084, as described, while the royal army marched along the present A44 on the other bank of the Avon. Under this analysis, when the

---

[26] His *The Chronicle of Walter of Guisborough* covers the period of English history from the Conquest (1066) to the nineteenth year of Edward III, with the exception of the years 1316-1326

royal army reached Fladbury three miles west of Evesham, Mortimer's division was detached, crossed the Avon at Cropthorne ford and followed de Montfort's army to Evesham. Edward and de Clare left the A44 and headed north to join the Alcester road at Norton, two miles north of Evesham. Edward left de Clare there and struck out north-east another two and a half miles, fording the Avon at Cleeve Prior.

If Edward were keen to conceal his presence and intentions then crossing the river at Offenham, in sight of the town, would have been risky with the possibility of de Montfort cutting and running before the trap was closed.

This was the most likely interpretation of the events of the day until Labordiere's New Account was discovered. Much of the earlier interpretation remains. The Montfortians left Kempsey and approached Evesham along the B4084. The Marcher army pursued him along the A44 on the other bank of the Avon. At Mosham Meadow the army came to a halt so that the long column of men straggling back along the Worcester road could assemble ready to be deployed.

10. Mosham Meadow

The *New Account*, supported by de Nangis's account, tells us that:

'Meanwhile, Sir Edward and Sir Gilbert de Clare, Earl of Gloucester, had knighted several men in the meadow called Mosham between Craycombe and Evesham.'

Craycombe can be identified on a modern OS map (OS Grid Reference: SP006474) on the bank of the Avon at the foot of Craycombe Hill a short way to the west of the hotel, retirement village and BBC Centre at Wood Norton. Mosham Meadow is an area of ancient water meadow between Craycombe and Wood Norton.

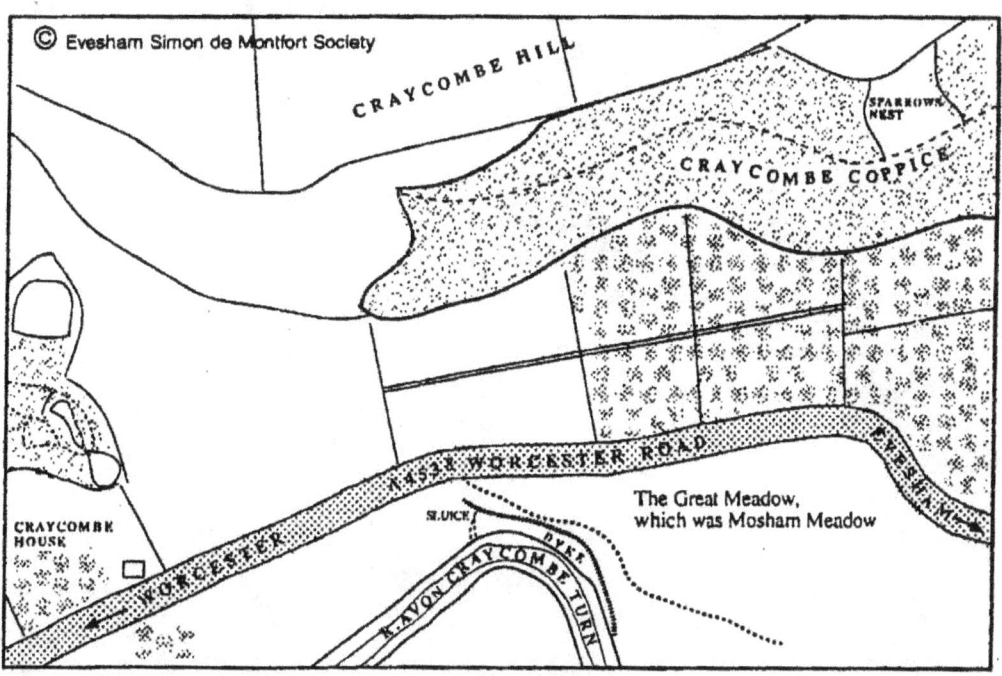

07 The location of Mosham Meadow (Source: The Simon de Montfort Society)

On the approach from Worcester the lords and knights would not have been riding their *destriers* or 'high horses' which were reserved for the battle and not to be tired on the march. Instead the members of the mounted élite rode palfreys, their ordinary travelling horses. Nor are they likely to have been wearing full armour all the time, to avoid sapping the strength of the men. As they were in dangerous territory they would probably have worn their hauberks and carried their shields and

08 Two views of Mosham Meadow (author's photographs)

swords, with their lances and helmets in the hands of their squires and any remaining pieces of armour on their pack horses.

They would not have put on their helmets or taken up their lances until within sight of the enemy. The squires would have ridden ahead of their knights, leading the baggage horses. At Mosham Meadow the squires would have helped their knights to don the rest of their armour before deploying onto Edward's chosen battlefield.

It was here that the *New Account* adds a new detail about Lord Edward's involvement in Earl Simon's death. Did Edward want his godfather, former ally and uncle by marriage, dead? Guisborough plainly states that Edward was away from the battlefield when Earl Simon was killed with the obvious implication that Edward was not involved in de Montfort's death. However, the *New Account* says that when Lord Edward and de Clare arrived at Mosham Meadow they:

'... had chosen and designated twelve of the strongest and most intrepid men-at-arms; and they knew that they were to kill the Earl of Leicester and break through the ranks forcibly and rapidly in such a way that they would look at no one not let anyone come between them until they reached the person of the earl ...'

There is only one interpretation of this passage: the writer believed that Edward had deliberately formed a 'death squad' to kill de Montfort. If this was so, then Edward acted contrary to knightly ethics.

Having drawn up his men Edward moved to The Squires.

11. Evesham and the Battlefield

I am going to take a look at the contours of the ground and the various viewpoints offered to the commanders, the form and lie of the land that dictated to some extent the deployment of the two forces and influenced the decisions to defend or attack. The nature of the ground at Greenhill decided the Marchers' minor tactics and gave them an idea of where to position the various types of soldier. We will need an idea of the capacity of the battlefield to accommodate the frontages of the battles, and to allow the execution of manoeuvres, before we look at the deployment and operation of the armies.

It is also useful to know what the condition of the ground was likely to have been in on August 4th 1265, the presence of crops, shrub, trees, ploughed ground and other factors affecting movement. As the battle spilt down the hill and into Evesham itself there is a need to examine the built environment, too. All of which is leading up to me saying that I am going to invest a few pages describing Evesham town, the village of Bengeworth and Greenhill on August 4th 1265, paying special attention to the strategic features present on the day.

We are fortunate in having only a geographically restricted area within which to place the Evesham battlefield: somewhere on the slopes or at the top of Greenhill. At the level of the Offenham crossing of the Avon, Greenhill is 1.6 kilometres (1,750 yards) from river bank to river bank. A little south of this line, on the geographical crest of Greenhill when viewed from Evesham town, it narrows to 1.5 kilometres (1,640 yards). What I am about to write is based on a series of assumptions, which usually sets alarm bells ringing. However, please bear with me while I develop a basis for a possible model for the deployment of the Marcher forces.

Meadows lay along the narrow flood plain of the Avon while open fields may have encompassed much of the remaining area. There is some evidence of ridge and furrow adjacent to Abbey Manor House on aerial photographs taken in the 1940s, but it is unclear how extensive the open fields were or even if this ridge and furrow is of medieval date. To the north, in Lenchwick parish, an area of heath is recorded on an eighteenth-century map, and David Cox has argued that Greenhill may have been common pasture in the thirteenth century.

In the medieval period a single bridge at the south-east side of the town led across the river. From the town the main road led north to Alcester, ascending Greenhill. Branching to the north-west below the hill was the route to Worcester which, at least in 1675 and thus well before the turnpike was created, skirted the lower slopes of the hill and then continued along the north side of the Avon to Worcester. It appears since to have moved slightly lower down the slopes below Abbey Manor due to imparking around the house. On the parish boundary at the north of the parish the Salt Street ran from the Worcester road on the west up onto Greenhill along the line now known as The Squires. There it crossed the Alcester road and ran down what is now Blayney's Lane to cross the Avon over Offenham bridge.

First, a look at the battlefield as it is today.

A Tour of the Evesham Battlefield

Approach Evesham from the north along the ancient B4088, rather than the modern A46, and you will be roughly following the route the young Simon de Montfort intended to take from Kenilworth via Alcester from Arrow, past Dunnington and through Iron Cross, Harvington and Norton to Twyford. Here, at a roundabout on the crest of Greenhill, the road known locally as 'The Squires', part of the A44, joins the Alcester road. The original course of The Squires that Edward's army would have ascended to reach the top of Greenhill, ran a little to the east of the present A44. Part remains.

Turning south to descend Greenhill the first thing you will notice is housing development on both sides of the road. To the east of the road the development is much deeper than the ribbon development to the west, particularly as the road approaches the foot of Greenhill. Near the top of Greenhill, just past the tollhouse at the end of the original 'Squires', Blayney's Lane joins on the left. This is now a pleasant little road that once led down to the Twyford ('Two Ford') crossing place and the island that became known as 'Dead Man's Ait', where it is possible that one ford led from the western bank to the island and a second ford led from the island to the eastern bank, which is now mostly merged with the western bank.

Some authorities claim that part of the Marcher army, having crossed the Avon at Twyford, ascended the hill up Blayney's Lane. A stroll down the lane will take you past the housing and onto agricultural land from which you have a excellent view of the western side of the battlefield. Looking east across the fields you might be able to make out the Bridge Inn that stands on the far bank of the river, slightly to the south of the former crossing place. There is a footpath into the centre of Evesham from here but if you follow it take good boots, especially in wet weather.

Back on Greenhill a small brown heritage sign almost at the top of Blayney's Lane points the way to the 'Evesham Battlefield', in reality only to the four-acre Battlewell conservation site; the whole of the hillside was covered by the battle. The site is at the end of a narrow track that is suitable only for vehicles with adequate ground clearance. It is unmade and normally used only by agricultural vehicles.

The Battlewell site occupies four acres and is returning to something like the condition it was in on that morning in 1265. From it there are excellent views across the eastern half of the battlefield and a marked footpath will take you down to the Worcester road, a continuation of the road the Marchers travelled in pursuit of the Montfortians. Much of the route is permissive so, if you visit, please treat the land with respect. Land use has changed since the thirteenth century and intensive agricultural methods have removed most of the orchards that once stood there and put the scrubland under the plough. The Simon de Montfort Society and The Battlefields Trust have jointly erected an information board near the western entrance to the site.

The deep pit in the ground, waterlogged in wet weather, near the information board is reputed to be the Battlewell itself. Tradition has it that the place where Simon de Montfort died was marked by the appearance of a miraculous spring. However, investigations show that this pit is lined with brick and seems to have been used as an agricultural sump to capture water run-off since the eighteenth century. Did a Georgian farmer reuse the sacred well to store water? There are strong local traditions about the site. However, looking at the development of trees on the site suggests another reading. Other than the trees planted to thicken the hedges and the ancient variety fruit trees planted by the Simon de Montfort Society as part of the Battlewell stewardship agreement with Natural England, the trees on the site seem to have taken root where they can find water all year round. Clumps of trees may indicate the Battlewell, assuming that it was filled in by order of Edward I in a vain attempt to suppress the cult of Simon de Montfort, unofficial saint.

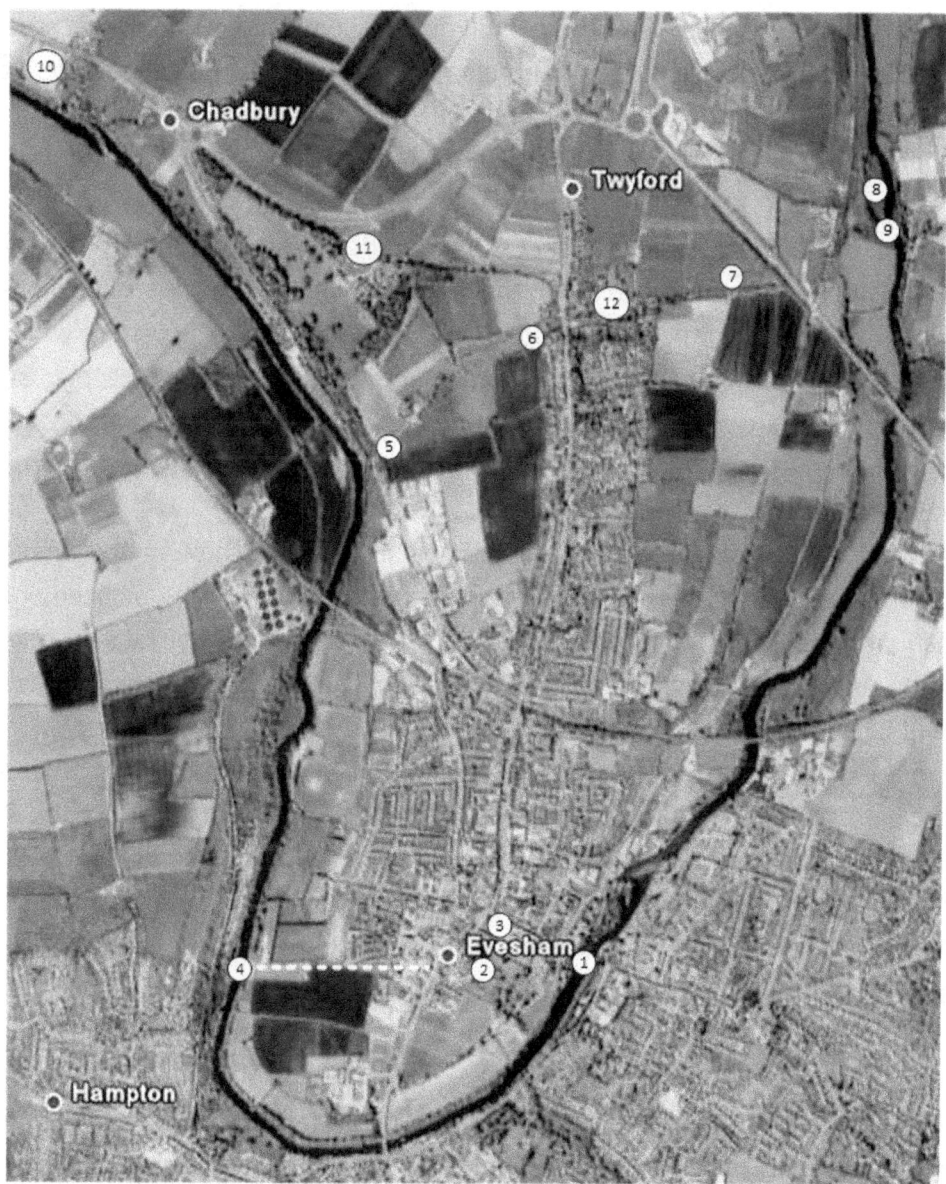

1. Bengeworth Bridge
2. Abbey bell tower
3. St Lawrence's church
4. Abbey foot ferry
5. Obelisk
6. Battlewell
7. Silvedstone
8. "Dead Man's Ait"
9. Twyford bridge/ford
10. Mosham Meadow
11. The Squires
12. Blayney's Lane

- - - - - Site of Evesham Abbey's 12 foot defensive wall

09 Key points of the Battle of Evesham (source: Geomaps)

The road continues to descend Greenhill down a gentle slope until it reaches the former Greenhill School, a pleasant Georgian house to the east of the road. Here the slope becomes appreciably steeper and the road descends for a short distance through a cutting. The ground on the western side of the road is higher than that on the eastern side.

The centre of Evesham is located at map reference NGR SP 038438 in Wychavon District, situated at the junction of the A435 and A44 with extensive modern development to the north, east and south of the historic core. The picture we have of thirteenth-century Evesham comes from analysis of topographic data, published and unpublished archaeological reports, museum collections, primary and secondary historical sources plus historical maps and field data recorded by several project teams.

Most of these materials are in the care of Worcestershire Archive and Archaeology Service, which service has also been responsible for much of the archaeological investigation of Evesham. Other investigations have been carried out by private individuals such as the members of the Rudge family and organisations such as the Vale of Evesham Historical Society.

For the medieval period the available information has been analysed and mapped and drawn together to provide a model of the development of Evesham. The archaeologically-relevant information has been recorded as part of the County Sites and Monuments Record, including specialist assessments of artefacts, standing buildings and documentary sources providing a detailed archaeological framework. The historic core of Evesham contains buried archaeological deposits with the occasional projection above ground of historic buildings. The surviving documentary sources are only moderate in quantity for our period.

Evesham in 1265 was a busy and thriving little town clustered around the great Benedictine abbey of St Mary and St Ecgwine and taking advantage of its position at a strategic crossing place over the River Avon between London, Oxford, Worcester, Hereford and the Welsh Marches. Most of the settlements set up during the period c. AD 500-700 were built on or near riverbanks, providing a permanent source of water. Built inside an easily defended loop of the River Avon, Evesham Abbey benefitted from the proximity of the river and from excellent soil for its own home farm, the Barton.

Evesham lay within the Feckenham Forest which, at its greatest extent, covered most of Worcestershire. To the west it reached as far as the Fore Gate in Worcester; to the north it enclosed Bromsgrove and Redditch and spread as far as The Lickeys. The forest was not entirely wooded ('forest' in this context meaning 'managed land', not necessarily 'wooded land'). The forest was managed for game and timber and seems to have consisted of coppices, lightly wooded pasture, scrubland and cleared fields, providing a model for the Evesham battlefield.

The town sits between 25 metres and 40 metres (75 feet and 100 feet) above sea level and developed on terraces on either side of the river. The area within the loop of the river was divided into the parishes of All Saints and St Lawrence while the parish of Bengeworth lay east of the medieval crossing of the Avon, joined to the town by a bridge built by Evesham Abbey to make the town a favoured crossing point of the Avon.

The minster church of Evesham was established around AD 700 by Ecgwine, bishop of Worcester, possibly on the site of an old sub-Roman British church. Ecgwine's church collapsed and was rebuilt around AD 970 with a new church, dedicated to the Holy Trinity, built between 1017 and 1037 by Earl Leofric (husband of Lady Godiva). Between 1054 and 1055 the Benedictine abbey was reconsecrated, enlarged and equipped with a shrine to the canonised Bishop Ecgwine. The abbey still formed the focal point of the town in 1265.

In 1055 King Edward (the Confessor) granted a port and market at Evesham, which developed its market to sell to pilgrims visiting the shrine of St Ecgwine, and the townspeople were involved in the river trade. Evesham did not have the status of a borough in Domesday Book although there seem to have been a body of reasonably well-off townsmen who may have been market traders. The original medieval marketplace was Merstow Green in front of the main gate of the abbey and now tastefully converted into a car park, the scene of the annual ancient Mop Fair.

The Norman abbey and town developed hand-in-hand. From 1078 the abbey was comprehensively rebuilt by Abbot Walter, the first Norman abbot of Evesham. The mid-eleventh century church was demolished and the crossing and chancel of a new church were built on its site. It was these abbey buildings that Simon de Montfort would have known.

By the late eleventh and early twelfth centuries Evesham had developed into a sophisticated settlement housing weavers and fullers, carpenters and smiths, parchment makers (a very lucrative trade so close to an abbey), bakers and cooks, vintners and butchers and, inevitably, millers. A document dated to the late twelfth century refers to inhabitants of 'the new borough' (*de novo burgo*) apparently a speculative urban development by the abbot and chapter of Evesham Abbey. The same document records a total of 234 tenants of the abbey and divides the town into four quarters: *Evesham, Ruinhulle, Berton* and *Nova Burgus*. The precise extent of these four districts is unclear.

The abbey's new development was laid out as burgage plots. A burgage was a town rental property (to use modern terms), owned by a landlord. The burgage tenement usually consisted of a house on a long plot of land with a narrow street frontage.

Some burgage plots were split into smaller additional units and at Evesham the original plots became subdivided into half-, quarter-, eighth- and even sixteenth-plots. The basic unit of measurement was the perch which was 5.5 yards (5.03 m) and the plots within Evesham can still be identified today because they were in multiples of perches. The properties in those streets named above still adhere to the medieval burgage plan and the layout can be seen clearly.

The area to the north of Bridge Street still shows signs of the original modified grid plan of the new town (Evesham's street plan did not universally correspond to the classic model of a grid plan), supporting the view that Evesham was laid out as a planned town centred on a large funnel-shaped marketplace, today's High Street, running northwards from the abbey precinct. In contemporary documents this area was called the *Altus Vicus* or *Magnus Vicus* (High Street or Main Street).

Documentary evidence shows that the present Bridge Street and Cowl Street existed in 1265 (Bridge Street was probably the site of the 'town conduit' that figures in de Montfort's legend). Oat Street, which crosses the end of Cowl Street, was not built until the fourteenth century, providing a northern boundary for Evesham in 1265.

1265 - The Murder of Evesham

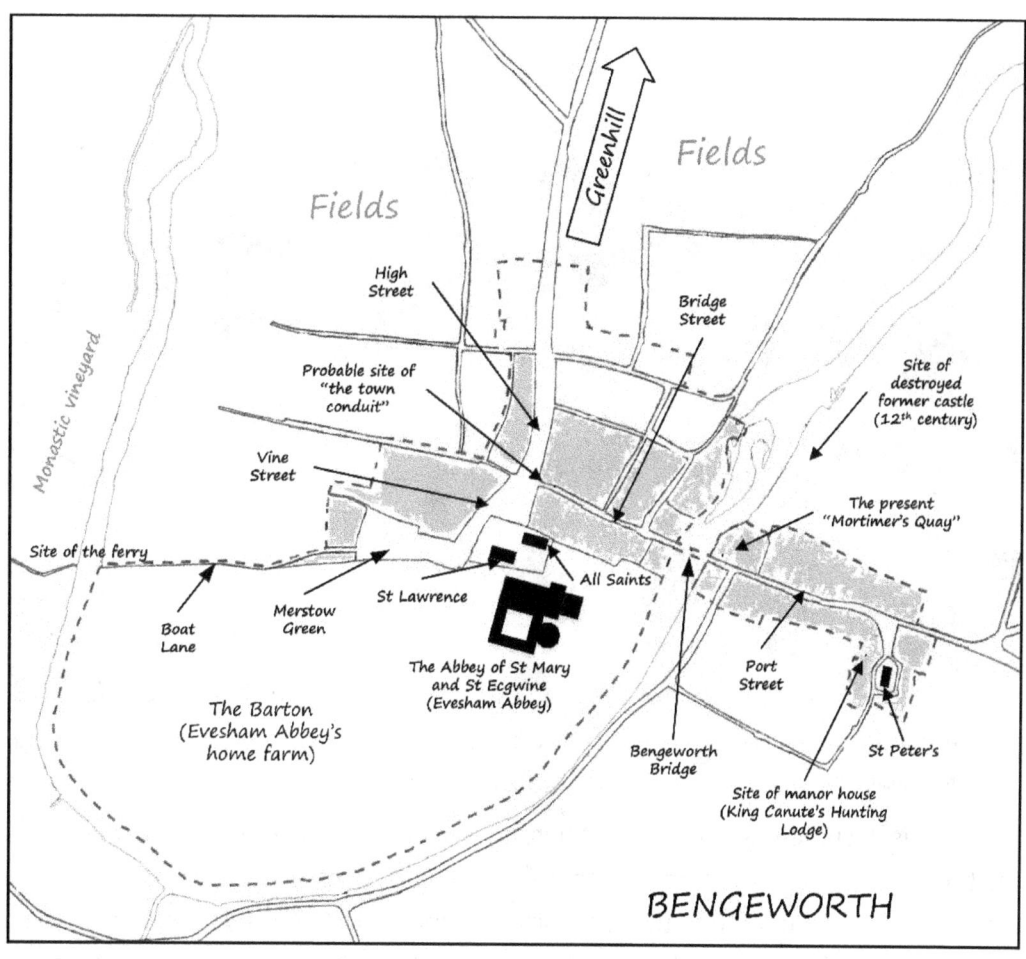

Sketch map of medieval Evesham

- - - -   Limits of medieval Evesham

Areas known to have been inhabited in 1265

10 The layout and extent of Evesham in 1265 (source: author)

11 No 31 Cowl Street, Evesham, was originally built in AD 1210 and would have been the home of a prosperous townsman (author's photograph)

There is documentary evidence of burgages from the early thirteenth century and the town held a weekly market and three annual fairs. Evesham's population in 1200 was over 1,000 souls, around the same size as Winchester's. The two parish churches, All Saints' and St Lawrence's, were built in the twelfth century within the abbey churchyard. By 1265 two separate parishes had developed around the churches, with the town crystallising around the parishes.

The abbey continued to dominate the town and its outlying estates, governing the town through two bailiffs appointed by the abbot. The local economy had developed serving the abbey community and relieving pilgrims of their pennies. However, thanks in part to speculative development by the abbey, the town had diversified with a trade in woollen cloth developing from the twelfth century. By 1265 Evesham had dyers finishing cloth and had developed a trade in manufactured goods including caps, gloves and stockings.

The estate of Bengeworth east of Evesham on the outside of the loop of the River Avon, played a controversial role in the battle. In the Domesday Book Bengeworth was divided between the Abbot of Evesham and Urse d'Abitot, the Sheriff of Worcester. The lower part of Bengeworth (nearest the river) passed into the ownership of the de Beauchamp family, the hereditary sheriffs of Worcestershire, who illegally built a 'castle', or fortified manor house, near the bridge in the mid-twelfth century. During King Stephen's civil war Bengeworth Castle was stormed and destroyed by the Abbot of Evesham's men and the moated site was still empty in 1265.

The parish church of St Peter was at the centre of the little settlement of Bengeworth. A visit to Church Street in Bengeworth, where terraced cottages huddle round the site of the original church of St Peter, provides something of a feel for medieval Benegworth. If you make that visit, look out for the cottage that preserves the remains of Bengeworth Manor, originally built for the early eleventh-century Danish king, Canute.

Rivers were the most important features in the landscape of 1265. We have seen how Earl Simon's movements were circumscribed by the Severn and he came to Evesham to avail himself of its crossing point to put himself on the same side of the Avon as the younger Simon. The actual banks of the Avon were not suitable for military manoeuvring. The river was deepened and straightened in the seventeenth century to improve navigation because Evesham was handling cargoes trans-shipped onto barges at Bristol. The main stretch of the river was later canalised on the orders of Henry Workman, a Victorian mayor of Evesham, to provide pleasure gardens, which form an excellent venue for regattas, angling contests and river festivals. In 1265 the banks of the river were less well defined and, in flood, impossible to detect, with numerous rivulets and areas of marshy floodplain on both sides. The floods of 1998 and 2007 provided an idea of how the medieval river would have looked. See figure 12.

An unruly river meant that crossing places would be militarily valuable. However, Evesham Abbey originally built the bridge for commercial reasons. A river crossing was often a place of trade and exchange. Roads converged on bridging points which were points of contact between communities or areas. At the head of the bridge other facilities for travellers developed, including accommodation in inns and at the adjacent monastery.

12 The River Avon, in spate during the July 2007 floods, gives an idea of its width and appearance in 1265 (author's photograph)

Most medieval rivers in England, if left in their natural state, were fordable at various points and the Avon had some fordable points. Where there was limited movement of people and goods the occasional necessity to use a ford or a ferry would not have been seen as a serious difficulty. Place names can often give a clue to the location of former fords. 'Twyford', at the eastern edge of the battlefield, suggests that there were once two fords or crossing places there.

The right to operate a ferry and to retain the income from it was a common manorial monopoly (in this case operated by the abbot of Evesham). Chain ferries, where a rope or chain is stretched across the river and used by the ferryman to haul a flat-bottomed boat across, were common. A ferry of this kind was in operation at Evesham in 1265 and its successor is still in regular use at Hampton Ferry. If its medieval predecessor were similar, then it would have been a sturdy punt drawing 450 millimetres (18 inches) of water and with 250 millimetres (10 inches) of freeboard when fully loaded.

13 This bridge at Tilford, Farnham, Surrey was built in 1128 and is a scheduled ancient monument. Bengeworth Bridge in Evesham is likely to have been similar, with multiple arches. Thirteenth century bridges seem to have had wooden rails like these (source: Pixabay)

Usually this load consisted of members of the monastic community crossing the Avon to work on the terraced vineyards on the opposite bank of the river. It was not a realistic method of moving large numbers of men and horses across the river so had negligible military value.

Bridges constructed during the Romano-British period continued in use as there are records in the archives of various monasteries of them being repaired. In 1130 a bridge of this type stood where the current Abbey Bridge of 1928, rebuilt in 2013, spans the river. In that year the bridge was removed when the abbey's home farm, the Barton, was enclosed by a twelve-foot-high defensive wall leaving only the town or Bengeworth bridge and the ferry, and the small bridge at Twyford, as places where the river could be crossed dry-shod.

Fords could be made impassable by high water; ferries were disabled by floods so Evesham's good bridge was a magnet for hauliers and travellers. Most early medieval bridges were quite narrow. Volumes of traffic were low and often it was not thought necessary to allow for two carts or wagons to pass in opposite directions. In 1265 few bridges had stone parapets. These were added to Evesham's bridge in the later Middle Ages. However, some had wooden railings or barriers as a safety measure, particularly where flocks of animals were likely to be driven across.

Until recently the bridge at Twyford was thought to be a clapper bridge, a type of bridge common anywhere that had quarries producing large slabs of stone. However, clapper bridges – structures with dry-stone piers and massive stone slabs laid along the top to form the roadway – are not a common feature of the Vale or the Cotswolds and most of the surviving clapper bridges are no earlier than the fourteenth century.

The crossing at Twyford had almost certainly been in use for centuries before the medieval bridge was built. The land on the right bank of the river at that point had been called Twyford since at least c. 1020 when it was referred to as *Twyforda* in a life of St Ecgwine that can confidently be dated to that period. 'Ford' indicates a crossing place and 'twy' means that there were two 'fords' at the site. These might have been side by side or they might have been consecutive crossings that used an island that has since been lost or destroyed as a mid-point. The former seems more likely.

At that point the river was crossed by a road that was certainly in use in the early eleventh century. The 'salt street' (called *sealtstret* in a charter-boundary copied in an Evesham Abbey cartulary of around 1200) was part of a network of tracks and roads used to carry loads from the great salt-producing centre of Droitwich. Salt had been extracted at Droitwich from the Iron Age onwards and the salt streets may have been Roman or even pre-Roman. Whichever it was, this was an ancient and well-used crossing.

The first known reference to a bridge at Twyford appears in the records of William of Berton's trial for murdering John the Deacon of Littleton at the 'bridge of Twyford' in August 1285. The existence of a bridge in 1285 does not prove that it was already there in 1265; however, on packhorse routes it was common to find bridges adjacent to fords to provide a dry crossing for pack animals that might otherwise roll in the stream to cool off or, laden with salt, to lighten their load.

14 The Twyford bridge may have resembled the packhorse bridge at Rearsby, Leicestershire, without the brick coping (source: Pixabay)

Research in the past 50 years points to Twyford having a packhorse bridge, a more sophisticated structure than a clapper bridge. Packhorses bridges, often with many of the features of full-size bridges but in miniature, are easy to recognise, usually very narrow allowing only a single file of animals to pass, in one direction, at a time. They usually had a very low parapet, or none at all, to accommodate the loads slung across the animals' backs.

When G.E. Parkes examined the remains of the bridge in 1975 he found that the roadway would have been around 2 metres (6 feet 6 inches) wide, perfectly aligned with the course of the old salt street (now called Boat Lane at Offenham). The bridge probably had three arches, the centre one around 8 metres (25 feet) wide and the outer ones perhaps a little narrower, erosion having interfered with the banks of the Avon at that point, making measurement uncertain. Built in an area that was prone to flooding the bridge may have been approached by a causeway at each end.

The land between the edge of the town and the foot of the slope of Greenhill seems to have been divided into cultivated plots worked by townspeople. There may have been small enclosures delineated by banks and ditches up to the lower slopes of Greenhill, intended to keep livestock from straying and some of these might have been used as impromptu defences during the retreat, although none of our accounts mentions either enclosures or any of Earl Simon's fleeing army making use of them.

The slopes of Greenhill itself were not used for cultivation. A landscape by William Robert Earl, painted in 1825 and currently on display in the Simon de Montfort Room of the Almonry Museum in Evesham, looks down Greenhill and shows a terrain little different from the way it looked in 1265: open scrubland, the occasional clump of stunted trees (figure 15). In 1265 this would have been common land, used for grazing the townspeople's animals and for collecting firewood.

There are traces of a ridge and furrow system in the north-western corner of the Battlewell conservation area, just visible in the aerial photograph, figure 16. This patch of agricultural land may have been worked by the people of the disappeared settlement of Twyford village.

We are lucky in Evesham in knowing where the battle was fought, which is rare for such an early battle. You will find the battlefield on OS Landranger 150 and OS Explorer 205, Grid Reference: SP039455 (403950,245530). The battle seems to have been fought across the 55 metre and 60 metre contours on the side of Greenhill facing the town. Put simply, it was fought north of the town on or near the top of Greenhill and overflowed into the town during the pursuit after the Montfortian army broke.

Battlefield Archaeology

As I said above, understanding historical topography, what the terrain was like at the time of the battle, is important. However, so is an archaeological investigation. The analysis of found artefacts, the gleaning of relevant information provided by the position of found artefacts, along with an appreciation of excavation revelations and material, is useful when reconstructing a 750-year-old battle.

15 'Evesham from Greenhill, Worcestershire', William Robert Earl, 1825, on display in the Almonry Museum, Evesham (Permission of Evesham Town Council)

Analyzing patterns of fallen shot indicating areas of engagement and intensity of shooting, backtracking via knowledge of ranges for position of firing units etc., as pioneered by Glenn Foard and Tim Sutherland might tell us a lot about the Battle of Evesham.

Unfortunately, there has been very little discovery of artefact evidence on the Evesham battlefield, largely because medieval battlefields, particularly in the days when men-at-arms wore mail armour rather than harnesses of plate, were picked clean of everything of value by human scavengers after the battle. Armour was very valuable. In today's terms, the mail shirt worn by Lord Edward at Evesham would have cost around £250,000. The lords and barons would have been carrying the equivalent of £150,000-£200,000 on their backs and even ordinary knights would have worn armour costing around £100,000 in 2020 terms. So armour was handed down, modified and re-used. It would be like finding a battlefield littered with Ferraris, Bentleys and Aston Martins with the keys in the ignition; they would not have been there the following day.

The same was true with weapons; even broken weapons could be repaired or modified, so they too were harvested. Arrows and crossbow bolts were pulled out of the ground, trees and bodies, and even boots, belts, cloth armour and breechclouts had a value, so they were taken. After an army of expert scavengers had passed over a battlefield there would be nothing left but naked corpses. After all, looting the dead was part of the pay and benefits package of a medieval soldier! Contrast this with a battlefield from, say, the English Civil Wars where bullets, roundshot, pieces of armour, saddlery and similar detritus keep turning up these days and where casualties were buried in their clothes. You should not expect to find many remains of armour and weapons on a thirteenth-century battlefield.

On the other hand, you would expect to find the mortal remains of the unsuccessful combatants, which were usually buried close to the spot where they fell. Records in state and private collections testify to the number of dead so somewhere there are around 3,000-4,000 bodies (plus the remains of horses killed in the battle). There are references in old books, such as Tindal's magisterial history of Evesham, suggesting the existence of mass graves. These possible sites are marked on the model of the Battle of Evesham in the Simon de Montfort Room in the Almonry Museum but nobody has yet turned up a host of hurriedly interred corpses. Or, if they have, they have kept quiet about it, probably out of respect for the honoured dead, and small blame to them for that. However, if anybody does happen to turn up 3000 dead Montfortians in their garden I would be very pleased to hear about it.

Battlewell

The extent of the four-acre Battlewell site is outlined in figure 16. 'Battle Well' (two words) was first recorded in 1272-3 as a spring where miracles had taken place and as the place where de Montfort died.

16 The Battlewell conservation area is outlined in white (source: Battlefields Trust)

The present site has been identified as the Battlewell since the fifteenth century. It was recorded on the six-inch Ordnance Survey map: Worcestershire XLII.SE in 1885 and on a map of the parish in 1827. There has been some twentieth century development in the area but this has not impinged on the Battlewell (one word) site which, at the time of writing, has been leased from the Rudge Estate by the Simon de Montfort Society who have managed it under a stewardship agreement with Natural England. A visit to the Battlewell field is the recommended starting point for anyone interested in a detailed reconstruction of the historic terrain and investigation of the battle archaeology. The Simon de Montfort Society, aided by the Battlefields Trust and supported by the Worcestershire Archaeological Service, is working to restore the site to something like its condition in 1265. There is already an information panel on the site linked to a self-guided trail, clearly signed by way marked posts, which takes visitors over the general area where the battle was fought.

As mentioned earlier, the limited archaeological investigation that has been possible at Battlewell has identified a ridge-and-furrow system (top left of the outlined area) on the higher, better drained, contours of the hillside with scrubland between that and the edge of the town which would have begun roughly where Swan Lane now stands, behind a band of gardens. This ridge-and-furrow has provided a problem for investigation of the battlefield. Furrows running along contours restrict soil creep. Our furrows run down the contours, accelerating and promoting soil creep to such an extent that the archaeological trace is some three metres (roughly ten feet) below the present ground level.

The land on the Battlewell site has not been under the plough for many years and even modern deep ploughing is unlikely to turn up any artefacts of the battle. North is to the top of the photograph. Abbey House stands in its own grounds north-west (above and to the left) of the Battlewell site in the photograph. Sir James Ramsay sited the battlefield in the grounds of Abbey Manor with Simon's 'forlorn band' drawing themselves up for a last stand on a level spur some 300 x 200 metres (330 x 220 yards) to the south of where Abbey Manor now stands.

In the photograph 16 the spur is concealed by the dense belt of trees south of the house. Ramsay does not give any sort of authority for this deployment beyond 'local tradition' (unattributed). A search of local sources has failed to reveal any ancient tradition to support Ramsay's view. Nevertheless Mr E.J. Rudge erected a monument (the 'obelisk') on the spot in 1845. This too is hidden by the trees.

Conversely, the tradition that Simon was killed at 'Battlewell' can be traced back to the earliest extant sources. None of the available accounts support Ramsay; they all have Simon making a dead set at the Marcher line and trying to cut his way through. As Byrne pointed out, assuming the earl was heading up Greenhill either to join his, supposed, son's forces or to try conclusions with the Marcher lords, he would then have had to march left, across the front of the Marcher Army, descend into the ravine between Battlewell and the spur and climb out onto the plateau while Edward and his cohorts sat quietly and did not interfere.

12. The Armies Deploy

A battle was usually regarded as a risky last resort to be used when every other way to defeat the enemy, or at least drive him to seek terms, had been exhausted or when a battle could be forced on an inferior enemy from an advantageous position with the advantage of surprise. Both considerations applied at Evesham, so Edward was confident of ending the revolt in a decisive battle.

Ramsay had de Montfort deployed on the ridge where the Obelisk now stands. The arguments for dismissing this interpretation were presented by Burne. Various more recent interpretations of the battle have suggested the approach of the royal forces from several different directions, the army being split by Prince Edward. Young and Adair[27], broadly following Burne, have all the troops approaching from the north east, having crossed the river at Cleeve Prior. Mortimer is then shown advancing on the east side of the Avon to Bengeworth bridge to close off de Montfort's line of retreat. Edward approaches across Offenham bridge and de Clare southward along the Alcester road to deploy on Greenhill, just to the north of the Battlewell. Smurthwaite and Seymour[28] also have a similar deployment. David Carpenter followed a broadly similar deployment but with Mortimer approaching Bengeworth from the west, on the Pershore road. It might have been considered unlikely, given that the numbers of troops involved, that Edward would have split and thus weakened his army in this fashion.

The *Evesham Chronicle* says that it was near Siveldestone that Edward divided his forces into three divisions and ascended the hill. David Cox has demonstrated that Siveldestone is almost certainly Siflaed's stone, a boundary marker on the late Saxon boundary of Evesham, a short distance to the west of Offenham bridge. It is described by Tindal and by Ireland in the eighteenth century and, though removed by the early nineteenth century, its position can be clearly identified. But this could be a fairly general identification of the location of the army being at the northern edge of the parish.

---

[27] Young, Peter and Adair, John, Hastings to Culloden: Battles of Britain, 1996
[28] Seymour, William, Battles in Britain 1066-1746, 1979 and Smurthwaite, David, The Complete Guide to the Battlefields of Britain, 1993

Figure 17 shows a profile of Greenhill along the axis of Greenhill Road. The numbers of metres show the height of the battlefield above sea level at that point and correspond to the contours on the current series of OS maps (the town of Evesham stands at 35 metres above sea level). The point of this diagram is to explain the difference between a 'false' or 'military' crest and a 'real' or 'topographical' crest.

Looking from the viewpoint of a man standing at the foot of Greenhill the real crest – the topographically highest point of the hill - is invisible, masked by the false crest.

The contours of the battlefield

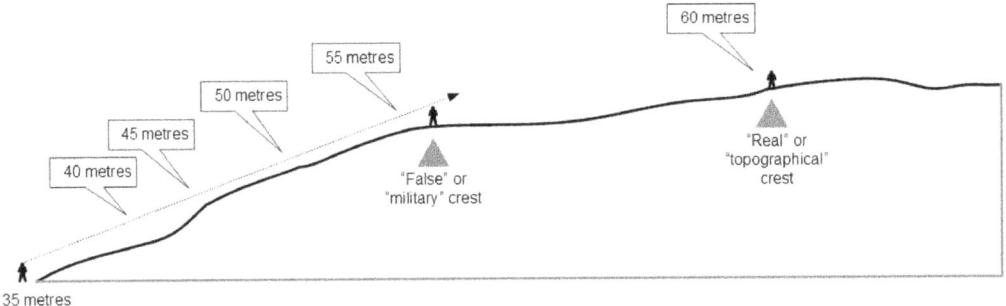

17 Section through Greenhill, not to scale (source: Joya Snowden)

Greenhill has and had a convex slope with its contour lines widely spaced at the top and closely spaced at the bottom. If Edward positioned himself at the top of the swell of the convex slope – on the topographical crest – he would have had no observation of most of the slope or of the terrain at the bottom; for that he would have had to advance to the military crest. On the other hand, the Montfortian army, attacking up a convex slope, would have had a more difficult task on the lower slopes and would not be able to see what was waiting behind the military crest. However, they would have an easier time on the higher slopes.

To understand the deployment of the royal army we have to understand not only the height of Greenhill, but also the degree and configuration of the hill's slope. Looking at the contour lines on an OS map Greenhill is not particularly steep (although it can feel like it when taking a party of visitors from the town to visit Battlewell) but neither is it gentle, particularly on the lower slopes.

To complicate matters there is evidence, based on soil sampling and analysis of contemporary written accounts from the seventeenth century onwards and some Victorian photographs, that the slope of Greenhill has changed in 750 years. In 1265 the slope would still have been convex but the military crest has slumped some 200 metres (220 yards) since then, in the opinion of the Geomorphology Department of Birmingham University.

18 Tony Spicer of the Battlefields Trust leads a party of walkers up the lower slopes of Greenhill (source: Battlefields Trust)

Composition of the battles

Traditionally Anglo-Norman cavalry deployed in divisions that were territorially based or under the leadership of a particular magnate. Lewes was an exception; other than a small mounted bodyguard for each baron the king concentrated all of his cavalry on the royalists' right flank and gave Edward the task of delivering a right-hook knockout. He succeeded in driving off the battle of Londoners opposite

1265 - The Murder of Evesham

him but then threw away his advantage by chasing them 5-6.6 kilometres (3-4 miles) beyond the battlefield, leaving his father to lose the battle in his absence.

Each division of horsemen would have been divided into *échelles* (squadrons). It is not clear how the squadrons were fitted into the battles but contemporary practice in Europe was to divide the squadrons into *conrois* (troops) of 20 to 24 knights or sergeants riding in close formation in two or three ranks, knee to knee.

Battles fought entirely by mounted men were rare. Most battles, as at Evesham, were fought by a combination of horse and foot. Tactics varied according to terrain and circumstances but there were two common deployments of Anglo-Norman armies. In one the horsemen advanced in close ranks with infantry archers and crossbowmen on their flanks to kill or wound the enemy's horses. This was a useful deployment if the army had plentiful archers and crossbowmen. Alternatively, the horsemen drew up in two or three ranks, with the better-equipped and mounted men in the first two ranks, with the foot drawn up behind with the spearmen in front, the archers and crossbowmen behind them to shoot over or between them in support and the axemen and swordsmen in the rear to cut down anyone who broke through.

The foot soldiers formed a mobile fortress behind which their horsemen could retreat to rally and reform, pick up a new lance and change horses, so gaps of one to two bowshots (200-400 metres or 220-440 yards) were left between battles. Most modern accounts implicitly accept that the three battles at Evesham were configured in this way. However, as I will argue in the next section, it was not unknown to have battles composed entirely of horsemen alongside battles entirely of foot soldiers, as had happened at Lewes in 1264, and this was the way the Marcher army chose to deploy on Greenhill.

Deployments

To see how Edward might have drawn up his army start with a fairly common (for the thirteenth century) deployment: three divisions or battles combining horse and foot. There is no evidence to suggest that the three battles would have been made up of equal in numbers; however, for the purpose of this model, bear with me and assume that each battle combined 2800 foot and 450 horse, one-third knights and two-thirds sergeants and lighter horse. Deploy the foot eight deep, giving each battle a frontage of around 860 metres (940 yards). This compact body of spearman, archers, axemen and swordsmen formed a solid base of manoeuver for the horsemen who formed up in front of their foot. The knights drew up in a single line, nearest to the enemy, spanning the full width of the battle, followed by a line of better-equipped sergeants and then by a third line, this time of poorer sergeants and other light cavalry. On a cramped battlefield we might expect the gap between the battles to be 200 metres (220 yards).

The 'traditional' deployment

The 'traditional' view of the Marcher deployment has them on the level ground at the crest of Greenhill on a line with the crossroad where the road currently called 'The Squires' crosses the Alcester Road and continues to the crossing at Twyford. If the three battles were deployed side-by-side, either abreast or in echelon, with a 200 metre (220 yard) gap between each, they would occupy the full 1.5 kilometres (1,640 yard) width of the battlefield. The central battle would sit astride the saddle of Greenhill; however, the two outlying battles would be invisible to one another and only partially visible to the central, linking, battle. Edward would have recognised that situation. He had been in the same position at the Battle of Lewes in 1264 and the dislocation of the royal forces had been a factor in their defeat.

Burne depicts de Montfort deployed immediately to the south of Battlewell and Edward's army just to the north. Young and Adair, followed by David Carpenter, have Edward just to the south of Battlewell. By way of comparison Burne has Edward and de Clare deploying their battles line abreast across the battlefield, reducing the depth of the battles to extend them further toward the river on either side, with de Mortimer's battle blocking de Montfort's line.

Deployment on the 'military' crest

David Cox places the initial deployments well down the slope, following the *Westminster Chronicle* which says that Edward was a stone's-throw away when de Montfort reached the top of the hill. If this was true, and giving due regard to the topography of the hill, then the action took place just to the north of the brow of the hill, the 'military crest'. This view was shared by Tindal.

The English Heritage analysis

English Heritage have all three battles on Greenhill with one battle forward to slow and entangle de Montfort's force, a second behind and to the east of the first battle to outflank de Montfort and close the trap with a third force held well back as a reserve.

The nobility were often led to disaster by their arrogance. The sense of honour that remained in some commanders made them, on occasion, abandon a favourable position to fight a 'level field' or to scorn a flank attack or ambush in favour of a head-on attack. Does this explain Earl Simon's apparent decision to ride up a steep hill with a numerically superior enemy poised at the top rather than investigate the possibility of outflanking Edward's position, escaping to the high ground at Bengeworth astride the road to London or barricading his force behind the stout walls of Evesham Abbey to await reinforcements?

Snowden's view

I drew up my view of the Marcher deployment (figure 20) to answer one question: if Edward had drawn up his battles to take advantage of terrain why not use it and charge downhill against the Montfortians as they laboured uphill? My idea is that Edward's forces were ordered as they were at Lewes: apart from a mounted bodyguard, Edward's and de Clare's divisions were entirely composed of infantry with the cavalry concentrated under de Mortimer's command.

In this scheme of deployment I too am following the *Westminster Chronicle*, which says that de Montfort's army, coming up the hill, saw their enemies no more than a stone's throw away. This suggests that Edward's army was deployed just behind the military crest, well forward of the summit of Greenhill, probably with the commanders forward at the crest to observe the Montfortian army's approach. This would seem logical: above the 55 metre contour the slope becomes gentle and even. Edward's greatest advantage would have been gained by preventing his uncle's army getting up onto this easier terrain. At this point in 1265 the battlefield was 1.5 kilometres (1,640 yards) wide from river bank to river bank. In figure 20 Edward deploys his forces with two battles, his own and de Clare's, partially astride the saddle of the hill but mainly occupying the slope on each side; a 200 metre (220

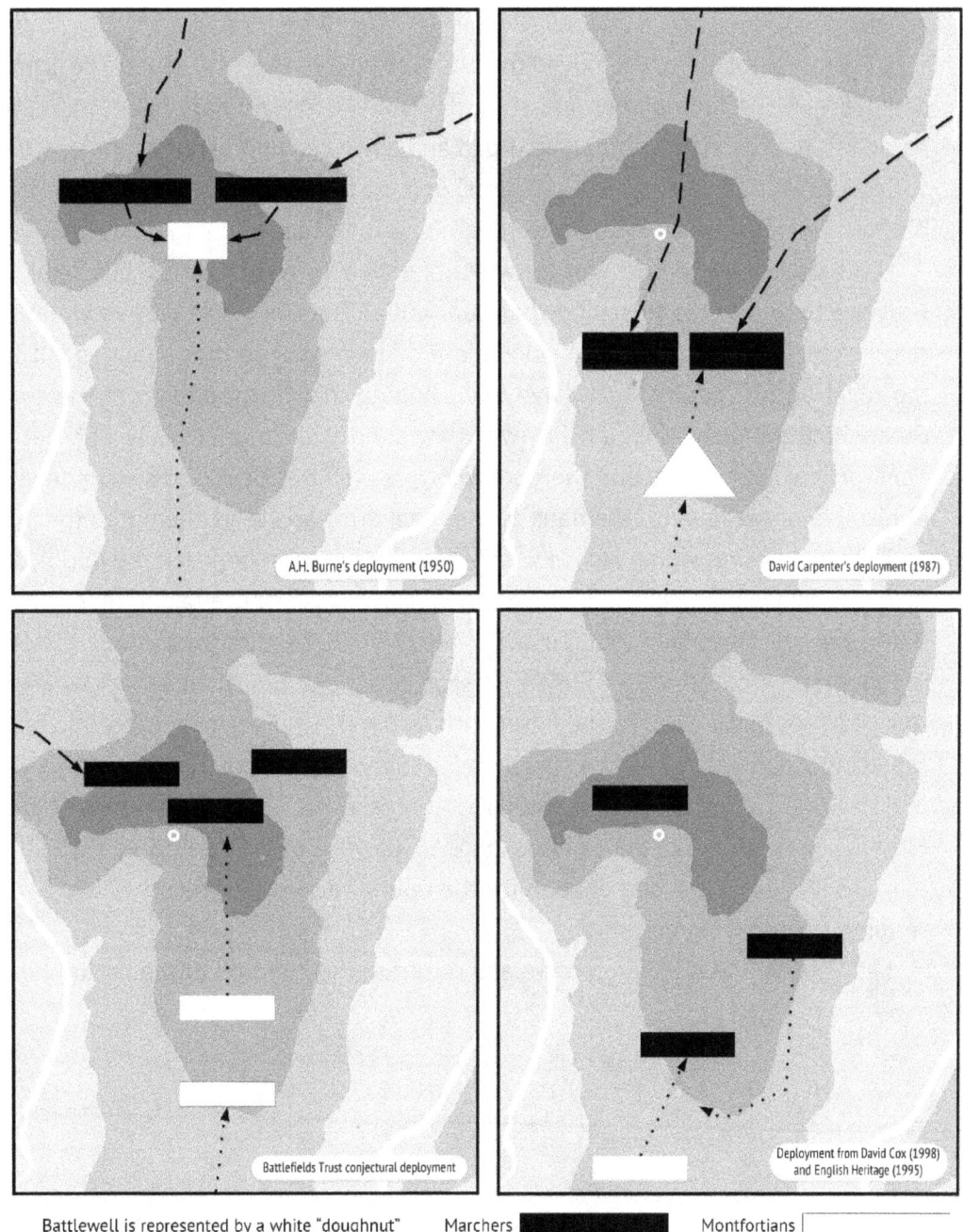

19 Conjectural deployments at the start of the battle (source: author)

yard) gap between them but the front-line battles close enough to coordinate their actions.

Edward and de Clare had moved their battles up the road now called The Squires, deployed on the hilltop then marched downhill to the military crest. Mortimer's battle fell back along the Worcester Road and advanced up the rear slope of the hill to take up position 400 metres (440 yards) or more behind the forward battles, giving his horse enough room to get up to speed for a full-blooded charge.

His battle covered the gap between the two forward battles but remained invisible to anyone approaching that gap uphill. The front-line battles would not reach as far as the river on each side; might de Montfort use those gaps to outflank the royal army? Edward may have been hoping that he would. From the top of Greenhill the Marchers would have had an almost interrupted view of what the Montfortians were doing and their battles were well positioned to sweep down on either side of the hill into the flank of the rebel army and drive them into the river.

This deployment would also reconcile the contradiction between the initial clash taking place well down the slope with the climax of the battle taking place around Battlewell and Dead Man's Ait. To anticipate the next chapter for a moment, Robert of Gloucester states that Earl Simon's assault pushed the royal army back, causing a rout that was only halted by the intervention of Warin of Bassingbourne who rallied the fleeing Marchers. If this were so then Earl Simon would have been through, clear and heading full tilt up the Alcester road. Instead he was counter-charged by de Mortimer's cavalry and the fighting bogged down around the top of the hill, de Mortimer holding him long enough for the rallied royalists of the other two battles to turn about and close the trap.

Let us leave the discussion there and return to the morning of the battle.

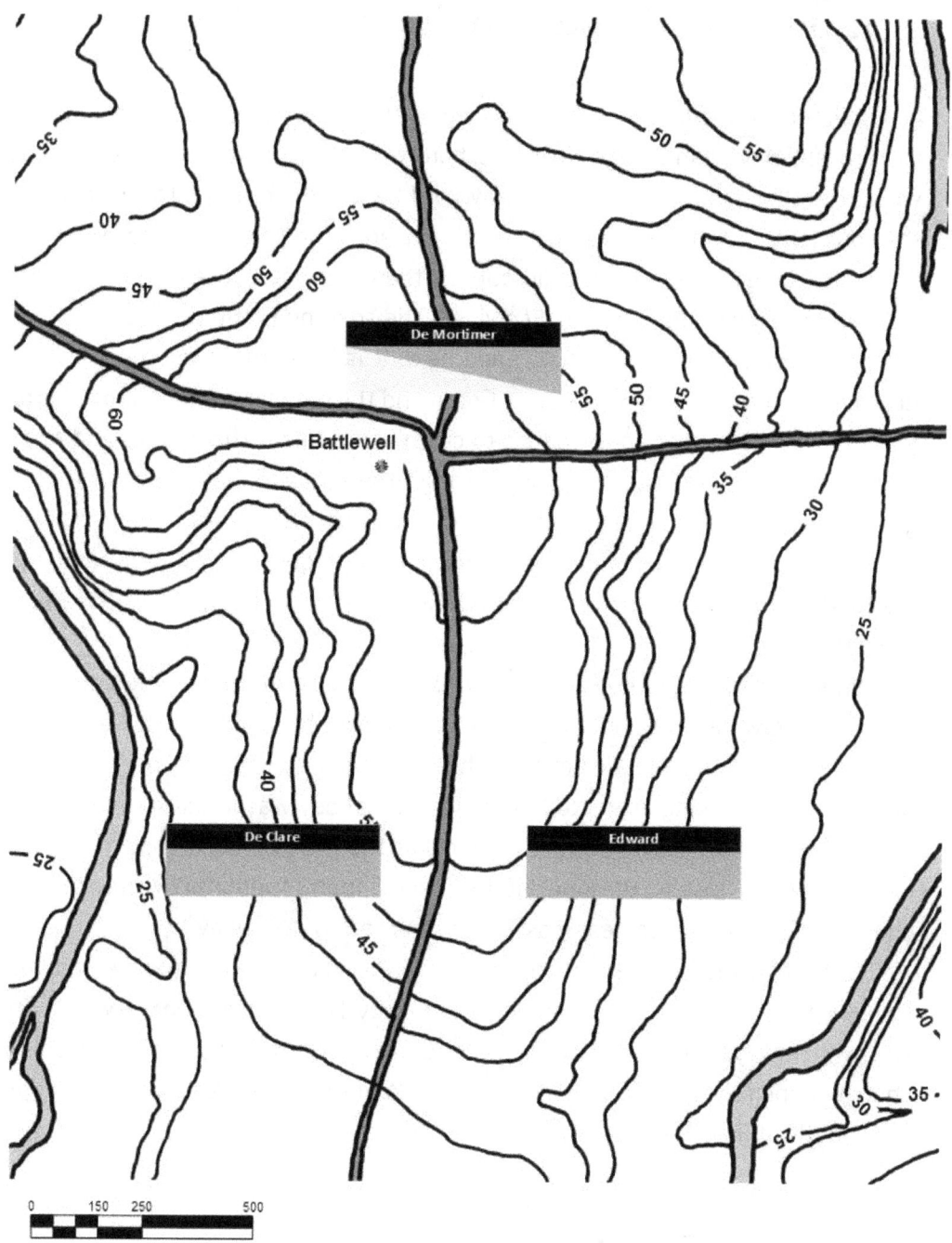

20 'Snowden's view', two battles of infantry deployed forward as bait with the Marcher horsemen held in reserve to deliver the fatal blow (source: author)

13. The Murder of Evesham

As Simon's army filtered into town across the bridge that stood close to where the present Workman Bridge links Evesham with the suburb of Bengeworth, they would have faced an uphill climb that would have brought them to the junction of the southern end of the present High Street and Vine Street, at that time Swine Street, the beast market that stood outside the great gatehouse of the abbey of St Mary and St Egwin's (or possibly 'Ecgwine' - the spelling is still debated).

There is no record of what happened next. It is likely that the foot soldiers and non-noble cavalry settled in Merstow Green and the old marketplace, looked around for food and ale or took their chance to catch some sleep. The knights and nobility seem to have ridden into the abbey through the processional arches of the great gatehouse because they rode out through them again at the start of their journey up Greenhill. The present gatehouse, converted long ago into dwellings, dates from the fourteenth century, replacing the gateway that Earl Simon would have passed through.

Bishop Walter de Cantilupe, one of Earl Simon's leading ecclesiastical supporters, had either travelled with the Montfortian army from his residence at Kempsey or a messenger had summoned him from his residence at Blockley, because he was present when the king asked to hear mass. The abbey was in interregnum, lacking an abbot, so ecclesiastical politics meant that the abbey church could not be used for the service[29]. Instead the king, Montfort and Simon's supporters visited the parish church of St Lawrence to hear mass, then returned to the abbey.

The occasion is commemorated by a vivid Victorian stained-glass window in St Lawrence's. The church is currently maintained by The Churches Conservation Trust; you will find details on *visitchurches.org.uk* (check the access information). The church is open every day and the excellent volunteers will be more than happy to tell you the story.

---

[29] There was an abbot-elect in the person of William of Marlborough who had been elected by Evesham Abbey's chapter in 1263. However, the disturbances had prevented him from travelling to Rome to have the election confirmed by the pope.

1265 - The Murder of Evesham

There are various accounts of how Earl Simon learned of Edward's approach. Guisborough provides some charming details: Nicholas, de Montfort's barber, evidently well versed in heraldry, saw the enemy approaching and recognised Montfortian standards among them. Some writers have taken this display of the banners captured at Kenilworth as a deliberate ruse to draw Earl Simon away from the abbey and into a trap. Guisborough relates that Simon was unsure so he sent Nicholas up the abbey bell tower to get a better look. When Nicholas saw the three battles approaching Evesham from different directions, he realised his error. Rushing back to his master Nicholas reported: 'We are all dead, for it is not your son as you believed', diplomacy not being the stock in trade of a medieval barber.

Could Simon's barber have recognised the banners on Greenhill from Evesham Abbey? This is one of those teasers that history throws up every so often. It sounds unlikely but it might be true. So, we tried it. The current abbey bell tower is half the height of Nicholas's perch but provides a good view of Greenhill over the top of the later development of the town. Having set up banners at Battlewell I ascended the tower on a clear summer morning and I could not pick out any of the details of the banners with unaided vision. So, I used the 8x50 binoculars I had brought with me. Even with the aid of Karl Zeiss's finest optics I could not say for certain which banner belonged to whom. So the answer, according to experimental evidence, is 'no, Nicholas could NOT identify the banners on Greenhill'. Although Nicholas could not have identified the individual banners carried by the army on the hill, he could certainly have got a feel for the deployment of the Marcher army.

If the story is anything other than pure invention then I offer this possible explanation: Earl Simon was too old a hand at warfare to neglect to station cavalry pickets up Greenhill, even if only to keep an eye open for young Simon's approach. Normally pickets operated in pairs, so that if anything happened one could stay to continue the observation while the other galloped off with the news. Fooled by the Montfortian banners a rider was sent to the abbey with the news that the reinforcements were approaching. On entering the abbey he gave the news to Nicholas who insisted on delivering the glad tidings himself, in expectation of a reward, as was the custom.

21 The Simon de Montfort window in St Lawrence's church, Evesham (author's photograph)

On the other hand, I believe that it was just a good story, a nice detail to add to Guisborough's account of the battle. I believe that the captured banners were borne aloft at Evesham not to trap Earl Simon but to taunt him: 'You think young Simon is on his way with reinforcements, but I've got news for you ...' Probably de Montfort learned of the enemy's approach in the usual way, alerted by pickets, by an observer in the abbey bell tower, or by both.

Guisborough, Gloucester and Rishanger all record de Montfort crying: 'may God have mercy on our souls for our bodies are theirs'. I suspect that he actually said something rather more terse and pointed.

The next question to answer is how quickly de Montfort was able to form his army up and head off to meet Edward. Wykes believed that the Montfortians were already 'booted and saddled' and ready to move so were in a position to set out without delay. Most other accounts suggest that Earl Simon was caught unawares. Osney has him still at mass. Simon sent his officers to round up his infantry and to get them into some sort of marching order while his horsemen put on the rest of their armour and mounted up.

How long did it take to round up a small medieval army and get them moving? In this instance it seems that the answer is no more than half an hour. The knights and nobles left through the great gatehouse. The other exit, known locally as Abbot Ranulph's gateway, which still connects the churchyard of All Saints church with the town square, was too narrow for mounted men.

Earl Simon was aware that his forces were heavily outnumbered. His army had been depleted by the loss of the Gloucester garrison, the desertion of de Clare and others at the time of Edward's escape, the surrender of hostages to Llywelyn and the usual dribble of desertion from fear, hunger or lack of pay. His body of Welsh infantry provided by Llywelyn were uncommitted to the cause and probably unenthusiastic.

There was evidently a debate of the best course of action, some counselling immediate action to catch Edward before he was properly deployed and others recommending fortifying the abbey precinct (which had a 4-metre or 12-foot wall, fragments of which are still visible in Boat Lane, but no ditch) and awaiting the arrival of young Simon. Yet others suggested that Simon should flee either back toward Hereford or for Oxford and London. If Earl Simon was cognizant of the fact that the royal army had arrived carrying his son's banners then he was unlikely to have relied on a passive stance.

22 This detail from the Simon de Montfort window in St Lawrence's church show's Nicholas, Earl Simon's barber atop the bell tower of Evesham Abbey and using his super-vision to identify the banners carried by the army approaching down Greenhill (author's photograph)

The New Account describes it this way:

Meanwhile, as the earl was discussing some other matter, someone said to him:

'Seeing how we have been hard pressed for some time now, and we have not slept or eaten for three days, and we and our horses are almost done for and exhausted, for this reason let us go into the church and the tower, which is very strong and can be defended, until our allies, who are still in different parts of the country, come to our aid, and until your army has recovered its strength.'

To this the earl immediately replied: 'No, fair friend, no. One ought to seek knights on the battlefield, and chaplains in churches.'

In an age when life was a fleeting possession and martial courage was exalted, the temptation for a great lord, when faced with death, to ride out and meet his fate with style must have been great, in the same way that the pride of the nobility often led them into well-documented acts of rashness. However, I do not believe that Earl Simon was tempted. While this debate was going on time was passing and eventually de Montfort decided that his best chance was to break out through the Marcher army and close with his son's army.

Simon's standard-bearer led the mounted men out on to Swine Street from the abbey compound through the processional archway in the abbey gatehouse. As he came through, the lance bearing Earl Simon's banner fouled the arch and snapped, which the author of the New Account took as an ill omen:

And as he came out of the Abbey gate, Sir Guy de Balliol shattered to pieces the lance bearing the standard against the top of the gate. Then the earl said: 'Now (?) God help us — now!'

The incident of breaking the standard is probably a literary convention with no basis in fact, although Simon's supposed words correspond very well with an understanding that he had reached the final crisis of a long and eventful life.

The chroniclers are certain that the battle took place during a sudden summer thunderstorm; however, they cannot agree on the time that it started. One camp claims that it began at the first hour of the day: 0445 hrs; the other (including the Evesham chronicle) favoured the third hour, which began at 0715 hrs.

23 Looking through Abbot Ranulph's gateway from the churchyard to Evesham's market square. In 1265 the ground level was a metre (3 feet) lower (author's photograph)

1265 - The Murder of Evesham

Before leaving the abbey Earl Simon had had the king dressed in a spare harness of armour. His reasons have been debated ever since. A favourite idea among his detractors was the accusation that Simon was setting up Henry to be killed in his place. To what end? It would have removed Henry and instantly have transformed Lord Edward into King Edward, which would not have suited Simon's long term plans. He needed a live king in his own hands to give him some spurious authority. Simon's only route out of the trap was through the blocking force on Greenhill and the Marchers were not going to give the Montfortians an easy passage. There would be arrows, quarrels and spears flying, swords and axes flailing, uncontrolled, unfocussed, death everywhere. If Henry was to have any chance of surviving the dash through his own allies he would have to be armoured.

In 2010 the Simon de Montfort Society, Evesham Town Council and Wychavon District Council set waymarks into the pavement to lead visitors along the most likely route for Simon's little army to have travelled. Vine Street and High Street once formed part of the ancient network of salt roads and the best archaeological opinion we have is that Simon was following a route that was already 2000 years old in 1265. The route was slightly to the east of the present road in places and the markers pick out that route. For variety, a brief account of the battle with thumbnail biographies of the key participants is set into the pavement outside the present Iceland supermarket.

The New Account has Simon offering his knights a final chance to escape:

And when they came to the conduit of the town of Evesham, the earl addressed everyone together and said: 'Fair lords, there are many among you who are not as yet tried and tested in the world, and who are young: you have wives and children, and for this reason look to how you may save yourselves and them. Cross the bridge and you will escape from the great peril that is to come.'

And to Sir Hugh Despenser he said: 'My lord Hugh, consider your great age and look to saving yourself: consider the fact that your counsel can still be of great value to the whole country, for you will leave behind you hardly anyone of such great value and worth.' Straightaway Sir Hugh replied: 'My lord, my lord, let it be. Today we shall all drink from one cup, just as we have in the past.' And with these words they leave the town.

24 A bad omen! Guy de Baliol, Earl Simon's standard-bearer, breaks his banner on the arch of Evesham Abbey's gatehouse (source: Iris Pinkstone)

The 'town conduit' ran from the market place down the current Bridge Street to the river, providing a water supply for cooking and washing. From that position Earl

Simon would have had a clear view of the Bengeworth Bridge. If this passage is not simply another literary tool, intended to demonstrate the loyalty that Earl Simon inspired, then it shows that, at this point, the bridge was not blocked; it does not prove that the bridge was not going to be blocked. Could Simon see Marcher soldiers hurrying to block the bridge or was it simply what he would have done in the circumstances?

I cannot shake the idea that Edward, or de Mortimer, would not have left Bengeworth Bridge open and available as an escape route. The road through Bengeworth led to Oxford and ultimately to London. More immediately, the road rose sharply through the village to high ground where Earl Simon's little army might have made a stand and invited the Marchers to attack them. To detach and move a compact force of infantry from Mortimer's battle on Greenhill, crossing the river Avon by the bridge and fords at Twyford, and hurrying them down the eastern bank to the Bengeworth end of the Bengeworth bridge would have taken no more than thirty minutes (we timed it last year!).

Outside the town the fields and strips worked by Evesham's lay population lined both sides of the road from today's Swan Lane to the foot of Greenhill, forcing Simon's army to advance in a narrow column. As Simon escaped from the constriction of the town fields and enclosures he would have found room to deploy his men.

At what point did Simon's Welsh infantry desert him? Col. A. H. Burne describes Simon deliberately advancing toward Greenhill with his Welsh infantry in column and his cavalry as a spearhead. Other military historians have followed Burne; however, the *New Account* disagrees. I am going to follow the *New Account* because I believe that Simon could expect little help from his borrowed Welsh spearmen. The *New Account* is eloquent on Simon's angry rebuke to the commander of his infantry, Sir Humphrey de Bohun:

And Sir Humphrey de Bohun, earl of Hereford[30], who had been designated commander of the foot soldiers, withdrew and - remained in the rearguard; at which the earl of Leicester said: 'Sir Humphrey, Sir Humphrey: that's no way to conduct a battle, putting the foot soldiers at the rear. I know well how this will turn out!'

---

[30] No, his father was still alive

It was normal battlefield practice, and on the march, for the infantry to be behind the cavalry to provide a solid base for them to fall back on and to rally behind, so what was Earl Simon saying here? My best guess is that he wanted his infantry in front of his cavalry for three reasons: he wanted them in a position where they could not easily flee or desert, where they could be driven forward at lance-point, if necessary, and where they could take the full force of Edward's charge, when it came. If so, then Earl Simon had little confidence in his Welsh infantry and was prepared to sacrifice them to blunt Edward's expected attack.

Although the *Evesham Chronicle* goes further and says that the Welsh infantry never left the abbey, it is difficult to imagine the Welsh deserting en masse. Some were still present on the crest of Greenhill, others were ridden down in the reddened water of Dead Man's Ait. Desertions from mass formations were gradual affairs, a slow but accelerating crumbling that usually began at the rear of the formation. The *Evesham Chronicle* is probably at least partially correct, some timid souls going into hiding rather than join the fray. Others would have split off and hidden in the town fields or turned back when they saw the strength of the force gathered against them. However it happened, Simon was going to have to rely on his own horsemen to take him through.

Standing at the foot of Greenhill, Simon would have seen, clearly visible on the brow of the hill, as it appeared to Simon, two lines of men with a 200 metre (220 yard) gap between the lines. There is no record of the composition of these lines of infantry but common practice from other battles suggests that the front three or four ranks would have been made up of spearmen endeavouring to present a hedgehog of spear points. Behind them archers and crossbow men would be deployed a little way back to give themselves room to shoot through or over the front ranks. And, behind them, would be the swordsmen, axemen and any others armed with cutting weapons, ready to contain any breakthrough. Faced with two solid phalanxes of infantry Simon would have been drawn to the gap between the battles. Even if it was too narrow for his cavalrymen to ride through unmolested it left the inner flanks of the two formations vulnerable to an expanding torrent of horsemen.

The view most consistent with the chronicle accounts is that Earl Simon formed his horsemen into a wedge or *cuneus* (figure 26), the standard formation for breaking through an enemy line, with his immediate affinity and bodyguard at the tip of the

25 This near-contemporary illustration seems to depict the Battle of Evesham with the Marchers charging from the left into the Montfortians on the right (unattributed, can anyone help?)

wedge and the less well-equipped horsemen lined up behind him to add weight and depth.

Aiming at the 200 metre (220 yard) gap between Edward's battle and de Clare's battle the compact force of Montfortian horsemen would have been able to sweep aside the flanking Marcher foot soldiers as they pushed their way into the gap and forced the Marcher line to bend backwards. If this were all then some at least of the Montfortians seem likely to have been able to break thorough to flee up the Alcester road and join forces with young Simon.

However, as the Montfortians pushed forward and appeared through the gap, de Mortimer ordered his horsemen into the charge and met the Montfortian advance, coming downhill with the advantage of the sloping terrain.

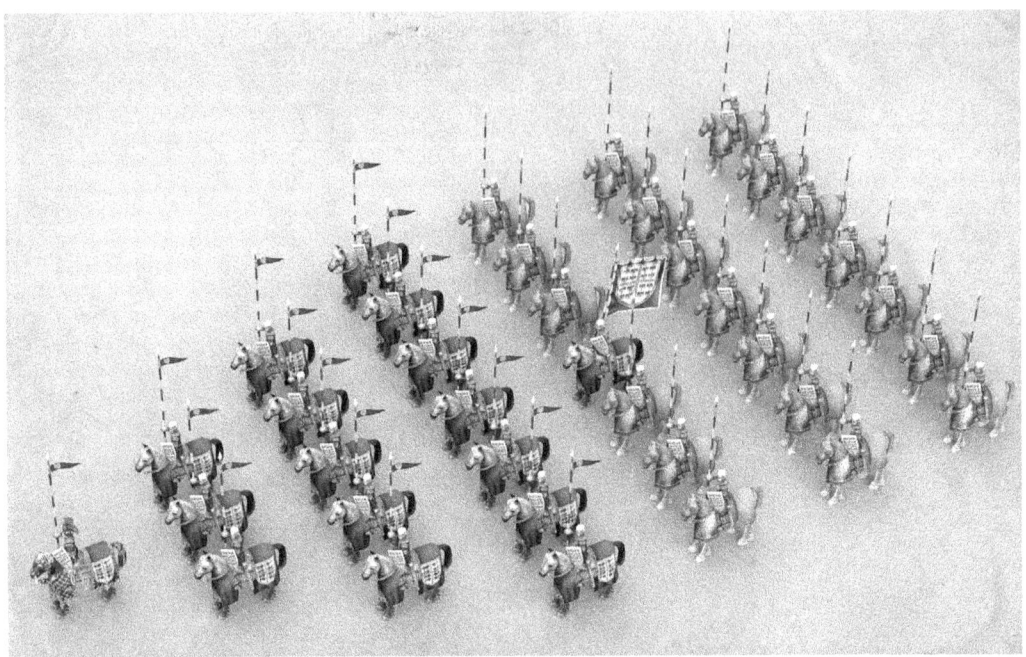

26 A 'cuneus' with the better armed and mounted lords and knights forming the wedge at the front and the less well-off knights and sergeants adding weight at the rear (source: Pixabay)

When cavalry fought cavalry the aim of the initial contact was to use the lance to unhorse an opponent – wounding him if possible – and leave it for the infantry or light horse to finish him off. The impact usually broke the lance. Even if it was not broken it became a liability once the opposing ranks intermingled so the knights would have dropped their lances and drawn their swords, axes or maces for the mêlée. Each knight would have spurred his horse forward, striking at each man as he passed rather than engaging in a prolonged one-to-one combat with a single opponent as this would have broken the momentum of the charge.

As de Mortimer's superior numbers stopped de Montfort's breakthrough and engulfed his little force Edward and de Clare pulled their battles together to close off any chance of escape.

It appears that Earl Simon's eldest son, named Henry after his uncle the king, was killed first, pulled down, stabbed to death or possibly beheaded. Simon fought on until his horse was killed under him, then picked himself up and fought on foot, surrounded by a shrinking ring of enemies who had dismounted to close with him,

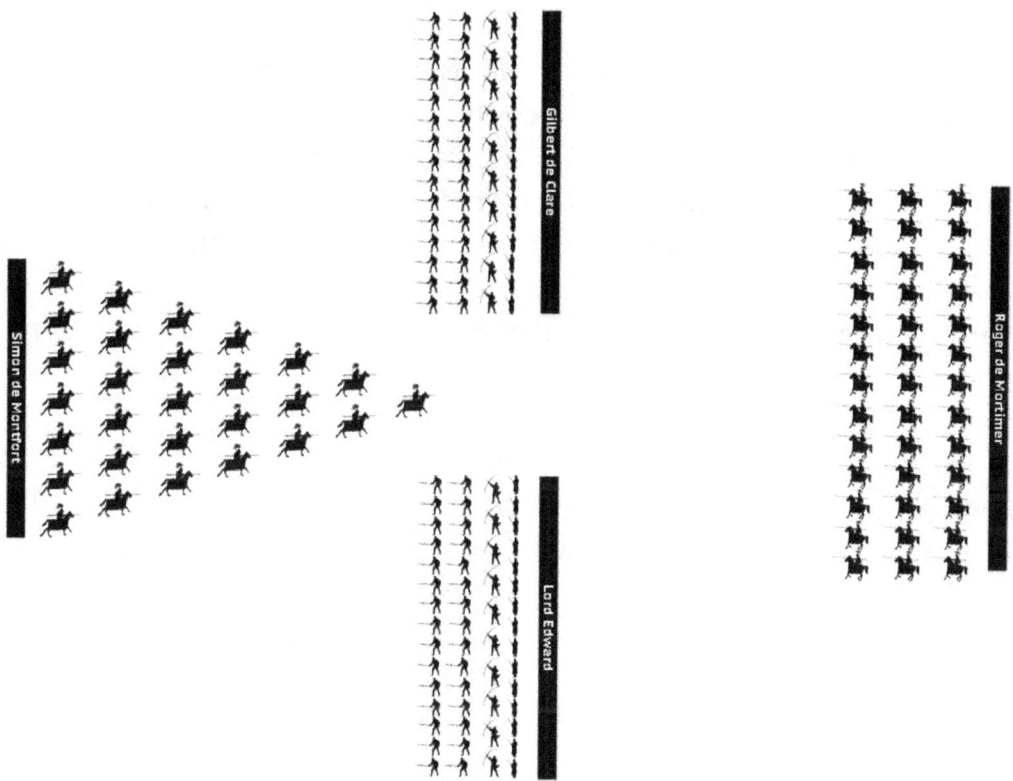

27 The crisis of the battle: abandoned by most of his infantry, Earl Simon led his cavalry wedge into the gap between the battles commanded by Gilbert de Clare and Lord Edward, driving the men on the inner edge of the battles back as he burst through to be met by a counter-charge by Roger de Mortimer, leading the bulk of the Marcher cavalry (source: author)

twelve in all, we are told, all chanting: 'Old traitor! Old traitor! It is impossible for you any more to live'.

Was this de Mortimer's 'death squad'? Labordiere's *New Account*, supported by de Nangis, tells the story of twelve stout men-at-arms being selected to capture or kill Simon. However, after that mention at Mosham Meadow, we lose track of this group. There would be a pleasing cyclical unity to the tragedy if they were the ring of enemies that finally laid him low.

Whoever these men were, Earl Simon was a doughty fighter and he left several of his attackers injured and bleeding. Inevitably, he was overwhelmed, disarmed and dragged to the ground. There are two accounts of what happened next and both provide evidence to support the assertion that Simon was murdered on the battlefield rather than killed in combat.

The Chronicle of Lanercost priory in Cumberland was written maybe forty years after the battle but may have been based on a first-hand account in a chronicle of 1297 written by Richard of Durham, a Franciscan Friar. The Lanercost account says that: 'his armour having been opened at the back someone plunged his dagger deep into the neck', which is as clear an example of a cold-blooded assassination as any I have found. This seems to be borne out by MS 3/23B, an anonymous manuscript currently in the College of Arms. Written in early fourteenth century the copy is faulty but the following can be read: 'with his pointed weapon someone [   ] the neck right through'.

The conclusion is that Earl Simon was pinned down while someone cut his throat. However, there is another possible interpretation of the reported facts. By 1265 a knight's armour was well enough developed to protect him from death during the normal course of a battle so, when a knight was unhorsed or surrounded, he would simply surrender and expect to be ransomed. It is clear that this was not an option for the senior Montfortians, and their deaths were a very deliberate act carried out by a group of men who would have had to hold both Henry and Simon down while removing enough of their armour to enable them to be killed with knives or daggers. Excavated remains of mediaeval knights and other men-at-arms show a considerable preponderance of head wounds as the cause of death either straight into the cranium or through the eye sockets, so this appears to have been a popular way to kill an armoured man.

The chaos on Greenhill nearly killed King Henry. Wearing borrowed armour, he was unhorsed and wounded. He was rescued by Adam de Mowhaut who recognised his voice and left him in the care of a body of his men-at-arms. Guisborough described it like this ...

All were therefore armed and animated for some time for the battle, but the king himself who remained all the time in the custody of the earl as a surety was, it is said, armed in the earl's own armour. So they advanced with their troops to fight for their country and before battle was joined the Welsh fled from Earl Simon and in crossing the River Dee [sic] many were drowned and the rest baptised again: thus battle was joined and many on the earl's side fell in this bitter conflict, but the king himself, struck on the shoulder, shouted loudly: 'I am Henry of Winchester your king, do not kill me:', for he was a simple man, peaceful and not warlike. Lord Adam de Mowhaut recognised him by his voice, also his son ran to his father's voice and handed him over to the custody of certain of his soldiers.

What happened next is repugnant to a modern mind but was by no means unusual in the Middle Ages. The accounts imply that a knight – the most reliable sources identified him as William Maltravers – cut Simon's head off at the neck, his feet below the knees and his hands below the elbows (see figure 28). The College of Arms narrative includes the detail that the earl's killers 'continued to inflict wounds all over the corpse long after it was dead' and we have the detail of de Montfort's corpse being castrated. When the monks of Evesham Abbey brought a 'broken ladder' to recover the corpse it was substantially still intact although bloody and hacked about. Someone (Maltravers?) castrated the corpse and hung the severed genitals on either side of the nose before stuffing them into the mouth of the severed head.

Wykes tells us that young Simon saw his father's head being carried past on the point of the spear, which caused him to withdraw from Alcester and return to Kenilworth where he remained inconsolable and refusing food for several days. It seems unlikely that no-one would have ridden the bearer down and killed him. However, whatever its immediate fate, Earl Simon's head was sent as a trophy to Lady Mortimer at Wigmore Castle.

David Carpenter has pointed out that Simon and Henry, de Clare and other leading figures in the revolt had to die to ensure their removal from the scene. It was not until the following century that political opponents captured in battle might be executed and, even at Evesham, Guy de Montfort was allowed to live. If they were not killed on the battlefield then they would have to be imprisoned and might yet form the core of future unrest. Battlefield executions untied a knotty political problem.

There was a personal element to it too, particularly between de Montfort and de Mortimer. Each had ravaged the other's lands. The particular significance of sending lady Mortimer Earl Simon's head and severed genitalia is obscure, and it had probably better remain that way. For most of the Marchers there was a motive of revenge: for the defeat at Lewes, the humiliation of Edward and the king and for the damage done to their personal properties by the Montfortians.

28 Simon de Montfort's corpse is dismembered (image reproduced by kind permission of The British Library)

As a footnote, there is an intriguing account of the death of Simon de Montfort in *The Templar of Tyre*, which is the name of a fourteenth-century historian and also of the document he wrote. In this version of events, Simon was not killed at Evesham, only captured, and Edward asks his cousin, Henry of Almain, what he should do with him. Almain advises him to behead Simon, otherwise there will be no peace or an end to the conflict. To avoid the outcry that would follow if he killed him after he had been captured, it should be made to look as though Simon fell in battle. So Edward waits until nightfall, chops Simon's head off, and has his body dumped on the battlefield. This interpretation is not supported by most of the contemporary sources; however, it would account for Henry of Almain meeting his own sticky end at Viterbo in 1271.

14. The Aftermath

The killing had not yet finished. Infantrymen and non-noble cavalry could not expect quarter. The different treatment of knights and commoners was often noted in medieval warfare (see chapter 15). What is significant at Evesham was an unprecedented loss of life among the knights and nobles. The complexity of landed relationships and the eagerness to profit from ransoms cut across political allegiances so fatalities were usually very few. It would have been a shock for de Montfort's men to discover that the rules no longer universally applied.

If the point of Edward's 'no quarter' order at Evesham was to remove the entire knightly and noble opposition to royal misrule it was only partially successful because it seems to have been partially ignored. It is likely to have been a matter of who surrendered to whom; neighbours on opposite sides would accept the surrender of one another, although there were exceptions. However, this did not excuse Edward from the contemporary opprobrium of having given the order.

For the infantry and non-noble cavalry there was no choice; they had to flee. There were two ways that they could go. Those who fled to the east raced downhill across ground made sodden by the storm, or along the road that led to the bridge and ford, funnelling themselves from Greenhill to the narrow crossing place of the Avon. Those who reached Twyford were caught around an island in the stream, locally called an 'ait' (these days it is called 'Dead Man's Ait') where they were ridden down as they floundered in the water or shoved one another off the narrow bridge. Those who made it across would have been pursued down the road and across country. If they had Welsh accents they could expect no mercy from the countrymen they encountered.

There was nowhere to run to the west of the battlefield although it would make an interesting 'what if' for a wargame for a party of survivors to make a last stand on the knoll where the obelisk now stands.

Those who retreated into the town would have been pursued by the bulk of the Marcher infantry, keen to see what plunder they could liberate, as well as by however many of de Mortimer's cavalry were not scattering fugitives from the hilltop. Those who made it as far as the edge of the town could have taken refuge in the ditches round the town fields and among the growing crops. Hunted down in fields and ditches they tried to find shelter in the town where they would have found every door barricaded. The slaughter spread through the town. There was no escape route. Some would have tried to swim to safety and drowned or been shot down in the stream. Before it was tamed in the seventeenth century the Avon was fierce and unpredictable; Evesham never needed defensive walls. The killing went on and on, wherever a fugitive was found, even inside the abbey precinct, church and crypt. The right of sanctuary was ignored.

Did any escape across the bridge to Bengeworth? Here I am going to stick my neck right out and say 'no, because it was blocked'. Some accounts have de Mortimer position his whole battle on the Bengeworth side to block the bridge and the present Mortimer's Quay commemorates this idea. But how could Mortimer be blocking the bridge and, at the same time, be killing Earl Simon on Greenhill? Obviously, by dividing his forces. It does not take 3,000-4,000 men to block a bridge. A couple of hundred would do the job, 400 at most. From Greenhill to Workman Bridge takes about 30 minutes on foot, crossing the Avon at the ford and bridge at Twyford and then doubling along the eastern bank to Bengeworth. A party of de Mortimer's men could have been in place well within the hour. They might have stayed in place until the climax of the battle and then have pushed up Bridge Street to join the fun.

The Last Hours describes it this way:

And then whatever was left of the knights, esquires, men-at-arms and foot-soldiers, if there were any, took flight and scattered completely and the others pursued them from every side and killed them. And such was the speed of their flight that some thought the water in the river (lit. 'the river of water') was safer than the land, with the result that a multitude of them drowned, and in that place where they thought to have refuge and succour they incurred danger and death. God alone knew how many of them there were.

Just as we have problems calculating the size and composition of the armies so we have challenges calculating the numbers of casualties. Richard of Durham's estimate of 7,000 Montfort infantry killed is a flight of fancy[31].

The number of knights and nobles who perished at Evesham has been exaggerated over the years with as many as 200 being quoted. We cannot be sure

---

[31] See *The Lanercost Chronicle* which, up to 1297, is a version of a lost chronicle of Richard of Durham

of the fates of all of the Montfortian knights and nobles at the Battle of Evesham; however we can be sure that no more than 30 or 40 were killed and these are shown in the following table. Even so this was an unprecedented loss of life among the nobility. It was, however, a tiny fraction of the total losses.

After the battle Walter de Cantilupe sorrowfully left Evesham for his manor at Blockley. He died in 1266.

As the pursuit spread out across the countryside Edward was reunited with his father. Slightly wounded, Henry would have been conveyed to the safety and comfort of the abbey to be cared for by the *Infirmarer* or other *medicus*. De Mortimer and de Clare would have joined the royal family while their men got on with stripping the corpses and rounding up the riderless horses.

Anketin de Martival	?	Richard de Havering	?
Baldwin Wake	Captured	Richard de Spetchesley	?
Fulk de Den	?	Richard de Grey of Codnor	Captured
Gilbert de Birteley	?	Richard Trussel	?
Gilbert Einesfield	Killed	Robert de Crevequer	?
Giles d'Argentin	Captured	Robert de Hardredishull	?
Guy de Balliol	Killed	Robert de Montfort	Captured
Guy de Montfort	Captured	Robert de Newton	?
Henry de Berham	Captured	Robert de Sepinges	?
Henry de Crammarvill	?	Robert de Tregor	Killed
Henry de Curson	?	Robert Doye	?
Henry de Hastings	Captured	Robert fitz Neil	?
Henry de Monmouth	?	Robert Motun	?
Henry de Montfort	Killed	Roger de Quincy	?
Henry the Forester	?	Roger de Roule	Killed
Hugh de Hopville	Killed	Roger de Rowley	Captured
Hugh le Despenser	Killed	Roger de Soulis	Killed
Humphrey de Bohun	Captured	Roger de St John	Killed
Humphrey de Bolesdon	?	Saer de Harcourt	?
John de Beauchamp	Killed	Simon de Montfort	Killed
John de Boseville	?	Stephen Soundan	?
John de Inde	Killed	Thomas de Ardern	?
John de la Haye	?	Thomas de Astley	Killed
John de St John	Killed	Thomas de Caleye	?
John de Vescy	Captured	Thomas de Cranesly	?
John Dive	?	Thomas de Hestelel	Killed
John Fitzjohn	Captured	Thomas Menill	?
John Passelow	?	Walter de Crespigny	Killed
Robert de Rowley	?	William de Boyton	?
Matthew Breton	?	William de Burmugham	Killed
Nicholas de Segrave	Killed	William de Mandeville	Killed
Peter de Montfort	Killed	William de Manners	?
Peter de Montfort jnr	?	William de York	Killed
Ralph Bassett of Sapcote	Killed	William Devereux	Killed
Ralph de Normanville	?	William Malteyn	?
Ralph de Otterden	?	William Marmion	?
Richard de Berham	?	William Perons	?
Richard de Coleworth	?	William Tressell	Killed

15. Chivalry at the Battle of Evesham

During the Middle Ages there were attempts, primarily by the church, to limit the scope and bitterness of war by developing theories such as the 'Just War'. The development of the theory of Just War followed the growth of monarchical power because the core tenet of the theory was that only a prince could legitimately declare a Just War. However you define the word 'prince' (and there was a great deal of confusion and dispute among medieval lawyers) Earl Simon's revolt was not Just War whereas Edward's suppression of that revolt was. In reality the idea of Just War did little to limit war between princes, both of whom would have persuaded themselves of the righteousness of their cause and neither of whom would cast themselves in the role of aggressor, and both of whom would have been fighting the Just War. Something similar happens today; war is not prevented but both sides have clear scripts for their propaganda.

During the high Middle Ages the rules of war became clearer, although they were often no more than rationalisations of the way things were, making a virtue of current practice. We need to understand these conventions to be able to judge Edward's actions at Evesham. There was an undoubted sense of what was honourable conduct and this was part of the code of chivalry. There were atrocities and the code was broken, but these incidents were regarded as scandals and were commented on harshly.

The Roman church held a central place in society and the thoughts and actions of lords and knights, as well as the common people, were greatly influenced by the framework of moral authority that it created and maintained and from which few were exempt. The Church's tacit support for Simon de Montfort's rebellion might seem surprising to modern minds that associate the Church with peace and reconciliation. The support of leading churchmen and moralists such as Grosseteste was a tribute to Earl Simon's patronage and moral standing.

The idea of laws and conventions of war dates from ancient times but, in the medieval west, the Church's preachings against the horrors of war and the diffusion of Christian values in a military society, seem to have had some influence. The Church's hold on the consciousness of the entire community is hard to imagine in these godless times; however, military men (in particular) always liked to remain in God's good books. They might shortly be despatched to meet Him. Fighting men would try to hear mass or make confession before going onto the battlefield; failing that, the cross-guard of a sword had to serve as a makeshift cross for a personal devotion.

However, we should not give too much weight to the Church's influence. Among the knightly classes the anticipation of a hefty ransom was probably a stronger incentive to mercy than any Christian precept, and knights had a community of self-interest. The senior combatants, the élite cavalry, were landowners who, with scattered holdings, were frequently neighbours of their current enemies or related to them by marriage. Neighbours could find themselves on opposite sides; moreover, the victor of today may be tomorrow's defeated, so informed self-interest and self-preservation inclined men to extend the courtesy of surrender and ransom, at least in their own class.

Knights were depicted in contemporary literature as paragons of matchless courage and ideal morality. However, knights reacted in combat in much the way that men will in any age. They might have felt braver than others because they were well armoured. They provided mutual support and encouragement by advancing in close formation and peer pressure (to coin a phrase) reinforced ideals of honour, courage, loyalty and steadfastness. But courage was and is a volatile commodity and could evaporate in the fever of an infectious panic.

The knights - and even the non-knightly cavalry - lived in a chivalric world where laws and conventions limited war and a beaten enemy could usually expect to surrender and be ransomed. On the other hand, the infantry on the losing side had no ransom value or family connections to protect them so they usually came off badly in retreat. Fighting between cavalry and infantry was frequently bloody. When mounted troops broke infantry they did not scruple to ride the fugitives down and massacre them, as happened at Evesham. The days when the cry was: 'save the commons; kill the nobles' belong to the later wars of York and Lancaster.

The different treatment of knights and commoners was often noted in medieval warfare. Knights naturally expected that they would not receive chivalric treatment from commoners and were careful to surrender to their own class. The ignominy of capture by an inferior often set defeated knights looking for an equal to surrender to.

Battle tried the relationship between idealistic chivalry and harsh military reality. On one hand some traditional scholars, such as Huizinga[32] and Kilgour[33], have argued that knights and their commanders left their chivalric aspirations behind them when they ventured onto the battlefield. Chivalry was a peacetime fantasy with negligible influence on the conduct of military operations. It was useful for rallying the troops, for inspiring speeches before battle was joined and it helped to reconcile the warrior to the Church, but it was forgotten as soon as it threatened to interfere with winning the battle.

On the other hand, there has been a growing consensus among scholars in recent years that this view is unhelpfully cynical, pointing to instances where fighting men of the knightly classes adhered to the tenets of chivalry even when it was inconvenient to do so and other occasions, where excessive dedication to the ideals of chivalry provoked warriors into rash and foolish actions. The rules were sometimes bent, occasionally broken in the heat of battle but there was a general agreement that chivalry remained the central pillar of military honour. Nevertheless, combatants in the middle ages seem never to have fully resolved the tension between their desire to fight chivalrously and the need to win. For them war was a way of life and the warrior caste drew their identity from their shared culture. The basis of that culture was chivalry so any deviation from the norms of chivalry in pursuit of victory was likely to taint the victor.

Ethical considerations had a limited influence on the conduct of the war but, when great issues were at stake, horrific conduct was common and treason could always be held up as the justification for a massacre. It was not unknown for one party to an agreement to break his word but even when he had an excuse - for example that the oath did not count because the other party belonged to a different religion - this would be disapproved of. Conversely, looting a town that had been taken by storm and massacring its population was perfectly acceptable conduct.

---

[32] Huizinga, Johan H, The Waning of the Middle Ages, 1924
[33] Kilgour, Raymond, The Decline of Chivalry, 1937

Throughout his military career Edward was rarely merciful to defeated enemies. His severity could be justified by the situation - possibly, arguably - but it was hardly chivalric and certainly not Christian.

If the Labordiere manuscript is accurate then Edward had little confidence in his knights' willingness to transcend the code. So much so that he formed his 'death squad' of a dozen men he could trust to do his bidding led by a man with a profound grudge against Earl Simon: Roger de Mortimer. It was less the lack of justification than the sheer savagery of the atrocity that earned the disapproval of the monastic chroniclers. Certainly, the continuator of Matthew Paris thought that when the victorious royalists beheaded and dismembered Earl Simon's corpse, they were breaking the knightly code.

Edward would not have wanted to publicise the existence of his 'death squad'. It would not have been recorded in official documents and (to my current knowledge) only the two accounts make reference to it. It is unlikely that a monastic chronicler would have relished placing himself and his institution in danger by writing about an incident that redounded so much to Lord Edward's discredit. So, where did this information come from?

It may have been a source close to Edward or de Clare who overheard the discussion. It may have been one of the twelve nominated to assassinate de Montfort. Tony Spicer makes a strong case for Guy de Montfort, who was wounded and captured at the battle, hearing rumours about a 'hit squad' or remembering that his brother, Henry, had asked for quarter and been refused, and putting two and two together. He may even have been taunted with his father's murder by one of his captors. If so then this would go a long way towards explaining Guy's actions in 1271 when he murdered his cousin, also called Henry, son of Richard of Cornwall inside the sanctuary of the *Chiesa di San Silvestro* (*Chiesa del Gesù*) in Viterbo. Guy would have confided his suspicions to his younger brother, Amaury, who was a priest and well-placed to make a record of what the family would have regarded as a crime.

16. Tony Spicer's Alternative View

In the 1960's Tony Spicer studied history at Bristol University and the London School of Economics where he wrote a dissertation for his Master's degree on: *The Battle of Poltava, 1709*. He subsequently qualified as a solicitor and practised in Worcester for over 20 years. Reviving his interest in history later in life he joined the Battlefields Trust as a founder member in 1992.

Over the years Tony has organised a number of walks for The Trust. Living in Malvern, local battlefields such as Worcester and Evesham came to be walked most frequently and he wrote a book about the Battle of Worcester (*The Battle of Worcester 1651*, published in 2002 by Paddy Griffith Associates [ISBN 0-9521488-5-4]).

In 1996 Tony led a walk round the Evesham battlefield after the Simon de Montfort Society's annual wreath-laying ceremony and this walk has been repeated each year since then. Tony has used these walks, and other private ones, to try to reconcile the ground with the mediaeval sources. He is candid about doubting that we will ever know exactly what happened at the Battle of Evesham and he does not claim that his theory is necessarily better than any of the others; he does, however, maintain that it is an arguable alternative.

What follows is a slightly amended version of an article that appeared in *Battlefield,* The Journal of Historic Places of Military Conflict, in association with the Battlefields Trust, Volume 8 Issue 4.

Every year, usually the first Saturday in August, The Simon de Montfort Society holds a wreath-laying ceremony in Abbey Park in Evesham in memory of the death of Simon de Montfort at the Battle of Evesham in 1265. I have for several years led a walk round the battlefield after the ceremony and also visited the battlefield on other occasions.

1265 - The Murder of Evesham

When Simon de Montfort found himself cut off and outnumbered in Evesham on August 4th 1265, it is usually assumed that he marched his troops out of the Evesham in column straight up what is now the modern High Street on to Greenhill to attack the enemy there. My walks round the battlefield have made me wonder whether Simon de Montfort may have taken another route out of Evesham, so that the battle, while ending in the traditional place around Battlewell on Greenhill, actually began on the flat expanse of land to the east.

The fascination with the Battle of Evesham, is not so much the battle itself, which was so one sided that it was little more than a massacre, but the strategic approach. How was it that Edward managed to surround his enemy in the loop of the River Avon and how was it that such an experienced soldier as de Montfort allowed himself to be trapped?

To understand how the protagonists found themselves in the area, we need to go back a year. De Montfort had won the battle of Lewes in May 1264 but had done so with the assistance of Gilbert of Clare Earl of Gloucester who, although only twenty-two, was probably, after de Montfort himself, the most powerful baron in the kingdom. Following the battle, de Montfort held both Henry III and his son Lord Edward as his prisoners and effectively ruled the kingdom in the king's name. In January 1265, he held his famous Parliament in London which for the first time included 'Commoners' who were not members of the nobility. But shortly afterwards, he fell out with Gilbert of Clare who departed to his lands in Gloucestershire. De Montfort followed him to try to effect a reconciliation. He did not have an army, but more of an armed court, including the King and Lord Edward.

Negotiations followed at Gloucester and Hereford but came to nothing. On May 28th, Lord Edward escaped and took refuge at Wigmore Castle with Roger de Mortimer, one of de Montfort's most bitter enemies. Whereas Clare's dislike of de Montfort could be described as political, with Mortimer it was personal for each had ravaged the other's lands. Warfare broke out. Edward, Mortimer and Clare combined and raised an army, usually estimated at around 10,000 men, which controlled the eastern side of the Severn. De Montfort, in Hereford, similarly raised an army but his task was more difficult because he was away from his main sphere of influence. He did however hire some spearmen from Llewellyn of Wales. The other thing which he did was to send messages to his son Simon, who was in Sussex, telling him to raise

1265 - The Murder of Evesham

an army and come to his assistance. Various manoeuvres and attempts by Simon senior to cross the Severn followed, but the end of July 1265 finds Simon senior still at Hereford, the royalist army in Worcester and Simon junior arriving at Kenilworth which was a de Montfort stronghold.

Thereafter, events moved rapidly, by anybody's standards. Although, from some accounts, an extra day was involved, the most likely diary - incredible as it seems - is as follows:

- **Friday July 31st:** Simon junior arrives at Kenilworth.
- **Saturday August 1st:** Spies inform Edward that the nobility in Simon's army are sleeping in the grounds of the Priory in the town, outside the protection of the castle. In the afternoon, Edward with his army sets off for Kenilworth.
- **Sunday August 2nd:** Edward beats up Simon junior's quarters at Kenilworth, capturing banners and important prisoners. The same day, Simon senior, no doubt hearing about Edward's departure from Worcester on the Saturday, marches from Hereford, crosses the Severn and occupies Kempsey about three miles south of Worcester.
- **Monday August 3rd:** Edward returns to Worcester from Kenilworth. Simon senior spends most of the day at Kempsey but departs for Evesham in the evening.
- **Tuesday August 4th:** Simon senior arrives at Evesham about 5 am. The royalists arrive at Evesham sometime between then and 9 am. when the battle starts.

Our first puzzle concerns Edward's brilliantly successful attack on Kenilworth. Intelligence had reached him that the nobility in Simon's army had decided against roughing it in the castle but had pitched their pavilions and tents in the grounds of the Priory. A visit to Kenilworth in the summer and comparison of the beautiful grounds of the old Priory with the forbidding castle can make one understand why. With hindsight, Simon junior's negligence seems appalling, but at the time, an overnight march by Edward's army from Worcester must have seemed beyond comprehension.

According to A. H. Burne, in his book *The Battlefields of England*, it is thirty-four miles from Worcester to Kenilworth, and this figure seems to be generally accepted. However, looking at the map of principal west midland roads in D. C. Cox's *Battle of*

Evesham - a new account and assuming that Edward went via Barbourne and Droitwich (there is Chronicler evidence to support this) and avoided Warwick, I estimate the distance at over forty miles. Warwick Castle had been taken by John Gifford, governor of Kenilworth castle, for de Montfort earlier in the Barons war and partially destroyed and although the situation is confused by Gifford changing sides, Warwick castle does not seem to have been restored to the Royalist cause until well after the Battle of Evesham. It therefore seems unlikely that Edward would risk taking troops through Warwick in the middle of the night which might alert de Montfort sympathisers.

Unfortunately, we know so little about how Edward's army was mobilised, how it was organised, fed, equipped and trained. Some clues however can be found in *The Welsh Wars of Edward I* by John Morris which tells of the period only a dozen years later. Here is an extract from a list of soldiers presenting themselves for the campaign of 1277:

    4 archers, with bow and 25 arrows each.
    1 archer with a bow and 2 arrows
    1 archer with a bow and an unspecified number of arrows
    1 archer with a bow without a cord
    1 sergeant to carry the king's bows
    7 boys with horses of low value, sacks and spits
    6 men with spades or axes, etc.

Applying this sort of scenario, it does not take much imagination to realise that many of the recruits turning up for the Evesham campaign would not have been suitable for a forty-mile march and dawn attack and I cannot believe that Edward took his whole army or even most of it, overnight, to Kenilworth. I think he took only a relatively small detachment of his best troops which is important because it has a bearing on what happened later.

There is some information in the chronicles which supports this. While some accounts simply say that Edward took his army to Kenilworth, others imply that only part was used. Most say that Edward and Clare went to Kenilworth but make no mention of Mortimer. It would be logical for Edward to take Clare with him. Firstly,

Clare is likely to have had the nucleus of the division of experienced men which he commanded at Lewes, and secondly, bearing in mind that Clare had fought against Edward only the previous year, Edward would want to keep an eye on him. But of Mortimer, there is no mention and it is my suggestion that his part of the army did not take part in the attack on Kenilworth. There is mention in the chronicles of a surprise attack and rapid movement which again would be consistent with a smaller force. Guisborough says that the force hid in a deep ditch near the castle and heard the sound of troops coming towards them (which in fact turned out be foraging party) which put them in fear of discovery so that they mounted their horses and put lances in their hands. There is no mention of infantry, and the fear of discovery suggests a smallish force totally dependent upon surprise for success. Although my knowledge of Kenilworth is not extensive, I was not able to find evidence of a deep ditch near the castle capable of hiding an army of 10,000 men.

The chronicle which gives most support to part only of the army going to Kenilworth is the *Evesham Chronicle*. It describes how Simon junior 'hurried with his men towards Kenilworth where not many days later he was plundered most shamefully. For, about the festival of James the apostle, Edward the first-born son of the King and Gilbert of Clare, Count of Gloucester and William of Wales and other temporal lords then in the City of Worcester pretended to march towards Shrewsbury and as a precaution sent their horse trappings with the foot soldiers towards that place. When they came to the road which veered towards Kenilworth, they took that route.' This implies that the raiding party slipped away north of Worcester and the rest of the army, mainly foot, continued on the Shrewsbury Road until sufficient time had elapsed to make it impossible for anybody to warn Kenilworth, and then retraced their steps to Worcester.

At Kenilworth, Edward's raid was a success except that he failed to capture Simon junior, doubtless an important objective. The surprise was total and from the above passage, it may be that it was unheard of at the time for men of quality to be attacked while asleep, unarmed and defenceless, by others of their own class which may have been partly responsible for the decision to sleep in the open in the first place. This may also be the reason why relatively few casualties are reported, most of the magnates who were attacked, being made prisoner. Simon junior is usually described as escaping, partially dressed, by means of a boat over the lake which is between the Priory grounds and the castle although one chronicler says that Simon junior in fact slept in the castle. Edward's success was to capture banners, horses and a number of the leaders of Simon junior's army which, although not destroyed, was thoroughly disorganised and its morale severely dented.

The apparent departure of the royalist army for Shrewsbury on the afternoon of Saturday August 1st was doubtless reported quickly to Simon senior in Hereford by his spies. It may be that Simon senior smelt a rat, but he had been trying to cross the Severn for weeks and had to make the most of this opportunity. Either the same day or early on the Sunday morning his army set out from Hereford, succeeded in crossing the Severn and spent Sunday night at Kempsey, about three miles south of Worcester, a tough journey of twenty-five miles. At this stage he must have intended to march straight on to Kenilworth, skirting Worcester to the east and then taking the Alcester road (modern A422). If he had intended to go directly from Hereford to Evesham, he would surely have crossed the Severn further south than Kempsey.

From Henry III's roll of oblations, which appears to be the strongest source (relevant extract in *The Battles of Lewes and Evesham 1264/65* by David Carpenter) Simon senior spent Monday 3rd August or at any rate most of it at Kempsey. According to the Westminster Chronicle and Guisborough, Simon senior was ignorant of the Kenilworth fiasco. We do not know why he stayed at Kempsey for so long but my guess is that he tried to renew his march to Kenilworth, skirting Worcester to the east to go via Alcester but found that there was far too much royalist activity in and around Worcester to enable him to do so. I think that by that time, the infantry which had pretended to go towards Shrewsbury had returned to Worcester and that there was also in Worcester Roger of Mortimer and his marcher forces. Simon senior was forced to change his route and make a more circuitous journey via Evesham. I think it was still his intention to go to Kenilworth after Evesham rather than attempt arrangements, which could well have gone wrong, for his son to meet him at Evesham.

There is virtual agreement over Simon senior's route from Kempsey to Evesham. He went from Kempsey to Pershore, crossed the Avon there and then continued south of the Avon to Evesham where he crossed the bridge into the town where his army could enjoy the hospitality of the Abbey. By contrast, there is considerable disagreement over the royalist approach. I have usually given a talk about the various theories during my Evesham battlefield walks and can summarise them as follows.

The first theory, that of e.g. C. Oman in his *The Art of War in the Middle Ages*, is that Edward divided his army at Worcester into three divisions, under himself, Clare and Mortimer. Mortimer took the same route as Simon senior, Clare took the Worcester/Evesham Road which keeps to the north of the Avon (modern A4538 turning into the renumbered A44), north of the Avon ending up on Greenhill a mile or so north of Evesham and Edward cut across along the modern A422 via Inkberrow to cut the Alcester Evesham Road (now the B 4088) and then went south to Green Hill to join Clare. Oman's principal authority for this is a strong source, the dramatic and a detailed account of Walter of Guisborough:

'...... he [Edward] proceeded towards Evesham on the third day and having divided his army into three divisions, he himself with his men from one side, the Count of Gloucester from another and Roger of Mortimer came from behind. And so Edward the son of the King came from the northern side as it were from Kenilworth to Evesham, and so that he should not be recognised from afar, put up first the standard of Simon junior and of the rest of those that he had captured, so that by this deception he could occupy the hill first and have the best position. When he saw this, Nicholas the barber who was the Earl's lookout, a man expert in the recognition of arms, seeing the armed men coming from afar said to the Earl 'Here come many armed men from the north, and as far as I can see from afar, they appear to be your standards.' And he said 'It is my son. Do not be afraid but go and have a closer look so that we are not by chance taken by surprise'. He did not then know what had happened to his son. The look-out therefore went up himself to the top of the bell tower of the Abbey where they had taken hospitality and clearly recognised the standards of the king's son from one side, the other standards having been discarded, and the standards of the Count of Gloucester from another side and similarly the standard of Roger of Mortimer from the west and from behind; he shouted to the him and said ' We are all dead..........' '

Nicholas was evidently not a man to mince his words or break bad news gently.

Although Oman relied principally on Guisborough, this three directional approach is supported by other Chroniclers, e.g. Trevet who says that Edward approached the town of Evesham from one side and from two other sides came the Earl of Gloucester with his division and Roger of Mortimer with his host, and in particular by the Evesham Chronicle which says the Count of Leicester was cut off from every side so that he must either surrender immediately or give battle with his forces. The assumption on the face of it therefore is that the three royalist divisions set off from Worcester by different routes.

However, there were objections to this theory. From a military point of view, it was argued that a capable commander such as Edward would not have divided his forces until the last possible moment. It was also pointed out that there was another route to Kenilworth along the east side of the Avon via Bidford and that Edward would need to block that too. The chronicler support for this is a line in Trevet 'and Edward, moving from Worcester, the river having been crossed next to the town which is called Clive, intercepted with his army the route of the father towards the son who was in Kenilworth Castle and that of the son to the father.' Clive is usually taken to mean Cleeve Prior and for example J. Ramsay in his *Dawn of the Constitution* argued that Edward had gone from Worcester across to Cleeve Prior, crossed the Avon there and then marched along the east bank to Offenham, where he divided his forces, sending Mortimer on to block the Bengeworth bridge so that Simon senior could not escape that way and with his own division and that of Clare going back over the Avon via the footbridge at Offenham and taking up the position on Greenhill.

Ramsay's view is the main basis for the theory that the battle itself centred on the hillock, where the obelisk is now, over to the west side of the battlefield. According to Ramsay, Simon senior realised what was happening, and tried to reach the Greenhill crossroads before Edward's army but was pushed to the west by the weight of numbers coming up Blayney's lane from Offenham and was forced to take up his position around the obelisk area, which was the best he could find in the circumstances and at least gave him some higher ground. This does not seem unrealistic to me but of course it depends upon the crossing of the Avon by Edward at Cleeve Prior.

Other historians have had similar views, albeit with reservations and variations as to how Edward got his troops together on Greenhill with Mortimer blocking the Bengeworth Bridge from the south of the Avon. I do not want go into these in detail because new evidence shows that the Cleeve Prior theory is probably wrong, but the reader will find it in many of the accounts of the Battle of Evesham. However, in 1988, D.C. Cox seriously challenged the Cleeve Prior crossing theory in his book *The*

Battle of Evesham, a new account. He argued that the logistical problems involved in crossing at Cleeve Prior and organising a three directional approach were too complicated for a thirteenth century army. His view was that 'the river having been crossed next to the town which is called Clive' referred to Simon senior's earlier crossing of the River Severn at Clevelode and that 'Clive' was the hamlet of Clifton on the east bank of the Severn opposite Clevelode. Edward had simply taken the old road, north of the Avon from Worcester until he was near Greenhill just north of Evesham and then divided his army into three divisions. He interpreted the position of Mortimer 'from the west and from behind' as meaning that Mortimer's division was behind and to the west of Edward's, when the royalist forces deployed on Greenhill.

Cox's view necessitates the Bengeworth Bridge being left open to Simon de Montfort, and might have remained a minority one but for a document which subsequently came to light and gave strong support to much of his argument. It is dated about 1330 but appears to be a copy of an earlier version by somebody who had access to witnesses of the events of the time. It is set out in full as *The last hours of Simon de Montfort: A New Account* in *English Historical Review vol. C X V (2000)* p 378, and I summarise the points where it differs from other chroniclers.

1. It was suggested to Simon senior that his army should defend itself in the abbey precincts. Simon refused 'No, fair friend no. One ought to see knights on the battlefield and chaplains in churches.'

2. As the army came out of Abbey Gate Sir Guy of Balliol shattered the lance bearing the standard against the top of the gate. The earl said: 'God help us now'.

3. When they came to the *'lavour'* of the town Simon addressed his followers to the effect that some of them, particularly the younger ones, could escape over the bridge.

4. Edward and Gilbert Clare had knighted several men in a meadow called Mosham between Craycombe and Evesham and had designated 12 men to seek out and kill Simon de Montfort. They then came up the hill, (i.e. Greenhill) in three divisions.

5. Simon saw the Earl of Gloucester's banner coming up alongside over towards the river.

6. Simon was killed by Roger de Mortimer.

1265 - The Murder of Evesham

As with other chroniclers, the author of the *New Account* gives verbatim detail of what Simon de Montfort supposedly said prior to the battle. It is difficult to know what to make of this. We do not know who the witnesses were and there must have been more than one as the same person could hardly have been at the '*lavour*' with de Montfort and in Mosham meadow with Edward. The words supposedly said could have passed through several people before reaching the chronicler. The more sententious phrases attributed to him may well have been influenced by the circumstances of his death with his admirers eager to preserve, no doubt quite sincerely, what they thought would have been his last words. On the other hand, this was the chroniclers' way of telling their stories, so I am assuming, particularly where a practical matter is concerned, that something of that nature was said or discussed.

Of the six points mentioned above by far the most compelling is the information that Edward and Clare were together in Mosham meadow before the battle. This meadow has been identified as being between the River Avon and the Worcester/Evesham Road (A 4538 recently renumbered A44) and below Craycombe Hill. 'Meanwhile Sir Edward and Sir Gilbert de Clare, Earl of Gloucester had knighted several men in the meadow called Mosham between Craycombe and Evesham'. This is strong evidence that Edward and Clare had simply marched along the road from Worcester to Evesham and had not been involved in any complicated manoeuvres of crossing the Avon at Cleeve Prior and recrossing it at Offenham.

At first glance, point 3 seems to confirm that there were no royalist troops south of the Avon and that the whole army was with Edward and Clare in Mosham meadow. 'And when they came to the *lavour* of the town of Evesham, the Earl addressed everyone together and said 'Fair Lords there are many among you who are not as yet tried and tested in the world and who are young; you have wives and children and for this reason look to how you might save yourselves and them; cross the bridge and you will escape from the great peril that is to come." This, on the face of it, indicates that the bridge was not blocked by Mortimer's men and that de Montfort's army could have escaped over it. However, I do not think it is as simple as that. I cannot believe that De Montfort would simply have allowed Mortimer to march up to the bridge on the other side of the river and block it. I suggest that the bridge was still held by de Montfort's army, probably with pickets on the other side of the bridge to defend it if an attack came from that direction. It would be quite possible for some of the 'Fair Lords' to escape over the bridge on an individual basis. Probably Mortimer remained some way off and would need time to prepare an attack on the bridge. But what de Montfort's army could not cope with was a simultaneous attack from the royalists on Greenhill. If the army tried to cross the bridge to the south east, it would be attacked in the rear from Greenhill and in the flank by Mortimer's division, probably cutting the army in half. De Montfort did not see much future in being besieged in the Abbey and so chose to lead his army out against the royalists on Greenhill where at least he could fight them in the open and have some control over what went on.

Otherwise, if there was nothing stopping de Montfort from crossing the bridge to the south east, it is difficult to see why he did not do so. He did not need to flee towards London but simply to move onto the higher ground near Bengeworth, less than a mile away, where at least he would have a decent defensive position and an open route along the east side of the Avon to send messengers to Kenilworth. By doing so, he would be putting the bridge between himself and his enemies and, while he may not have been able to actually demolish it, he could have made it difficult to cross and thereby gained himself valuable time. Also, where at point 1, there was discussion of the army defending itself in the Abbey, there is no mention of the Bengeworth option, which implies that it was not available.

Point 6 is also consistent with Mortimer being on the south of the Avon. The new account is the only one that actually says that Mortimer killed de Montfort but other chroniclers say that his head and private parts were sent to Lady Mortimer. This could only really have happened had Mortimer or his men killed de Montfort and captured his body. If Edward did want Simon de Montfort killed and organised his assassination squad accordingly (and this is debatable because other chroniclers suggest that he would have spared him if he could; indeed he spared Simon's son Guy who was wounded in the battle). Edward would hardly have allowed such mutilation of the body of his godfather and uncle by marriage had he been able to stop it. If Mortimer's division had been with the rest of the royalist army to the west and to the rear of Edward's division it is unlikely to have been at the heart of fighting. If on the other hand it had been south of the bridge then as soon as de Montfort's army marched northwards it would have been a simple matter to take the bridge, brushing aside any rearguard left by de Montfort, whose likely priority would be sanctuary in the Abbey, and then use the mounted men to charge after de Montfort (and Mortimer hated de Montfort) and attack him in the rear.

The next question is how Mortimer's division came to be south of the Avon. Was this part of a master plan or did it just work out that way? What follows is mostly speculation, but on the previous day, de Montfort was in Kempsey trying to break out past Worcester towards Kenilworth. On my reconstruction, Mortimer did not go to Kenilworth but was at Worcester and able to stop him. Doubtless there was skirmishing between the armies and then de Montfort, unsuccessful in his attempt to get through, slips away towards Evesham. My guess is that Mortimer followed him. Mortimer, as head of a Marcher army would have been used to acting independently and expected to do so. In Wales the law of the March would have applied. This basically meant that what land you conquered you kept but that if you needed help from the King to keep it, then such land belonged to the King. The law of the March would not apply in Evesham, but maybe Mortimer pursued the same concept. If he defeated de Montfort's army, then he was entitled to the spoils. This independent action may have been specifically pre-arranged with Edward, or more probably, when Mortimer realised that de Montfort had left for Evesham, he was not going to let him get away and followed his route, leaving messages in Worcester for Edward and Clare that he had done so.

So, on the Monday evening we have de Montfort slipping away towards Evesham via Pershore with his army, and Mortimer, once he realises what is happening, follows him. At Evesham, de Montfort makes his fatal decision to cross over the bridge to the comfort of the Abbey where he can get the provisions he needs for his troops, also perhaps influenced by the King's desire for spiritual as well as bodily refreshment. But there may be another reason for crossing the bridge into the town. De Montfort is aiming for Kenilworth, he has to cross the Avon somewhere and better the bridge here than some ford higher up. Perhaps he suspects that he is being followed by royalist forces, in which case, he can put the river and the easily defended bridge between him and them.

So, de Montfort crosses the Avon into Evesham, spending longer there than he intends, with his army exhausted and his men queuing and jostling to get something to eat. The King is not hurrying, either because he is not naturally inclined to do so or because some royalist sympathiser in de Montfort's army has got wind of what is likely to happen and tipped him off. De Montfort then learns the appalling news, not only that Mortimer is approaching from behind him and threatening the bridge but that there are royalist forces north of Evesham as well. At first, the only visible forces are on Greenhill and there is another route out of Evesham which goes alongside the River Avon. It is a short cut, avoiding Greenhill. De Montfort marches out in that direction. Humphrey de Bohun wants the infantry in the rear but de Montfort is having none of that and moves the infantry up on the right alongside the river with the river protecting its right flank. The cavalry are on the left, protecting the infantry. A rear guard has been left to hold the bridge against Mortimer.

But Edward has anticipated this. From Mosham meadow, he has sent Clare north east with his division over towards the river using the cover of a small but longish hill so that he cannot be seen until he is near the river and then advances rapidly towards de Montfort's army. Clare's division crashes into de Montfort's infantry near Siveldeston. It is too much for de Montfort's Welsh spearmen, who have probably had little enthusiasm for the venture once east of the Severn. They abandon the battle and try to flee over the footbridge at Offenham. Some escape, most are either drowned in the river or cut down nearby in what came to be known as Deadman's Ait.

Deserted by their infantry, the cavalry try to continue alongside the river. But the enemy is too thick. De Montfort looks towards Greenhill. The enemy line is thinner there, because of the transfer of troops towards the river. It is his only chance. His cavalry charge up Blayney's lane and the eastern side of Greenhill. At the top, they force back the troops in Edward's division, who are taken by surprise. But these rally and de Montfort's cavalry is held. Gradually the overwhelming numerical superiority of the royalists begins to tell, and their line, reinforced by some of Clare's troops from the east, starts to encircle de Montfort's cavalry. The final blow comes as Mortimer's division, brushing aside the defences at the bridge, storms up Greenhill and smashes into the remains of de Montfort's army from the rear. De Montfort and his entourage are killed by Mortimer's men, and the battle breaks up into a series of rolling mauls with the rest of the de Montfort magnates either being killed or captured depending on into whose hands they fell.

But what actual evidence is there of this interpretation of the battle? I suggest the following.

1. One of the chroniclers, Nicholas Trevet says that both armies met in a large plain outside the town *'in campo extra oppidum spatioso'*. This may on the face of it sound like chroniclers' verbiage, but if you walk out of Evesham via Mill Street and Common Road you will indeed see before you a spacious plain stretching from Greenhill to the River Avon. Common Road turns into a footpath which links up with Blayney's Lane, by then also a footpath, at the Evesham bypass. On the other side of the bypass the footpath continues to the Avon and then along its west bank. Did this footpath exist as a road at the time? In his study of ridgeways, which were the great through roads of the time, Dr Grundy, (who incidentally took the standard view that de Montfort had marched up Greenhill, which was the Ridgeway) also pointed out that there could be 'summer ways' where people took a short cut in the summer which was denied to them by a the wetness of the ground in the winter. I suggest that the road out of Evesham by the Common Road was such a summer way and there is some evidence from a study of the Evesham Civil War defences that a road existed there in the seventeenth century. So, if de Montfort did take this route, he would soon find himself in a great plain outside the town and where he could at least see where the enemy was attacking from as opposed to marching up the ridgeway to Greenhill and trying to guess what was over the other side.

2. The wash-house incident in the new account. I quote from the Norman French. *'E quant il vindrent au lavour de la vile de Evesham, le conte communement dit a touz......'* The translation in English Historical Review translates *lavour* as conduit with a note that it could mean washing place in the alternative. I am not an expert in Norman French but in modern French 'conduit' is exactly the same word. *'Lavoir'* in modern French means wash-house. I would have thought therefore that the more likely translation was wash-house. In a town with a river, would you not expect to find the wash-house by the river? I suggest that it was on the outskirts of the town in the area of what is now Mill Street and Common Road.

3. According to Wykes, Edward divided his army into two divisions, the first one under himself, and the second under Clare. It was only the first division that could initially be seen at a distance by the de Montfort army; the second division was hidden by a small intervening hill. It is usually assumed that the small intervening

hill was Greenhill on the basis that there is no other hill, but as Edward's division was on Greenhill, it is rather difficult to see how Clare's division could be coming from a different direction and yet hidden by the same hill. But in fact, there is another hill further back from Greenhill on the road from the A4538 (recently renumbered A44) to Lenchwick. From a distance, it looks more like a long ridge than a hill although when you walk up it, it is steeper than it looks! There is also another hill at Twyford. The point is that they are directly between Mosham Meadow and the Avon to the east which is the way that Clare would have been likely to have gone if he was to block the route along the river which I suggest that de Montfort took out of Evesham. If he kept his troops just behind these hills then for much of the time his division would have been out of sight of de Montfort's army. One of the things which Simon de Montfort supposedly said before the battle was 'by the arm of St James they approach wisely; but they learnt this method from me, not from themselves'. If de Montfort did say that, I wonder if he was referring to moving troops out of sight of the enemy. I think he may have done something like this at Lewes, using the ridges in the Downs to hide his troops while he moved them into the position which he wanted, and according to John Morris, his father used the same technique in 1213 at the Battle of Muret during the Albigensian Wars. So perhaps de Clare is now using the same trick which he had learned from de Montfort at Lewes.

4. Although the new account says that the royalist army came up the hill in three divisions, it goes on to say that de Montfort saw the Earl of Gloucester's banner coming up alongside over towards the river. This is consistent with Clare blocking de Montfort's escape route and clashing with him at Siveldeston near the river.

5. A passage in the Evesham chronicle refers to Siveldeston as a place of significance at the beginning of the battle, going on to say that Humphrey De Bohun and all the Welsh foot soldiers fled. Siveldeston was an old boundary stone, in Blayney's Lane about 100 yards west of the Offenham footbridge. It disappeared during the nineteenth century, but it would have been about 20 yards east of the modern bypass.

6. Tyndall, writing in 1794, was informed by a farmer of many bones having been found in Deadman's Ait and also around the area just to the west of it. At that time Deadman's Ait was an island in the Avon opposite Offenham although it has now

merged with the west bank. The bones were never dated, and it has been suggested that they could have come from a Saxon burial site. Nevertheless, the location is entirely consistent with the Welsh spearmen fleeing from Siveldeston to Offenham Bridge, prevented by the bottleneck from crossing it there, and attempting to swim across the river with consequent heavy casualties.

7. In 1757 Dr Richard Pococke was told at Evesham that the battle was in the Evesham Kenilworth Road and in Blayney's Lane. A small point perhaps, but evidence of a local tradition of fighting in Blayney's Lane.

So I hope that there is enough evidence to persuade the reader to consider this reconstruction as an option worth thinking about next time he or she visits the Evesham battlefield. Make your way out of Evesham via Mill Street and Common Road and along the footpath into the *'campo spatioso'*. In front of you – north-west and to your left is Greenhill with Edward's soldiers on it. In front of you, slightly to the right and north east is Clare's division coming up alongside the River Avon towards you. Behind you, probably out of sight behind the Abbey Tower - but you can sense the danger - is Mortimer and his host of Marchers. The enemy really is coming at you from three directions.

17. The End of the Revolt

Simon de Montfort died at Evesham but the ideas of the reform movement did not, continuing to frustrate the royal revival. Fleeing Evesham and fearing for their lives, those still loyal to de Montfort's cause occupied his former stronghold of Kenilworth Castle, and the Isle of Axholme in north Lincolnshire. Henry, heavy-handed as always, confiscated the lands of all of the Montfortians. With nothing left to lose 'The Disinherited' proved tougher opposition than Henry had expected.

Between May 24th and December 20th 1266 the full might of the Crown was turned against the lingering insurgents at Kenilworth in what was to become one of the longest sieges in English history. Mining the walls was impossible because of the water defences. The besiegers used siege towers and catapults and even tried an amphibious assault in barges across the Great Mere. It was rumoured that the defenders had kept the gates of the castle open as a gesture of defiance and as an invitation to the royal forces to enter a killing ground.

Several attacks were launched by Montfortian men-at-arms on the siege lines, causing much damage and loss of life. This was one reason why men-at-arms were as important to the defence of a castle as were crossbowmen and archers. Yet food was equally important, and lack of provisions was a major reason that the defenders asked for a truce, saying that if no help came within forty days they would surrender and be allowed to march out with full military honours.

Eventually the reformers capitulated. Unsettled by the ferocity of the opposition to him Henry outlined a process of rehabilitation in the *Dictum of Kenilworth*, promulgated on October 31st 1266. Those who wanted to reclaim their lands could do so for a fine, determined by the nature of their involvement in the 'disturbance of the realm'. The *Dictum* represented a loosening of attitudes; however, its terms were still harsh.

Sir John de Deyville[34] and his men would not accept the *Dictum* and, in April 1267, his mentor, Gilbert de Clare, having betrayed Earl Simon, now changed sides again

---

[34] John de Deyville was one of the leaders of the so-called *Disinherited*, the expropriated former rebels, who continued the fight into 1266. He plundered **Sheffield** and burned down **Sheffield Castle**, escaped from defeat at the **Battle of Chesterfield**, plundered **Lincoln** (where he murdered Jews and

and occupied London, where de Deyville joined him. Faced with the prospect of a renewed civil war, Henry offered further concessions. After sundry adventures de Clare surrendered London but he had achieved his objective: with peace finally restored Henry was careful not to provide further fuel for revolt. Magna Carta was not challenged again and passed into the constitution during the reign of Edward I.

Simon de Montfort has, for many years, being held as the 'Father of Parliament'. By summoning knights and burgesses to the Parliament of January 1265 Simon set a precedent and laid the foundations for a future House of Commons. However, it was left to Edward I to establish the house as a mechanism for raising extraordinary revenue, funds extra to normal government requirements such as those needed raise an army, and to enact a thorough overhaul of local government on the lines of the 1258-9 settlements.

---

destroyed their records), and led a group of the Disinherited people to the Isle of Ely from where they raided to Cambridge and Norwich. One of the more colourful Montfortians.

18. Evesham Today

There are only a few physical reminders of 1265 in Evesham. The slope where Earl Simon kept his appointment with destiny has been partially clad with houses and the contours of the slope have shifted in 750 years. There are a total of fifteen medieval buildings or other structures in Evesham. Of the great abbey of St Mary and St Ecgwine that dominated the town scarcely one stone remains on top of another: a few stretches of wall, a cloister arch and an ancient gateway. The adjacent twin parish churches, originally built in the twelfth century, are largely Victorian restoration. The great gatehouse, now converted into apartments, was rebuilt in the fourteenth century. The town's bell tower was built under the Tudors, not the Plantagenets, but may have replaced an earlier *campanile*. The bridge that Earl Simon's army crossed to enter the town has been replaced by another, slightly to one side of the site of the medieval bridge. There is hardly a stone, wall, tree or field that survives unchanged from 1265.

Nevertheless, for such an early battle, Evesham is relatively well understood and the battlefield itself lies within a restricted area clearly defined by very distinct terrain features, including the river Avon. Although some parts of the battlefield cannot, at present, be accessed one can gain a reasonably good feel for the character of the terrain and the possible positioning of the forces from the Battlewell Conservation Area.

The town of Evesham is well organised for the tourist. There are several car parks close to the centre and there are various pubs, cafes and other facilities. There is also plenty of information, some free and some for sale, including town maps, a town trail and a battlefield trail available from the Tourist Information Centre in the Almonry Museum. This includes a leaflet on the Battle of Evesham produced by the Vale of Evesham Civic Society and the Simon de Montfort Society. Following the trail round the early centre of medieval Evesham it is still possible to capture something of the flavour of the town in 1265.

Parts of the Almonry, itself a patchwork quilt of architectural styles stretching back to 1134, were in existence at the time of the battle and Earl Simon would have ridden past them on his way into Evesham abbey and again on his way to Greenhill.

29 The Almonry Museum and Heritage Centre, Abbey Gate, Evesham. The Simon de Montfort Room lies behind the large mullioned window on the left of the picture (author's photograph)

The museum contains the Simon de Montfort Room, opened by the speaker of the House of Commons, Sir Harry Hylton-Foster, in 1965 to commemorate the 700th anniversary of the battle.

The abbey precinct is a remnant of the open space of the Saxon and mediaeval abbey precincts. The area stretches down to the river Avon and includes St Lawrence's church (where Simon heard mass on the morning of the battle), All Saints church, the bell tower, the remains of the west wall of the north transept of the abbey and a cleared area at the rear of the abbey gatehouse where the cloister stood in 1265. The buildings stand at the highest point of the site above the river within a substantial area of green space, broadly corresponding to the sacred enclave of the original Abbey is. Although little remains of the thirteenth century, the Almonry Museum probably occupies the site of the original Almoner's House of Evesham

30 Evesham High Street with the detached *campanile* of Evesham Abbey in the background. Greenhill lies behind the photographer (author's photograph)

Abbey. Between the marketplace and the abbey precinct is an original gateway, which has been confidently dated to 1138.

Merstow Green is a former marketplace and the housing area of the original Saxon settlement opposite the entrance to the Abbey. Although today's buildings date mainly from the sixteenth and nineteenth centuries many of them replace or remodel earlier buildings. Narrow roads and lanes leading up the former marketplace are surrounded by a mix of cottages and tenements that were occupied by the tied tenants of the Abbey. The layout of narrow roads and lanes and the triangular shape of the former marketplace along with the grain of small narrow linear plots, the small-scale tightly packed buildings and the presence of some timber framed buildings, date back to the earliest settlements in Evesham. Vine Street, the marketplace and the lower High Street were planned mediaeval extensions to the earliest Saxon settlement at Merstow Green. This area includes a former main marketplace of the town and its main thoroughfare. The buildings here date from as early as the fifteenth and sixteenth century and the majority would date to the eighteenth and nineteenth centuries, again either replacing or remodelling much earlier buildings, as is evident from the medieval beams that appear on the exposed ends of some buildings. Whenever they were built these buildings still reflect the frontages of the original mediaeval burgage plots that had been in place in 1265. There is a continuous line of buildings down each side of this area broken only by an occasional gap. Walls and buildings still define plots at the rear of the area.

Bridge Street is part of the mediaeval town and almost certainly pre-existed the development of the town centre as a principal route from the river crossing from Bengeworth to the earliest Saxon settlement. The former Crown Hotel, now Marilyns Nightclub ('Mazza's') stands in place of an early mediaeval inn. The narrow street climbing steeply up to the Market Square from the river is currently lined with commercial premises. Buildings date from the fifteenth century although, again, the majority are eighteenth and nineteenth-century buildings, most of them containing the fabric of medieval buildings. Individual buildings sit tight against each other with an occasional gap between buildings. The frontages of the buildings on Bridge Street correspond either to the original burgage frontage, to a multiple of burgage frontages or to a fraction of burgage frontages so the mediaeval street plan is still very much evident and easily identifiable.

Perhaps the most evocative area of central Evesham is Cowl Street, an area that is part of the grid of narrow mediaeval streets to the rear of the High Street and Bridge Street and where there was a tightly-packed community of workers cottages, workshops and other domestic and commercial buildings. Many historic buildings have gone; however much of historic plot definition is still present. The remaining historic buildings and narrow lanes still give a good sense of history and the character today is still that of a street of modest buildings with a run of small domestic premises at the Bridge Street and Cowl Street having Georgian frontages on mediaeval buildings. Further along Cowl Street one cottage has been restored very much to the condition it would have been in when originally built in the reign of King John.

It would be a mistake to neglect Bengeworth. The mediaeval plan of this suburb is evident, with tightly packed linear plots on both sides of Port Street. The name refers to the inland port that once stood at the foot of the street. Some of the buildings have visibly earlier origins with timber framing apparent in rear, side and internal walls. Historically a main thoroughfare, the street is still heavily used by motor traffic. This again is a narrow, steeply sloping, street. Church Street is a quiet, mainly residential, area where the vacant site of the old church occupies a tranquil setting of small cottages on sites that were filled by small buildings in 1265. The church of St Peter would have stood in the centre of the square at that time with, to one side, the remains of the building that we now know was a hunting lodge used by King Canute and his immediate successors.

Greenhill remains surprisingly intact; the course of the battle can easily be traced on the ground and it is possible to get a good feel for the terrain and the general position and movement of the forces. Currently, there is footpath access through the Battlewell conservation area along a planned trail. The Simon de Montfort Society and the Battlefields Trust have provided an interpretation panel.

The Simon de Montfort Society is a heritage and educational charity, founded in 1987. Among its objectives the Society seeks to protect and preserve the site of the Battle of Evesham and this was given a boost when, after lengthy negotiation, the Society was able to lease the Battlewell Field from the Rudge Estate. The field has been well preserved, despite changes in agricultural use over the centuries. In 1265 it would have been mostly open scrubland. In the north-west corner of the Battlewell field, there are the remains of a ridge-and-furrow system, which may be later than 1265.

Battlewell has been managed under an Environmental Stewardship Agreement, which enabled the Society to accept funds from Natural England to offset part of the cost of maintaining the field. This imposed certain duties on the Society, which was required to carry out capital works on the field, including installing sheep fencing with wooden field gates that can be operated from a wheelchair, hedgerow planting, pond restoration, scrub management, promoting wildlife on the field (such as installing bat boxes and nesting boxes in a derelict barn on the site) planting fruit trees to screen the field, to plan grassland management and to agree management

31 One of a series of customised pavement slabs on Evesham's High Street commemorates the Battle of Evesham (Source: the Simon de Montfort Society)

plans for the ponds. That the stewardship arrangement was so successful owes much to Clive Bostle, a trustee of the Simon de Montfort Society, who expended a great deal of 'blood, toil, tears and sweat' on the field.

There was a fear that the required capital works might change the character of the field or interfere with the archaeological trace. These fears were proved to be unfounded as Natural England and Worcestershire County Archaeological

Department provided advice and consultancy so that the Society was able to fulfil its obligations under the Stewardship Agreement without compromising the archaeology. Worcestershire Archaeological Service advised that the optimum way to display the site would be to restore it, in time, as close as possible to its condition in 1265 so that visitors can stand in the field, look across the uncluttered half of the battlefield and have a flavour of how it looked on the day. This is a much bigger challenge than it sounds; however, it is well under way.

The Battlewell lease does not permit intrusive archaeology on the site. Although there is documentary evidence of some structures on the battlefield, close to Battlewell, raised shortly after the battle, there is little solid evidence in ready-to-use form (there is plenty of evidence in scattered collections) so at the time of writing (2020) the Society is collecting and reviewing documentary evidence about the battlefield in general and Battlewell in particular to develop a hypothesis that could be tested by geophysical survey (surface scans by professional technicians) and later, if the necessary consents could be obtained, by a limited excavation. The Battlewell Pool, held by some to be the original 'Battlewell', has been dug out and cleaned as part of the continuing maintenance on the field. As part of that work the Society used the opportunity to investigate the original depth and contour of the pool and to see if there are any clues to its origin, although inconclusively so far.

Elsewhere in Evesham work continues to promote knowledge of the battle and understanding of the battlefield. The Almonry Museum and Heritage Centre at Abbey Gate was occupied by the Almoner of Evesham Abbey in 1265 and now contains the 'Simon de Montfort Room', refurbished by the Vale of Evesham Historical Society, dedicated to the Battle of Evesham. It was opened in 1965 by the speaker of the House of Commons when he and the Archbishop of Canterbury came to Evesham to dedicate a memorial to Simon de Montfort in the adjacent abbey park to mark the 700th anniversary of the battle.

Evesham High Street has been tidied up by Worcestershire County Council, supported by Advantage West Midlands and Wychavon District Council. The Better Welcome programme initiated by Advantage West Midlands and supported by Evesham Town Council, Evesham Market Town Partnership, the Vale of Evesham Commerce and Tourism Association (VECTA) and the Simon de Montfort Society augmented the refurbishment scheme with the aim of making Evesham town centre more tourist-friendly.

The Simon de Montfort Society was involved in designing areas of 'heritage pavement'. These are built up of half-metre square slabs bearing scenes from Evesham's history. Slabs telling the story of the Battle of Evesham have been installed in front of the Iceland supermarket on the High Street. A central slab depicting the chaos of a battle in pictorial form is flanked by a brief description of the battle and by other slabs showing the arms of the leaders of both sides and the battle, with brief biographies of each man. The shield designs were copied from 'Glover's Roll of Arms' drawn up in the middle of the thirteenth century, cross-referenced with illustrations in Matthew Paris. The slab depicting the climax of the Battle of Evesham bears the number '6' as it is intended to be the sixth point on a new town heritage trail. In addition, Battlefield Trail directional disks have been set into the pavements, leading visitors through the town centre and up Greenhill to the Battlewell site along the route we believe was taken by Simon de Montfort and his outnumbered army. In time it may be possible to provide further plaques or panels to identify key points of the battle within the town itself. Recently Evesham secured a long hoped for addition to its brown heritage signs, identifying 'Battle of Evesham 1265' and there is a signpost on Greenhill pointing to the concealed entrance to the Battlewell site.

It is an old chestnut that those born in a town are the last to appreciate its attractions. I was born in Barnsley (the mining town in South Yorkshire NOT the lovely village in Gloucestershire) and I certainly failed to see its attractions despite it being an ancient pre-Norman market town with a long and lively history. Coming to live in Evesham opened my eyes to the depth of interest of this lovely quirky little town and the important role that it has played in critical times in the history of this country. This book is one attempt to share this sense of wonder at Evesham's unique heritage.

32 The original Simon de Montfort memorial in front of St Lawrence's church, Evesham, where Earl Simon heard mass on the morning of the battle (author's photograph)

33 Abbey Manor stands on the western side of the ridge on which the battle developed (source: Battlefields Trust)

34 Built in 1842, Lord Leicester's Tower Stands on a wooded slope above the Worcester Road to the west of Abbey Manor. It is not on the battlefield (source: Battlefield Trust)

35 Built in 1845 by Edward Rudge, the obelisk monument does not mark the site of the battle either. Like Lord Leicester's Tower, its location was determined by landscape gardeners rather than by battlefield archaeologists (source: Battlefields Trust)

1265 - The Murder of Evesham

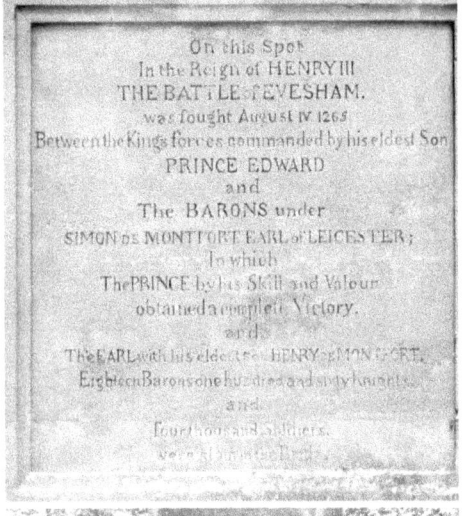

36 Details from the obelisk monument in the grounds of Abbey Manor (source: Battlefields Trust)

19. Epilogue

On October 26th 1265 Henry III invested his younger son, Edmund, with the earldom of Leicester along with all of the English lands formerly held by Earl Simon, disinheriting young Simon, who left Kenilworth Castle and joined the Montfortian rebels on the Isle of Axholme. Surrounded by a royal army the Montfortians 'sought peace from the king' at Christmas 1265. In January 1266, at Northampton, Simon junior agreed to abjure the realm. In return for leaving the country and causing no further trouble to Henry III it was agreed that he might draw an annual pension from the Honour of Leicester. However, he remained in custody until February 1266 when he slipped his leash and escaped to France via Winchelsea. In the spring of 1266 Simon was followed to France by his brother, Guy, who had escaped from Dover Castle.

In 1267 Amaury de Montfort petitioned Pope Clement to investigate the disposal of Earl Simon's mortal remains. The papal legate to England, Ottobuono, was ordered to investigate. Earl Simon was a good Christian and notable friend of the Church who had repented his sins on the morning before the Battle of Evesham and received absolution. He had been denied a church burial, imperilling his immortal soul. As only his torso had been recovered from the battlefield and hastily interred before the high altar of Evesham Abbey church, his head, limbs and genitalia having been distributed around England, a proper Christian burial presented practical difficulties.

The Battle of Evesham bred one remaining act of brutality. In 1271 Lord Edward, then on his way to the Holy Land to fulfil his vow to go on Crusade, sent Henry of Almain, son of his uncle, Richard, King of the Germans, to Italy to broker a peace between Simon de Montfort's surviving sons and Henry III. On the inauspicious date of Friday, March 13th 1271 Henry was hearing mass at the church of San Silvestro in Viterbo. Guy and Simon entered the church and Guy stabbed Henry to death, a reckless revenge for the killing of their father and brother at Evesham and for Henry's betrayal of the Montfortian cause in 1263. The brothers fled but remained in Italy. Simon died in a castle near Siena soon afterwards while Guy surrendered and was released into the custody of his former Lord, Charles of Anjou.

Henry III died on November 16th 1272, while Lord Edward was still in the Holy Land. In April 1275 Lord Edward, now Edward I, sent out the summonses for his first Parliament:

'We order you to cause four of the knights of your county with knowledge of the law and also six or four citizens, burgesses or other good men from each city borough and market town of your bailiwick to come there on the aforesaid morrow of the Sunday after Easter to consider at the same time as the magnates of our realm the affairs of that realm.'

Annex A. The Mind of a General

Tactics tended to be simple and well-tried. However, there was plenty of scope for a commander to make creative use of terrain and this was how the best commanders, such as Simon de Montfort and Lord Edward, earned their laurels. However, the tactics available to the commander of a small force (particularly if the force consisted of only one troop type) were circumscribed and Simon could rely only on a small cavalry force.

Warfare was not 'chivalrous' in the modern sense of the word. There was no equivalent to the Marquis of Queensbury's Rules and warfare was not regulated with the formality of an eighteenth-century duel. The 'way of the horseman', was composed of craft and violence. Ingenious trickery and underhand dealing were praised as was harshness to an enemy who had allowed himself to be tricked. The idea of giving an enemy a sporting chance would have astonished any thirteenth-century commander and there was nothing unchivalrous about metaphorically bringing a foe to the ground and then kicking him until he stopped trying to get up again. Cunning and brutality were qualities to be admired. Neither would a thirteenth-century commander have felt shame in refusing battle unless he had overwhelming odds on his side, as Edward had at Evesham.

Battles were rarely the all-cavalry scrums beloved of the movie makers. The heads-down tails-up cavalry charge was not the way the better commanders used their mounted men. They used their mobility for manoeuvre, holding back, feinting, switching position, probing for a weak spot which they would then charge into when they were confident of carrying the field. A medieval battle was a boxing match in which a big-swinging bruiser would have fallen to a flurry of short jabs to the jaw from his wilier opponent.

Vegetius counsels:

'But if ... you expect your cavalry to act with advantage against the enemy's infantry, your ground must indeed be higher, but level and open, without any obstructions such as woods or morasses',

As on Greenhill in Evesham.

Vegetius

It is possible to peep into the mind of a mid-thirteenth-century commander by way of a book. Most thirteenth-century aristocrats would have been able to read and most could write, too. Unlettered knights and lords had become the exception and learning had become almost as much a matter of pride as was military prowess. This made classics of military literature almost universally available to the aristocracy who would have discussed, criticised and followed them.

The most influential military treatise in the western world from Roman times to the nineteenth century was known by two titles: the *Epitoma Rei Militaris* ('Epitome of Military Science') and (risking confusion with Cato the Elder's work of the same title) *De Re Militari* (roughly translated as 'on soldiering'). Manuscript copies circulated widely during the time of Charlemagne and it was required reading for his commanders. Around AD 1000 Vegetius was the favourite author of Failques the Black of Anjou. Henry II of England owned a copy and his son, Richard *Coeur de Lion*, carried a copy with him on all of his campaigns.

Today there are some 150 manuscript copies in existence, dating from the tenth to the fifteenth centuries. The first printed edition was produced in Utrecht in 1473, by which time it had been translated into English, French and Bulgarian. It was first printed in English by Caxton, from an English manuscript copy, in 1489. It was still being quoted in western military academies in the twentieth century. Largely ignored by the Romans, for whom it had been written, the *Epitoma* simply became the military bible for generations of medieval commanders.

It might seem odd to a modern mind that Vegetius could have exercised such an influence in the Middle Ages. The book is full of references to formations, organizations, ranks and institutions that were several centuries out of date even in the author's day and thirteenth-century copies made few concessions to the changes that had occurred in the intervening 900 years. Nevertheless, the *Epitoma* contains a great deal that would have appealed to the medieval mind. There is a lot of practical common sense, not least the maxims collected in Book III and also scattered through the rest of the text. Book III deals with tactics and strategy and it was this section that had the major influence on warfare in the Middle Ages, in particular the 'General Rules of Warfare' in III.26, which became a military catechism for teaching the basic principles of warfare in a non-specific form that could be adapted to a variety of military situations. It was a toolbox for generals. To a thirteenth-century mind the antiquity of the writing gave it authority, so much so that it was frequently quoted in scholarly and philosophical works of the Middle Ages.

Lord Edward and Earl Simon would have read it, or have had it read to them, in Latin or French (the first English edition was not produced until 1408 when it was translated for Thomas of Berkeley). A number of translations were made into vernacular languages and frequent additions and adjustments were made to adapt it to the age of chivalry. Segments were reproduced to augment contemporary material on warfare.

Edward owned a copy, but we cannot be sure when he first saw a copy of the book. We know that during his stay at Acre in the Holy Land, after May 1271, his wife, Eleanor of Castile, presented him with a specially commissioned copy. The first translations from Latin into a vernacular language were into French, beginning with an Anglo-Norman translation by 'Maitre Richard' for 'Lord Edward', possibly for the future Edward II. If for Edward I, then Lord Edward may have had his copy as early as 1254-6. It is unlikely that such a fundamental part of his military education would be neglected as most military men would have had a copy available to them. However, the question is less important than it might seem. Even if Edward had never seen a copy of the *Epitoma* before the Battle of Evesham its teachings pervaded all military thinking. If you are interested in understanding medieval warfare then I recommend a close study of Vegetius.

Some more recent editions of Epitoma are listed in the bibliography. I recommend: Lang 1885; Andersson 1938; Stelten 1970 (Books I & II); Sadler 1572; Clarke 1767; Phillips 1944 (Books I-III); Silhanek 1972 (Books I & II).

Maurice's Strategicon

Vegetius was not the only influential military author studied during the Middle Ages. Although very much in second place behind the *Epitome* the *Strategicon* or *Strategikon* (Gr. Στρατηγικόν) was also a popular manual of war, written in the late sixth century and usually attributed to the Byzantine Emperor Maurice. It is a practical manual, described in its introduction as 'a rather modest elementary handbook for those devoting themselves to generalship.' It was written in an effort to codify the military reforms brought about by the soldier-emperor Maurice.

There is little consensus about the identity of the author of the *Strategicon*. Maurice may have written it or have only commissioned it. Perhaps the author was Maurice's brother Peter or another general of his court. The dating of the *Strategicon* is also open to debate. It may have been produced to codify the experience of the Balkan and Persian campaigns or those campaigns may have been carried out in compliance with the lessons of the manual. In any case it is considered one of the more important military texts of the medieval years. Later military treatises attributed to the Byzantine emperors Leo VI (*Tactica*) and Nicephorus Phocas (*De velitatione* and *Praecepta Militaria*) drew on the *Strategicon*.

The text consists of twelve 'books' on various aspects of the tactics, logistics and other military arrangements employed by the Byzantine army of the sixth and seventh centuries AD. The Byzantine armies of that era were predominantly cavalry forces so the *Strategicon* focuses on cavalry tactics and formations. However, there is an abundance of information about how to use infantry, the conduct of sieges, operation of baggage trains, springing ambushes and organising marches. Books VII and VIII contain practical advice to the General in the form of instructions and maxims. Book XI contains portraits of various enemies of the Byzantines, including Avars, Franks, Lombards, Slavs and Turks. There is even a list of military infractions and their penalties.

Annex B. Classic Interpretations

How Sir James Ramsay, Sir Charles Oman and Lt-Col A.H. Burne interpreted the accounts of the Battle of Evesham.

Ramsay

Sir James Henry Ramsay (1832-1925) was the tenth baronet of Bamff, succeeding his father in 1871. Ramsay made his life's work of writing the political history of England down to the end of the Middle Ages. He wrote *Lancaster and York* in 1892, *The Foundations of England* in 1898, *The Angevin Empire* in 1903, *The Genesis of Lancaster* in 1913 and, most relevant for this book, *The Dawn of the Constitution* in 1908. Ramsay has been characterised as a chronicler, who writes accounts of important or historical events, rather than as a historian, an analyst of historical events. Ramsay wrote in comparative isolation, little influenced by other historians; however, his narrative of the Battle of Evesham has been useful in researching this book.

Ramsay describes the raid on Kenilworth and lists ten barons and bannerets captured by Edward's men. He has the elder Simon crossing the Severn at Kempsey on August 2nd, resting on the Bishop of Worcester's land at Kempsey and then marching to Evesham, resting over the night of August 3rd/4th. Ramsay did not believe that Earl Simon had heard of his son's defeat and was intending to press on from Evesham to Alcester and beyond to meet his son. In a footnote Ramsay notes that Waverly, Osney and Rishanger had de Montfort's army resting at Kempsey overnight on August 3rd and arriving at Evesham on the morning of August 4th.

Edward had learned of de Montfort's crossing of the Severn and had hurried after him overnight on August 3rd. Ramsay's account of the route taken by Edward is: marching north toward Bridgnorth to confuse the enemy then wheeling to the east, crossing the River Avon at 'Cliue', which Ramsay believes was Cleeve Prior, then progressing along the left bank to Offenham where he re-crossed the river before ascending to the crossroads at the top of Greenhill to deploy his force.

On the morning of August 4th, having heard mass and eaten breakfast, Earl Simon's army was preparing to move off, and the vanguard was already in motion, when the approach of an unknown army was reported. The Montfortians were soon disabused of the idea that young Simon had arrived and Ramsay has Simon, not his barber, ascending the abbey bell tower to ascertain the situation.

Ramsay believed that Earl Simon urged Despenser and Basset to flee to safety because 'they may not have been aware that Mortimer was being sent down the river from Offenham to occupy Bengeworth Bridge in their rear'. Walter de Cantilupe blessed the Montfortian army and Earl Simon took his place at the head of his army.

Ramsay's Marcher deployment has Edward on the right of the line, de Clare on the left and de Mortimer crossing at Offenham and hurrying down the left bank to block Bengeworth bridge. Ramsay believed that there was a race for the top of Greenhill, Edward trying to deploy his two battles to block the Alcester Road while Earl Simon rushed to sweep the Marchers aside and escape to meet up with his son.

The Marchers won the race and Ramsay has the Montfortian army branching left onto the spur of land near the current Abbey Manor, a little promontory 275 metres (300 yards) by 185 metres (200 yards) marked by the obelisk that survives from Ramsay's day. Here Earl Simon formed his men into a ring for a last stand, their white crosses contrasting with the red crosses of the Marchers.

Edward turned his battle to face his uncle while de Clare crossed the Battlewell site, then ascended the spur to engulf Earl Simon's outnumbered and surrounded army. At this point the Welsh infantry, who had ascended the hill with Earl Simon, broke and fled before the Marcher ring closed and a desperate combat ensued. De Montfort, his son Henry and his chief supporters were deliberately butchered.

Oman

Sir Charles William Chadwick Oman KBE (1860–1946) was a British military historian of the early twentieth century, a pioneer in reconstructing medieval battles from the fragmentary accounts left by chroniclers.

1265 - The Murder of Evesham

His account of the Battle of Evesham begins with Earl Simon hearing of the resurgence of the royal cause in the west. De Montfort assembled a small army and hurried to the Welsh border, taking the king in tow, and sending instructions to his second son to collect a larger army and join him. However, Edward and de Clare trapped the elder Simon on the western side of the Severn, separating him from his reinforcements. The earl moved toward Kenilworth along the western bank of the Severn until he could slip back across the river, then reached Evesham, while his son had marched as far as the Montfortian stronghold of Kenilworth. The two parts of the Montfortian army were only a few miles apart but Edward and his army were between them and Edward was eager to defeat them in detail.

Oman describes Edward's raid on Kenilworth as a 'sudden and unexpected attack the prince surprised and scattered young Montfort's army under the walls of Kenilworth'. Edward then hurried back to attack the elder Simon. Earl Simon had reached Evesham and his men were camped in the town, surrounded by a deep loop of the river Avon. Edward and de Clare closed the narrow neck of this loop with their battles, while a third battle, led by Roger de Mortimer, crossed the river and blocked the only bridge which led, southward, out of the town. Oman assumes that de Montfort slept overnight in Evesham, so Simon woke to find himself surrounded. Forming his little force into a compact mass (Oman thought on a frontage of 50-60 horsemen), he rushed the royal forces formed up at the top of the hill to the north of Evesham and tried to cut his way through. Heavily outnumbered, the battle was 'a short sharp fight' and de Montfort was killed along with his eldest son Henry, Hugh Despenser, the Justiciar of England, and many of the knights and barons of the rebel party. King Henry had been dressed in Earl Simon's spare armour and rode in the earl's force where he was wounded and narrowly missed being killed by his own side.

Burne

Lieutenant-Colonel Alfred Higgins Burne (1886–1959) was a soldier and military historian. Burne based his analysis of battles and campaigns on the concept of Inherent Military Probability (IMP). He described IMP in this way: 'my method here is to start with what appear to be undisputed facts, then to place myself in the shoes of each commander in turn, and to ask myself in each case what I would have done. This I call working on Inherent Military Probability. I then compare the resulting action with the existing record in order to see whether it discloses any incompatibility with the existing facts. If not, I then go on to the next debateable or obscure point in the battle and repeat the operation'. In other words, where there is some doubt over what action was taken in a battle or campaign, Burne looked for the solution by estimating what a trained soldier would have done in the circumstances. The shortcoming with this approach is that it relies on a medieval military leader having a mindset that would still apply to the age of mechanised mobility, long range artillery and flat-trajectory small-arms.

Picking up Burne's account[35] on the arrival of the younger Simon's army at Kenilworth: he agreed with Oman that, after a sleepless night, Edward opted to attack the Montfortian army he feared least, and marched from Worcester to Kenilworth, arriving at the same time that a convoy of supplies was being admitted. Burne holds that most of young Simon's men were billeted in the town and were soon scattered, leaving a number of horses and thirteen banners in the hands of the Marchers. Edward rested his army at Kenilworth for the rest of the day (August 1st) before returning to Worcester where they arrived late on August 2nd.

Meanwhile Earl Simon had learned that Edward had withdrawn his pickets from the banks of the Severn (to reinforce his attack on Kenilworth, although Earl Simon

---

[35] Burne, A. H. (1950, reprint 2002) The Battlefields of England, London: Penguin

remained unaware of his son's defeat) and seized his chance to cross the Severn by boat close to Kempsey, an operation that would have taken most of August 2nd. Edward rested his returned army before pursuing Earl Simon's army.

Simon sent a message to his son summoning him to join his father then headed for Evesham, avoiding the more direct route via Alcester as that would have taken him too close to Edward's army at Worcester.

Edward divined that de Montfort would detour via Evesham, pick up the Alcester road and hurry north to meet the young Simon. Or were de Montfort's intentions betrayed by a spy? If Edward set out late in the afternoon of August 3rd he could reach Alcester that night, cross the river Avon at Cleeve Prior before dawn on August 4th and, dividing his forces, block both roads north: the Alcester road and the Stratford-upon-Avon road.

Burne rejects the notion that Edward was intending to trap Earl Simon's army at Evesham; his objective was simply to interpose his force between the two Montfortian armies. Having achieved this limited objective in the very early hours of the morning of August 4th, with de Clare's force on the western bank of the Avon and his own and de Mortimer's battles on the eastern bank, Edward found no sign of his quarry. He advanced south to try to gain contact with de Montfort. Just south of Offenham, where there was an old crossing place, Edward detached de Mortimer to continue south to block the bridge at Bengeworth, crossed the river at Offenham and then ascended Greenhill, probably up the current Blayney's Lane, where he regained contact with de Clare who was deploying on the top of the hill.

Edward pushed de Clare's battle to the right of the crossroads to make room to deploy his own battle on the ridge and had the captured banners brought to the front. The barber in the tower did not recognise the banners (which would have been impossible to do at that range and under the prevailing weather conditions) but he was able to see the Marchers forming up in battle formation, two battles abreast, thinly stretched with a 500 metre (550 yard) gap on each flank, covered by pickets, which news he conveyed to de Montfort.

The earl quickly concluded that his best chance was to charge the over-stretched Marcher line and formed up his army with the cavalry leading on a frontage of 137-183 metres (150-200 yards) with the king in full armour in the middle of the formation. As the Montfortians breasted the rise, 640 metres (700 yards) north of the current railway station they had their first sight of their deployed enemy. The time was around 0900 hrs. The sky had turned black and a tremendous thunderstorm broke.

At this point the infantry recollected the better part of valour and fled leaving the Montfortian cavalry to collide with de Clare's battle and push part of it beyond the line of the roads before they rallied and held the thrust. The two wings of de Clare's battle folded inward to engulf Earl Simon and his cavalry while Edward's battle moved right to complete the encirclement. With no escape and no quarter the Montfortians on Greenhill fought to the end while the fugitives fleeing toward Offenham were cut down in the stream of the Avon at Dead Man's Ait.

Annex C. English Heritage

This report is reproduced here with the kind consent of English Heritage.
English Heritage Battlefield Report: Evesham 1265
Evesham (4 August 1265)
Parish: Evesham, Norton and Lenchwick
District: Wychavon
County: Hereford and Worcester
Grid ref: SP039452

Historical Context

The Battle of Evesham was part of that period of instability and civil conflict which characterised the years 1258-1267, and which later became known as the Barons' Wars. Simon de Montfort's victory over Henry III and his son Lord Edward at Lewes in May 1264 did not bring lasting peace. Simon's government was threatened by rebellion on the Welsh marches, by the defection of his own followers and by the escape from captivity of Lord Edward.

After his escape from Hereford on May 28th 1265, Edward lost no time in coming to a military arrangement with Gilbert de Clare, de Montfort's erstwhile ally, and with William de Valence and John de Warenne. Assembling a considerable army, Edward and Clare moved against de Montfort at Hereford, seeking to block his passage eastwards across the River Severn. Edward first took Worcester and then advanced on Gloucester, capturing the town, but not at first the castle, in the second week of June. Thus denied his preferred route across the Severn, Simon struck south to Monmouth with the eventual hope of crossing the river at Bristol. Frustrated by the destruction of much of the shipping required for his army to cross the Severn, de Montfort returned to Hereford. There the strategic situation began to swing in his favour for his son, Simon, was advancing west from London with an army which threatened Edward and Clare's freedom of movement on the east bank of the Severn.

1265 - The Murder of Evesham

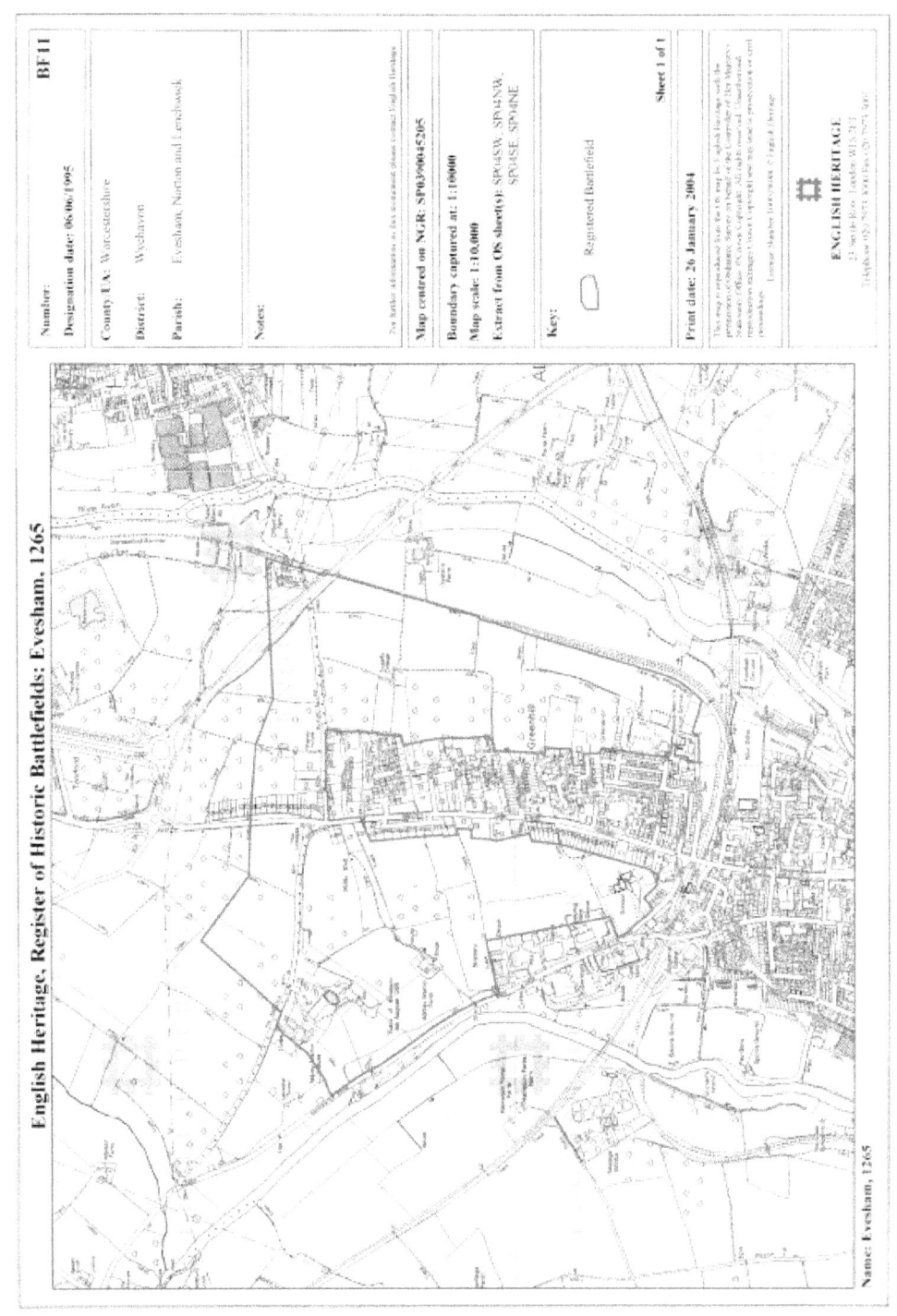

Although young Simon's progress was hesitant as he moved first to Winchester, then to Oxford and Northampton, he had reached Kenilworth by the end of July. His maneouvres had succeeded in relieving the pressure on his father for Edward had been forced to look to the defence of Worcester. Edward was also now the potential victim of a pincer movement by young Simon advancing on Worcester from Kenilworth, and de Montfort advancing from Hereford. To forestall this possibility Edward feinted towards Shrewsbury with a mounted force, and then fell upon young Simon's army in its tents at Kenilworth at dawn on August 2nd. Edward's victory was short and sharp and for the moment the ability of Simon's army to participate in the campaign was disrupted. Simon had part of his army safely within the castle and these troops survived the attack of Edward's lightly equipped force with little difficulty. We do not know, however, how large was Simon's remaining force. Returning in triumph to Worcester, Edward prepared to deal with de Montfort who was now once more on the east bank of the Severn and who, by the morning of August 4th, had reached Evesham.

Location and Description of the Battlefield

There is no dispute as to the general location of the Battle of Evesham. While Simon rested his army in Evesham on the morning of August 4th 1265, the Marcher army, by now deployed in three divisions led by Earl Gilbert, Roger de Mortimer, and Edward, was mounting the northern slopes of Green Hill barely a mile to the north of the town. The point at which the Marchers probably climbed the hill was near to a place named 'Siveldeston'. The name was derived from an ancient stone ('Siflæd's stone') located by the eleventh century on the 'salt street' which delineated Evesham's northern boundary or that of the abbey lands. The stone was positioned[1] on what is now Blayney's Lane near to the point at which the lane becomes a path as it meets the course of the dismantled railway line close to the banks of the River Avon. The spot was some 800 yards to the east of the crossroads on the crest of Green Hill where, in the words of William Tindal:

'just on the northern edge of the old road leading down to the river, a stone of about six feet in height, and apparently squared by art, is fixed to the ground....The place and figure of this stone have occasioned many to suppose it a memorial of the battle, and it has even, as I have heard, been described and engraved as such.'[2]

The stone was removed at some date before Tindal's death in 1804.

While Siflæd's stone can be used as a general reference to the location of the Battlefield it does not pinpoint the scene of the clash between Simon's troops and those of Edward. For this many writers have turned to a site known as 'Battlewell'. Very soon after the battle a cult of Simon and his dead supporters as miracle workers grew up and the scene of the Earl's death on the battlefield, together with his first tomb in the abbey church, became places of pilgrimage. In 1266, according to the monks of Evesham Abbey, a spring was discovered in miraculous circumstances by Piers of Saltmarsh close to the site of Simon's death. Earl Simon's well, as it became known, was soon the haunt of pilgrims seeking a cure from its waters and by 1448 Richard Fox, a monk of the Abbey of St Albans, could write that:

'where the battle and murther (of Simon) was is now a well, and grete elmes stande about the well; there is over the well an hovel of stone, and a crucifix and Mary and John'.[3]

By 1457 the site had become known, at least locally, as Battlewell and it was marked as such on the first Ordnance Survey map of Evesham produced in 1828. The well as marked by the Ordnance Survey still exists to the west of the Evesham-Alcester road (A435) and south of the Worcester road (The Squires), and it is reasonable to accept that it is the same well as that to which Richard Fox referred. Equally there is little reason to doubt that the fifteenth-century well was the same one that was 'discovered' by Piers of Saltmarsh in 1266.

By the end of the eighteenth century the continuity of interest in Battlewell had led to the belief that its site marked the centre of the Battlefield and the spot on which Simon de Montfort was killed. This narrow interpretation was espoused by, amongst others, E.J. Rudge who argued that the Battle occurred: 'on the rising ground immediately adjacent'[4] to the well. Rudge's father, the owner of Abbey Manor (built 1817), constructed an obelisk to commemorate the Battle in the grounds of his new home in 1821. Neither the obelisk nor the well should, however, be accepted as evidence that the armies fought the main engagement of the Battle of Evesham on the ground immediately to the south of the Worcester road and west of the Evesham road.

The Chronicle evidence, so far as it goes, suggests rather that after the Marcher army had deployed in three divisions, Lord Edward's column took up position in the centre close to the brow of Green Hill facing south. Roger de Mortimer's column was behind Edward and to his right, while the troops of Earl Gilbert were on the Prince's left and again to his rear. As Simon marched out of Evesham and ascended Green Hill he did not discover the full extent of the enemy's strength or deployment until he had gained the brow and was almost upon them. As Edward occupied the Barons in front, Gilbert swung his men round the right flank of Simon's force and attacked it from the rear. When Gilbert's men rushed forward they linked with either flank of Edward's column, thus completing the encirclement of the Barons.

The Landscape Evolution

The town of Evesham and the substantial abbey lay next to the bridge at Bengeworth, the only bridge in the area. Beyond the town the only road running north was probably on the same line as the present A435(T) leading out of the loop in the River Avon. Documentary evidence refers to 'East and West Fields' here which would indicate medieval arable open fields in this area. No field evidence, such as ridge and furrow, has been identified to support this, but given the era and the town close by, open fields are to be expected. The ridge along which the A435(T) runs drops down to the Avon to east and west and there was certainly meadowland by the river.

The open fields that lay to the north of Evesham had all been enclosed into regular hedged fields, probably by a Parliamentary Act, by 1827. Records show that adjacent open fields at Norton Lenchwick to the north had been enclosed by 1765 and Evesham's were probably enclosed around this time also. By 1885 the majority of the earlier hedged enclosed fields in the battlefield area had become orchards with the only orchard-free areas being around Abbey Manor Farm.

Green Hill retains its position of eminence above the town, but Evesham has spread northwards to encroach upon the hill with suburban dwellings. The area around Battlewell is surprisingly rural and quiet, with views south to the Abbey tower and west towards Charlton.

The old Salt Street running east to Offenham Ferry from the A435(T) is unfortunately cut by the new by-pass over which walkers must cross, (there is no bridge or traffic lights here) to the quiet oasis around the Offenham Ferry - Dead Mans Ait area.

The Battle: its sources and interpretation

When Lord Edward learnt that de Montfort was at Evesham he took steps, as the contemporary chronicler Mathew Paris recorded, to ensure that he would not reach Kenilworth.

Edward then returned from Kenilworth to Worcester, which is only three miles distant from the above-named manor; and Simon on hearing of his arrival there, went away with the king at nightfall, and took up his quarters in the town of Evesham where he awaited his unhappy destiny. For on the morrow, which was the day of the Finding of St Stephen, Edward moved from Worcester, crossed the river near the town of Claines, and cut off the approach of the earl to his son, who was in the castle of Kenilworth, and prevented all chance of the father and son meeting.[5]

De Montfort's position was grave for the morale of his men had been undermined by their weeks of short rations and fruitless marching in Wales, and the force he had recruited from Llywelyn ap Gruffydd was reluctant to fight. Moreover, de Montfort was now in a trap.

On the following day he drew near the town of Evesham on one side and the earl of Gloucester and Roger Mortimer came up with their respective forces in two other directions; and thus the earl of Leicester was hemmed in on all sides, and was under the necessity either or voluntarily surrendering, or of giving them battle.[6]

De Montfort's plan was still to attempt to unite his own force with that of his son Simon, and Edward's immediate task was to block the routes leading from Evesham to Kenilworth. The barons had a choice of routes, but the two principal roads that would lead them towards Kenilworth were to the north on the road towards Alcester, and to the north-east on the road towards Cleeve Prior. The former was the most likely route for de Montfort to follow and it ran over Green Hill, where Edward deployed his troops. The prince had taken the precaution of detaching Roger Mortimore and his force to approach Evesham from the west, thereby blocking any attempt de Montfort might make to escape in that direction or to the south.

Simon's only chance was to attempt to fight his way out of the trap, and link up with his son, and it is possible that Edward exploited this fact by ordering the banners lately captured from young Simon's army at Kenilworth to be displayed ahead of his troops as they approached Evesham. This ruse may have convinced de Montfort that his son was close at hand and thus encouraged him to march north out of Evesham to join this friendly force.

De Montfort was heavily outnumbered and he deployed his troops as a single column or wedge aimed at the junction between Gloucester's and Edward's troops on the Alcester road. As his army mounted Green Hill de Montfort launched it forward at the charge as heavy rain began to fall. It was a desperate strategy executed by a veteran soldier and it might have succeeded had not the wings of Edward's army swung in to attack the flank of the Baronial force. As it was, the momentum of de Montfort's wedge carried his force well into Edward's position and caused some panic among the royal troops. Many of the Welsh spearmen and foot soldiers with de Montfort had already been killed or had left the battlefield when Simon, to maintain the cohesion of his army, ordered his remaining troops to form a circle for all-round defence. Gradually the Barons were pressed into an ever tighter formation by the sheer weight of numbers of their opponents. Although de Montfort's army continued to resist for some hours the battle became a progressively bloody and one-sided affair, and both de Montfort and his son Henry were cut down with nearly 4,000 of their followers. Mathew Paris *(sic)* recorded de Montfort's final battle with clarity and brevity:

both armies met in a large plain outside the town, where a most severe conflict ensued; till the partisans of the earl began to give way, and the whole weight of the battle falling upon him, he was slain on the field of battle. At the time of his death, a storm of thunder and lightning occurred and darkness prevailed to such an extent, that all were struck with amazement. Besides the earl, there fell, in that battle, twelve knights bannerets; namely, Henry, his son: Peter de Montfort: Hugh Despenser, justiciary of England; William de Mandeville; Ralph Basset; Walter de Crespigny: William York: Robert Tregor; Thomas Hostelea; John Beauchamp; Guy Balliol; Roger de Rouleo; and a great number of others of inferior rank, such as esquires and foot-soldiers; the greatest loss being amongst the Welsh.[7]

Estimates of the casualties at Evesham are unreliable, but the fact that upwards of thirty knights were killed when to ransom was the normal practice, convinced contemporaries that the closing stages of the battle had been akin to murder.

Indication of Importance

Although their field army was destroyed at Evesham, the surviving Barons still held their castles and the war dragged on until 1267. Complete reconciliation came only in 1275 when the best elements of the Provisions of Oxford were encapsulated in the Statute of Westminster. Evesham had, however, freed Henry, and later Edward, from the need to accept ministers or councillors imposed upon them by others. As such the battle secured a political victory for the King, and while De Montfort himself has remained a potent symbol of liberty through later English history, it was the monarch's need for revenue which was to increase the power, permanency and influence of the Commons.

The Evesham campaign was a personal triumph for Lord Edward and it did much to establish his prestige and power as heir to the throne. Militarily he had shown maturity and strategic skill, though some of the credit here must also go to Gilbert de Clare.

Chronicles provide a basic record of the Battle and, although the deployment of the rival armies is still a matter of argument, the battlefield itself can be located with confidence. The growth of Evesham has covered much of the battlefield but the course of the fighting can still be appreciated on the ground.

Battlefield Area

The battlefield area boundary defines the outer reasonable limit of the battle, taking into account the positions of the combatants at the outset of fighting and the focal area of the battle itself. It does not include areas over which fighting took place subsequent to the main battle. Wherever possible, the boundary has been drawn so that it is easily appreciated on the ground.

The battlefield area embraces primarily the fighting on Green Hill, allowing space for the manouvres carried out by de Montfort's mounted troops, and the flanking movements by the royal army. The battlefield boundary therefore follows the line of the disused railway line on the eastern side, allowing for Earl Gilbert's role in the battle, runs parallel with Blayney's Lane and The Squires allowing for the starting positions of the Royal army and returns southwards via the Worcester Road to allow for the migration of the battle westwards to end around the Battlewell. The Register boundary excludes the more intensively built-up area along the spine of Greenhill in recognition of the impracticality of including such areas on the Register. Since this central axis was a key part of the battle, the full extent of the fighting is shown for illustrative purposes with a dashed line.

Notes

1. See Cox, D.C. The Battle of Evesham. A New Account. The Vale of Evesham Historical Society (1988).

2. Tindal, William History and Antiquities

3. Blaauw, W.H. The Barons' War including the Battles of Lewes and Evesham. 2nd. Edition (1871) p277 fn.1.

4. Rudge, E.J. A Short Account of the History and Antiquities of Evesham (1820).

5. Paris, Matthew (Matthaei Parisiensis), Monachi Sancti Albani, Chronica Majorca. Ed. H R Luard, Rolls series 1872-83.

6. Ibid.

7. Ibid.

© English Heritage 1995

Annex D. Received Wisdom

The title of this appendix, referring to the account of the Battle of Evesham published by the Battlefields Trust, is clearly written tongue-in-cheek, but with no disrespect intended. The Trust's account is an amalgam of the best research and blends the extant accounts, giving weight to the most reliable and discounting the more suspect. As such it is a yardstick against which to measure other accounts and I reproduce it here from the Trust's UK Battlefields Resource Centre (www.battlefieldstrust.com/resource-centre/medieval) with the generous consent of The Battlefields Trust.

The Evesham Campaign

Following his victory at Lewes in 1264, Simon de Montfort, Earl of Leicester, had controlled the kingdom. The king was 'under his protection', effectively his prisoner, as was Henry III's son Prince Edward. But de Montfort's position was precarious. There was a threat of invasion from Flanders, promoted by the queen, and unrest in the Welsh Marches. But it was the disaffection of his former ally the Earl of Clare that was the greatest problem. When two important opponents, Warenne and de Valence landed in Pembroke, and Prince Edward escaped from custody, they joined with Clare in building an army in the Welsh Marches.

With this army Prince Edward (later to become Edward I, one of the greatest military commanders of the period) seized the strategically important city of Worcester. In response, by the twelfth June 1265, de Montfort had begun to assemble his army at the other great strategic centre in the region, Gloucester. The fortified city controlled the lowest bridge over the Severn and from there he advanced into Wales to gain the support of Prince Llewellyn, bringing Welsh infantry into his army. But Edward attacked and took Gloucester, the castle surrendering on the 29th June. De Montfort was now in danger of being cut off to the west of the Severn.

To counter the threat, de Montfort's son, also named Simon, began to assemble an army in the south east. Meanwhile de Montfort manoeuvred in the Welsh Marches, trying to avoid being trapped by Edward's forces until he could march east to unite with the army which his son had raised. By the 16th July de Montfort was in Hereford. By this time Edward had retreated back across the Severn, to counter the approach of the army under de Montfort's son, which had reached Kenilworth by the 31st July. It was essential for Edward to destroy one or other of the rebel armies before they had the opportunity to unite.

The Battle of Evesham

The Battle of Evesham was fought on the morning of the 4th August 1265. The army of Simon de Montfort had probably not long entered Evesham when, from lookouts on the tower of the Abbey, news came of the approach of the royal army under Prince Edward. Taking the captive king Henry III with him, and despite being outnumbered more than three to one, de Montfort rode out with his cavalry, with his infantry in support, to engage the enemy.

Less than a mile to the north of the town, somewhere on the summit of Greenhill, de Montfort found the royal forces deployed in three divisions. He appears to have made a bold cavalry attack, perhaps in the hope of breaking through. At first some of the royal forces retreated, but then there was a counter attack and de Montfort's army, or at least his knights, were soon encircled. Unusually for a medieval battle, no quarter was to be given and de Montfort and most of his main supporters were cut down. It appears likely that the infantry had already broken and begun to flee, but if not then they were soon routed. The rebel forces were pursed mercilessly back into the town, the killing continuing right through the streets and even in the abbey itself. Though peace was not finally restored across the country for another two years, the Battle of Evesham had completely broken the rebellion, for almost all of its major supporters had been intentionally killed on the field.

Evesham is one of the few early battles for which a genuinely new primary source has been recently identified, one that has transformed our understanding of the event. This is now a battle where the broad character and location of the action is clearly understood and where the location of the action is fairly tightly constrained by the physical topography. Though there has been 20th century development in the area, a substantial part of the battlefield still remains undeveloped. This makes Evesham one of the few early medieval battles where a visit to the battlefield can

be very clearly focussed and a relatively secure outline of the battle provided. For the same reason it is one where there appears a high potential for detailed reconstruction of the historic terrain and investigation of the battle archaeology. Although parts of the battlefield are accessible, a new scheme is being developed which should greatly improve that access and provide the first on site interpretation.

The Armies and the Losses

Simon de Montfort, Earl of Leicester, commanded the rebel cavalry. The infantry was under the command of Humphrey de Bohun, Earl of Hereford. De Montfort's son Simon commanded the forces marching to his aid, but they never arrived at the battlefield, news of the defeat reaching them while on the march.

Prince Edward (later Edward I) commanded the royal army, with Gilbert de Clare, Earl of Gloucester, and Roger de Mortimer commanding the other two divisions.

There is limited evidence on the numbers engaged on either side but, according to Melrose chronicle, de Montfort was outnumbered at least 3 to 1. If this was correct then the Evesham chronicle's claim that de Montfort had more than 6000 Welsh and other infantry would mean that Edward's army was well over 18,000. Though well within the range of chronicle estimates for other battles it still appears excessive.

Losses

The report that few of Edward's men killed may be correct while the losses on de Montfort's side may have been far higher at Evesham than other battles of the period, because no quarter was to be given. However, the 7500 - 10,000 said by to have been killed is another example of the gross exaggeration of most of the medieval chronicles when recording numbers. The claim of 160-200 knights killed is also unsupported, although 36 names of the most important are recorded. The English Heritage report suggests perhaps 4000 of de Montfort's forces were killed.

The Battle

Montfort had arrived at Evesham at about 6:00am. News of the royal army's approach reached him in Evesham Abbey at around 8:30am. At first the royal forces were supposedly mistaken, by a lookout on the tower of Evesham Abbey, for the approach of de Montfort's son, possibly because Edward was carrying captured banners from the attack at Kenilworth.

According to the new account, de Montfort dismissed the advice that they should defend the Abbey church against the enemy and await the arrival of reinforcements. Neither would he retreat over the bridge to delay the action. After addressing his troops beside the conduit in the town, taking the captive king Henry III with him, de Montfort rode out with his cavalry to engage the enemy. The infantry, under the command of de Bohun, followed as a rearguard because, according to other accounts, the Welsh troops were reluctant to fight.

He presumably took the Alcester road north out of the town, which after less than a mile the road reaches the summit of Greenhill. The continuator of Matthew Paris says the armies fought on a 'large plain', and Greenhill does rapidly widen out into a quite extensive flat topped hill. The new account implies that de Montfort was already deployed on the hilltop when Edward's army advanced up the hill, from the direction of Worcester. He thus had the choice of ground, but was outnumbered by more than three to one. According to Guisbrough and Wykes chronicles Edward's battle was to the fore, but rather than the extensive separation between the forces depicted by Cox, this may simply have been the staggered deployment of battles such as those known for twelfth century battles (Verbruggen, 1997, 209). However the new account implies the royal forces more simply deployed, Prince Edward's division in the centre, with those of de Clare to his left and Mortimer to his right.

Some accounts imply de Montfort made a bold cavalry attack, perhaps in the hope of breaking through, attacking in a wedge formation along the Alcester road, between the two divisions of de Clare and Prince Edward. At first some of the royal forces are said to have retreated, but then there was a counter attack, with the wings of the royal army swinging around, encircling de Montfort's army, or at least his knights. According to the English Heritage report many of his infantry may already have been routed, but the suggestion that the encircled forces then sustained the action for 'some hours' seems highly improbable.

The new account clearly explains Edward's tactics. Mortimer and twelve of his knights had been given the task of breaking through the rebel formation and striking straight at de Montfort, to kill him and thus destroy his army's will to fight. According to Wykes, de Montfort brought his army together 'in a thick mass in the form of a circle' as a defence but very soon he and some twenty of his knights were killed, his body being hacked to pieces. Even the king himself, still held prisoner on the battlefield, was nearly killed in the mêlée.

After de Montfort's death his army broke and fled, some towards the river, many of whom were drowned; others were pursued across the fields and into the town, even in the abbey church itself. This execution is said to have continued until mid afternoon. Unusually for a medieval battle, no quarter was supposedly to be given and de Montfort, his son Henry and most of his main supporters were cut down, though some important prisoners were taken. De Montfort's son Simon, was still marching south from Alcester towards Evesham when he encountered fugitives for the battle.

Aftermath & Assessment

The night after the battle, it is said, de Montfort's body and that of his son and of Hugh Despencer, were brought down to the Abbey and buried before the high altar, while the others bodies of the slain were buried according to the king's orders.

The campaign and battle had been lost because de Montfort had failed to unite his forces. He had manoeuvred effectively for a time, almost long enough avoiding battle and to be able to reach his son's forces. However it had been Edward's ability to move quickly and strike unexpectedly, when they were divided, first at Kenilworth and then at Evesham, that proved decisive. The Evesham campaign showed Prince Edward's military abilities and provided important experience that would stand him in good stead in the famous campaigns he would fight in Wales and Scotland in future years as Edward I.

Though peace was not finally restored across the country for another two years, the Battle of Evesham had completely broken the rebellion, for almost all of its major supporters had been intentionally killed on the field. It was also decisive in giving the king his freedom to rule without the control of a council. Henry III was no longer restricted by the impositions of a Council.

However, because of his attempt to control the excesses of the crown through the use of parliament, de Montfort has long held an important place in English history. This veneration of the Earl had begun within a few years of the battle, with his tomb and the spot where he is said to have died becoming associated with miracles.

The Battlefield

Evesham and the battlefield are encompassed on three sides by the river Avon. Cox provides by far the best discussion of the historic terrain. However much remains to be done in reconstructing the landscape as it was at the time of the battle, for as the Lanercost chronicle says, de Montfort was killed in a place called Godescroft, indicating that there were enclosed fields somewhere on Greenhill in the 13th century, with significant implications for the interpretation of the terrain and the deployment of the armies.

Meadows lay along the narrow floodplain of the Avon while open fields may have encompassed much of the remaining area. There is some evidence of ridge and furrow adjacent to Abbey Manor House on the 1940s aerial photographs, but it is unclear how extensive the open fields were or even if this ridge and furrow is of medieval date. To the north, in Lenchwick parish, an area of heath is recorded on the 18th century map, and Cox has argued that Greenhill may have been common pasture in the 13th century.

In the medieval period a single bridge at the south east side of the town led across the river. From the town the main road led north to Alcester, ascending Greenhill. Branching to the north west below the hill was the route to Worcester which, at least in 1675 and thus well before the turnpike was created, skirted the lower slopes of the hill and then continued along the north side of the Avon to Worcester. It appears since to have moved slightly lower down the slopes below Abbey Manor due to imparking around the House. On the parish boundary at the north of the parish the Salt Street ran from the Worcester road on the west up onto Greenhill along the line now known as The Squires. There it crossed the Alcester road and ran down what is now Blayney's Lane to to cross the Avon over Offenham bridge.

Ramsay had de Montfort deployed on the ridge where the Obelisk now stands. The arguments for dismissing this interpretation were presented by Burne. Various more recent interpretations of the battle have suggested the approach of the royal forces from several different directions, the army being split by Prince Edward. Young & Adair, broadly following Burne, have all the troops approaching for the north east, having crossed the river at Cleeve Prior. Mortimer is then shown advancing on the east side of the Avon to Bengeworth bridge to close off de Montfort's line of retreat. Edward approaches across Offenham bridge and de Clare southward along the Alcester road to deploy on Green Hill, just to the north of the Battlewell. Smurthwaite and Seymour also have a similar deployment. Carpenter follows a broadly similar deployment but with Mortimer approaching Bengeworth from the west, on the Pershore road. It might have been considered unlikely, given that the numbers of troops involved, that Edward would have split and thus weakened his army in this fashion.

The Evesham chronicle says that it was near Siveldestone that Edward's divided forces into three divisions and ascended the hill. Cox has demonstrated that Siveldestone is almost certainly Siflaed's stone, a boundary marker on the late Saxon boundary of

1265 - The Murder of Evesham

Evesham, a short distance to the west of Offenham bridge. It is described by Tindal and by Ireland in the 18th century and, though removed by the early 19th century, its position can be clearly identified. But this could be a fairly general identification of the location of the army being at the northern edge of the parish.

Burne depicts de Montfort deployed immediately to the south of Battlewell and Edward's army just to the north. Young & Adair, followed by Carpenter, have Edward just to the south of Battlewell. Cox, followed by English Heritage, places the initial deployments further south still, referring to the London Chronicle which says Edward was a stones throw away when de Montfort reached the top of the hill. This has caused Cox, like Tindal before him, to suggest that the action took place just to the north of the brow of the hill.

Battlewell is however first recorded in 1272-3 as a spring where miracles had taken place and the site where de Montfort died. The site of Battlewell is recorded on the 1st edition 6 inch Ordnance Survey map in the late 19th century and the map of the parish in 1827, when buildings stood immediately to the south of the well. The site can be traced back to the 15th century. To encompass this tradition, Cox suggests that de Montfort may have initially pushed back the royal forces strung out across the hilltop. However it is even more difficult to accommodate the burials found in the 19th century or before at Deadman's Ait, by Offenham bridge, with deployment and action so far to the south. In support of a more southerly location for the action Cox refers to the Lanercost chronicle, which states that de Montfort was killed in a place called Godescroft. However Cox suggests this might be The Croft, where Croft Road now lies, though no record is known of this before the 19th century.

The newly discovered account however may enable an alternative interpretation. It seems to imply that it was de Montfort who deployed first and thus was able to choose the ground, for he viewed the enemy advancing up onto Greenhill. Deploying immediately to the south of the Battlewell would make sense, enabling him to use the valley here to provide some protection for his left flank. There is no other logical place for him to have deployed. If de Montfort did indeed choose the ground then Edward could not have deployed further south than The Squires.

Evesham is one of the few early battles for which a genuinely new primary source has been recently identified, one that has transformed our understanding of the event. This is now a battle where the broad character and location of the action is clearly understood and where the location of the action is fairly tightly constrained by the physical topography. Though there has been 20th century development in the area, a substantial part of the battlefield still remains undeveloped. This makes Evesham one of the few early medieval battles where a visit to the battlefield can be very clearly focussed and a relatively secure outline of the battle provided. For the same reason it is one where there appears a high potential for detailed reconstruction of the historic terrain and investigation of the battle archaeology. Although parts of the battlefield are accessible, a new scheme is being developed which should greatly improve that access and provide the first on site interpretation.

Archaeology of the battle

In 1794 Tindale published the report from a local farmer that 'innumerable bones' had been discovered at 'deadman's eyot', a small former island beside the site of Offham bridge, and also just to the west thereof. There is however no proof that these burials were actually associated with the battle. This had previously been reported by Brooke, in 1857, who also made reference to other human remains having been discovered near to Battlewell House, which is 500 metres (550 yards) to the south of Battlewell.

Brooke 1857

Brooke, Richard. Visits to Fields of Battle in England of the Fifteenth Century. London, 1857. 203-4

'THE FIELD OF THE BATTLE OF EVESHAM

As the Battle of Evesham was not fought in the fifteenth century, it would not have been noticed here, if it had not been for the circumstance of my having visited the field of battle a few months before this work was sent to the press. Very little information, however, respecting that sanguinary conflict, can be obtained by inquiry upon the spot.

On the 28th and 29th of May, 1856, I visited the field of battle, which was fought on the 4th of August, 1265, between the forces of King Henry III., under the command of his eldest son Prince Edward, and those of Simon de Montfort, Earl of Leicester, and the rebellious barons, and terminated in the defeat of the latter with great slaughter.

The battle was fought in the spot now enclosed fields, upon the elevated tract of ground, adjoining the turnpike road from Evesham in Worcestershire, to Alcester and Warwick, very near a house called Battle-well House (which stands on the left side of the road in going from Evesham), and also near the tollbar, called Battle-well Gate, and almost a mile and a quarter from Evesham.

A lane turns off from the turnpike road near the tollbar, towards the river Avon, by which the defeated forces are said to have fled, and to have attempted to descend to the meadows, in order to cross the Avon, at a place now called Offenham Ferry. The lane was, until about 1741, the great high road from Worcester towards London. An old man, named Thomas Price, who lives at the lodge of the mansion belonging to Mrs. Blainey, which is situated on the side of the turnpike road, opposite to Battle-well House, and, consequently, upon the spot where the conflict took place, and who has resided there most of his life, informed me, that many years ago, he recollected seeing a battle-axe, which, with some human bones, had been ploughed up in a field, close to Battle-well House. A bridge is said to have formerly stood at Offenham Ferry, and some appearances of masonry, seemingly of the pier of the bridge, may still be discovered at the ferry. Close to it the ground is a little raised, and that spot is called 'Dead Man's Height,' or 'Dead Man's Bank,' where human remains and fragments of weapons, are said to have been formerly discovered, as well as in an orchard very near there, called 'Twyners.' About two miles on the opposite side of the ferry, is a stone quarry upon a hill, at South Littleton, which was also in the line of retreat, and human bones, and parts of weapons, are said to have been found there, about thirty years ago.

In the beautiful grounds of F. J. Rudge, Esq., of Abbey Manor, near the field of battle, a small pillar has been erected with the following inscription:

>   ON THIS SPOT
>   IN THE REIGN OF HENRY III
>   THE BATTLE OF EVESHAM
>   WAS FOUGHT AUGUST iv 1265
> BETWEEN THE KING'S FORCES COMMANDED BY HIS ELDEST SON
>   PRINCE EDWARD
>   AND
>   THE BARONS UNDER
>   SIMON DE MONTFORT EARL OF LEICESTER;
>   IN WHICH
>   THE PRINCE BY HIS SKILL AND VALOUR
>   OBTAINED A COMPLETE VICTORY,
>   AND
> THE EARL WITH HIS ELDEST SON HENRY DE MONTFORT,
>   EIGHTEEN BARONS, ONE HUNDRED AND SIXTY KNIGHTS,

AND
FOUR THOUSAND SOLDIERS,
WERE SLAIN IN THE BATTLE.'

Visiting the battlefield

For such an early battle, Evesham is relatively well understood, with several detailed contemporary accounts. The battlefield itself also lies within a restricted in area clearly defined by very distinctive terrain features, including the river Avon. Although some parts of the battlefield cannot at present be accessed one can gain a reasonably good feel for the character of the terrain and the possible positioning of the forces.

Currently, through the Forestry Commission grants scheme, footpath access has been provided, from a car park accessed from The Squires, to the Leicester Tower and thence along, through the woodland on the slopes of the valley side to the Obelisk. To complement this excellent walk, the Simon de Montfort Society, with the support of Wychavon District Council, is currently preparing a proposal for the development of a battlefield trail with interpretation panels, which it is hoped will provide a link across land not currently accessible, to the Battlewell and then across to the Obelisk, would provide an excellent circular walk of the battlefield.

The town is well organised for the tourist. There are several car parks close to the centre of the town and various pubs, cafes and other facilities. There is also plenty of information, some free and others for sale, including town maps, town trail etc available from the Tourist Information Centre. This includes a leaflet on the Battle of Evesham produced by the Vale of Evesham Civic Society and the Simon de Montfort Society.

The Obelisk monument

The Obelisk monument was erected in 1845 by Edward Rudge. It does not mark the site of the battle. Its location, and that of the Leicester Tower, was determined by the landscaping considerations of the parkland laid out around Abbey Manor House in the 19th century. However the obelisk site will have given a good prospect of Greenhill and of the site of the Battlewell before the trees of the Wilderness existed to obscure the view.

The main inscriptions read:

> 'GreateLE'STER here expir'd with HENRY his brave Sonne,
> When many a high exploit they in that day had done.
> Scarce was there noble house of which those times could tell
> But that some one thereof,on this or that side fell:
> Amongst the slaughtered men,that here lay heap'd on pyles
> BOHUNS and BEAUCHAMPS were, BASETS and MANDEVILL's:
> HARDREDESHULL,CREPPINGS,LE DESPENSER,BALIOL,ROWELE,
> INDE. TRECBY, EINEDYELD, ASTLEY[36], YORK, BERMINGHAM, TROSSELL,
> SEGRAVES, and SAINT JOHNS,seeke,upon the end of all,
> To give those of their names their christian buriall.
> Ten thousand on both sides were la'n and slain that day;
> PRINCE EDWARD gets the gule, and beares the palme away.
> Drayton's Polyolbion'
> ON THIS SPOT
> In the Reign of HENRY III
> THE BATTLE OF EVESHAM.
> was fought August IV 1265
> Between the Kings forces commanded by his eldest Son
> PRINCE EDWARD
> and
> The BARONS under
> SIMON DE MONTFORT. EARL of LEICESTER;
> In which
> The PRINCE by his Skill and Valour
> obtained a complete Victory,
> and
> The EARL with his eldest son HENRY DE MONTFORT,
> Eighteen Barons one hundred and sixty knights,
> and

---

[36] Tony Spicer of the Battlefields Trust wonders if Thomas of Astley was an ancestor of Jacob Astley, a Royalist general who led his men to defeat at the Battle of Stow in 1646, just down the road from Evesham. If so, Evesham has not been very lucky for the Astley family.

Four thousand Soldiers,
were slain in the Battle.

The de Montfort Memorial

A monument to Simon de Montfort was erected in the Abbey Park, Evesham, in 1965. Its inscription reads:

HERE WERE BURIED THE REMAINS OF
SIMON DE MONTFORT, EARL OF LEICESTER
PIONEER OF REPRESENTATIVE GOVERNMENT WHO WAS
KILLED IN THE BATTLE OF EVESHAM ON AUGUST 4th 1265
THIS STONE BROUGHT FROM HIS BIRTHPLACE THE
CASTLE OF MONTFORT-LAMAURY IN FRANCE WAS
ERECTED TO COMMEMORATE THE SEVEN HUNDREDTH
ANNIVERSRY OF HIS DEATH
UNVEILED BY THE SPEAKER OF THE HOUSE OF COMMONS
AND DEDICATED BY
HIS GRACE THE ARCHBISHOP OF CANTERBURY
ON THE 18th DAY OF JULY 1965

Interpretation

There is good interpretation of the Abbey site itself in Abbey Park, Evesham, but no interpretation about the battle on the battlefield.

In the Almonry Heritage Centre there is the Battle Room, opened in 1965, on the 700th anniversary by the Speaker of the House of Commons, as a memorial to Simon de Montfort. It contains a battle plan, though its reconstruction of the landscape and especially the open fields of Evesham is inadequate. There is also some information about the battle, an iron axe head, found in the silt of the Avon near Offenham, which is said to be consistent with the form of the weapons likely to have been carried by the Welsh infantry. There are also arrowheads of the period, though apparently not from Evesham. The display is worth a visit but is now looking rather dated and in need of replacement.

The Battlefields Trust regularly lead a walk of the battlefield and The Simon de Montfort Society hold an annual wreath laying at the Abbey on or close to the anniversary of the battle. For more information on the Simon de Montfort Society

Battlefield Walk

Six miles. Starting from the Abbey Park in the centre of Evesham. There are several car parks near the centre. The route is partly along metalled footpaths beside roads, partly on un-metalled lanes and partly on well marked footpaths across pasture. Just one small area along the Avon bank can be boggy, especially after wet weather. There is a full range of facilities within the town of Evesham. The walk described here is meant to be used in conjunction with the Battlefield Explorer map, which can be downloaded from the left hand side of the screen.

If a much shorter walk is required then there is parking adjacent to The Squires which gives access to the walk to the Leicester Tower and the Obelisk. It is also possible to park on the old road beside the main road to Alcester, immediately to the north of the junction with the Squires.

Start from the Abbey Park in the centre of Evesham at the de Montfort Memorial just to the south of the tower of the Abbey church, overlooking the river Avon. This is not the tower from which, supposedly, de Montfort's barber saw the approach of the royal army, which was closer to the river. This is a detached Tudor *campanile*. The nineteenth century stained glass in a window in the north aisle of St Lawrence's church is worth a visit. Also keep an eye out for several interpretation panels around the grounds which describe the Abbey itself, giving a good impression of the character and layout of the abbey in the medieval period. Almonry Heritage Centre with its Battle Room is also just a short walk to the north west of the Abbey site.

From the abbey walk north along the High Street and north out of the town along the Alcester road, following the route taken by de Montfort's army up onto Greenhill. Today the suburbs of the town stretch right up to the battlefield, but in 1265 the town stopped just a short distance north of the market place.

Just after reaching the brow of the hill, opposite Croft Road, is Battlewell House. It has the name on a stone plaque on the brick wall beside the gate. This should not be confused with the site of the Battlewell. It was however close by here that burials were found some time before 1857 – possibly rebel troops killed during the pursuit. There is a small lane that gives access to the hilltop just to the south of Battlewell House, on the west side of the road, but this is not a public right of way.

Continue north. Just before Blayney's Lane, which is on the east (right hand) side of the road, is a footpath that leads to the left between the houses to the site of the Battlewell. This is not a public right of way, although it is hoped that the new scheme being developed by the de Montfort Society will soon enable public access to this key location on the battlefield. This is where, according to tradition, de Montfort fell. Close by a chapel appears to have been constructed in the medieval period but its exact site is not known. You are now probably just to the north of de Montfort's initial deployment a the beginning of the battle.

Continue north and turn left along The Squires. This is probably the location where the royal forces deployed, with de Clare's division to the east, Mortimer's to the west and Edwards perhaps across the line of the main road. The Squires footpath alongside the road is not well maintained and so, until the bypass is completed, care needs to be taken when walking here. Go past the entrance to Abbey Manor House. 200 metres further on there is a gateway on the left. If you look along the line of The Squires north westward you can see the wooded hills adjacent in the distance which lie close to the site of Mosham Meadow where Edward's army rendezvoused before marching on the final approach to the battlefield. De Montfort's army was probably already in battle array on Greenhill when Edward's three divisions march up this road, the old Salt Street, to deploy.

From here there are waymark signs that lead you to the Leicester Tower and the Obelisk. Having passed the Tower and gone through the trees, when you reach the stile where the path turns north east up the slope to the Obelisk, look to the south east. From here it is possible to see the tower of the abbey in the valley to the south east and further eastward the rise up onto the top of Greenhill and around to the east the site of the Battlewell is just visible at the head of the small valley.

From the Obelisk retrace your steps to the top of the Squires. Take Blayney's Lane on the other side of the main road. This leads you down the hill towards the site of Offenham ferry. The bypass now cuts across the line of the lane necessitating a slight diversion, Take great care when crossing the bypass. The path leads a short distance along the line of the old railway line. This is the site of the Siveldestone, the Saxon marker stone near which one of the accounts says the royal army deployed. Maybe the left wing of the royal army was indeed deployed well down the slop toward the stone. Take the path across the small pasture field towards the river. Deadman's Ait, which was once a small island encompassed by the Avon, is the tree covered land immediately adjacent to the river. On the other side of the river, close to the site of the medieval bridge which used to give access across the Avon to Offenham, is a pub, but sadly for the thirsty walker it is no longer accessible from this side of the river!

From here follow the path south along the bank of the Avon. There are good view of Greenhill across the meadows, giving a good feel for the steepness of the slope, though on this side of the Alcester road the whole of the hilltop has been built over in the 20th century. Continue along the path until it takes you back into Evesham. Take the first opportunity of a linking path that takes you up onto the main footpath from Oxstalls Farm as this is as easier walk along the last short stretch into the town and back to the starting point.

You will find Battlewell at SP/038455 on Ordnance Survey maps close by the not altogether accurately-placed crossed swords and 1265 of the battlefield symbol. Leave Evesham town centre by High Street and travel up Greenhill on the road to Alcester until nearly art the top of Greenhill. Just past the entrance to the Abbotswood private estate you will find a brown heritage sign on the right of the rload. You will need to keep a sharp lookout for it because it is very small and sometimes obscured. The sign will direct you to turn left into a rough track. Follow that track for 125 metres until you come to the gate of the four acre Battlewell Conservation Area. Once there you are in what all of the traditions recognise as the centre of the 1265 Evesham battlefield. The whole site is known as Battlewell and the name has attached itself to the entire area. If you visit Battlewell by car then it is a good idea to park in one of the nearby side streets and walk down the lane to the Conservation Area rather than risk your shock absorbers. If you prefer to walk up to Battlewell from Evesham town centre then you will have a walk of roughly one and a half miles. To help you to follow the route the Simon de Montfort Society has placed pavement route-markers that look like this ...

... starting near the Almonry museum.

Whether travelling by car, bicycle or on foot you will likely be retracing the steps taken by Earl Simon and his army on the morning of August 4th 1265.

The Battlewell site contains a deep, steep-sided, pool that has been identified as the Battlewell of Montfortian legend. Battlewell was never a well in the sense of a lined cylindrical shaft with a bucket on a rope. The name originally referred to a spring of water rising to the surface and feeding a pool. Both the Vale of Evesham Historical Society and the Simon de Montfort Society have examined the present pool and concluded that it is an agricultural sump fed by water run off from the surrounding fields, forming a tiny reservoir. There has been no sign of a spring and the pool does not sit on the Greenhill spring line. The presence of a brick lining, discovered when the pool was recently cleaned out, suggests that it may have been set up no earlier than the eighteenth century.

Annex E. 'My left foot ...'

After Earl Simon was killed at Evesham his body was dismembered and the portions were distributed across the country. In the days before mass media it was the only way to convince people that Earl Simon really was dead ('I don't believe he's dead! You're just saying that!' 'Oh yeah, well he's not going to get far without his right leg').

Robert of Gloucester described it this way, and fingered Sir William Maltravers as the man who did the dirty deed:

'And in the midst of all of it, it was tragic that Sir Simon, the old man, should have been cut to pieces, for Sir William Maltravers, and he deserves no thanks, carved off his feet and hands and most of his limbs. And, pitiful beyond belief, he cut off his privy parts and sent them to Dame Maud Mortimer. But no matter how they mutilated him, he did not bleed.'

David Cox supports the view that Simon's head, testicles in its mouth, was sent to Maud, wife of de Mortimer, at Wigmore castle. One theory explains the selection of Lady de Mortimer as the recipient of this grisly gift by looking back to the execution of her father by Llywelyn ap Iorwerth because of his adultery with Llywelyn's wife. This Llywelyn was the grandfather of the Llywelyn ap Gruffyd who had provided the bulk of Simon's foot soldiers for the battle and to whom Simon's daughter, Eleanor, was betrothed. Once satisfied that Simon was dead Maud returned the relic.

One hand made its way to Cheshire; the other may have been deposited in Evesham Abbey. One foot was sent to Llywelyn ap Gruffyd. Evesham Abbey retained the torso, recovered from the battlefield by monks of the abbey who buried it in the abbey church with the body of Henry, his eldest son, and that of Hugh le Despenser. A recent study has described how Simon's remains were enshrined to form the basis of the cult of Simon de Montfort, unofficial saint, which lasted, in one form or another, for fifty years. The Dictum of Kenilworth, sealed in October 1266, forbade anyone to venerate Simon as a saint and the annals of Osney abbey (among other sources) state that Earl Simon's remains were exhumed and disposed of in some secret place, since forgotten.

We do not know where Earl Simon's torso is now and we have documented information about only one other portion of the earl's body: one foot, encased in a silver boot-shaped reliquary. John de Vescy is credited with saving earl Simon's severed foot (reportedly his left foot) and taking it away to venerate.

This grisly relic eventually made its way to de Vescy's home at Alnwick Castle, was deposited with the community of Alnwick Priory and, after remaining there for some years, passed into the safe keeping of Durham Cathedral. The Simon de Montfort Society contacted Alnwick Castle and the staff there looked for it without success because, as we discovered, the relic had been brought there straight after the Battle of Evesham but had been passed on to Alnwick Priory almost immediately. At the Dissolution of the Monasteries by Henry VIII in 1539 it vanished. One legend held that it had been rescued by the staff of Durham Cathedral and was preserved in the cathedral's treasury, so we pursued our enquiries there.

The chapter clerk very generously enlisted the help of the Chapter's librarian, archaeologist and archivist, and of the Blue Badge Guides, to see if any of them could reveal its location. Sadly, none of them had any knowledge of the relic, so the enquiry moved on to the Bishop's Office at Bishops Auckland, following a lead that Alnwick Castle at one time belonged to the Bishop of Durham. The staff at Auckland Castle, the bishop's residence, had no record of the relic. The bishop was on the case but he was distracted by being translated to Canterbury and the palace has since been sold. However, we still have faint hopes that we might have welcome news.

Our greatest fear is that the relic ended as so many did at the Dissolution, thrown on a bonfire and the reliquary melted for its precious metal.

I must report that the Kenilworth History and Archaeology Society takes a different view.

This account is reproduced from *The Great Siege of Kenilworth Castle 1266* written by Harry Sunley, with assistance from Jan Cooper, on behalf of the Kenilworth History & Archaeology Society and published in 2011, with kind permission of that society:

SIMON'S BODY

WHEN SIMON DE MONTFORT was killed at Evesham, his body was mutilated. In the words of Richard of Gloucester:

And in the midst of all of it [the battle], it was tragic that Sir Simon, the old man, should have been cut to pieces, for Sir William Maltravers, and he deserves no thanks, carved off his feet and hands and most of his limbs. And, pitiful beyond belief, he cut off his privy parts and sent them to Dame Maud Mortimer: But no matter how they mutilated him, he did not bleed.

It is relevant to Kenilworth to attempt an audit of Simon's remains. According to Cox[37], his head, with his testicles in his mouth, was stuck on a spear and sent to Mortimer's wife, Maud, at Wigmore, Herefordshire. It is understood that Dame Maud was selected because her father had been hanged by Llywelyn ap Iorwerth (known as Llywelyn the Great) because of his adultery with Llywelyn's wife. This Llywelyn was the grandfather of Simon's ally, Llywelyn ap Gruffyd. It is said that she returned this gruesome present. One hand was sent to the wife of a Marcher in Cheshire, the other to Evesham Abbey, where it was venerated. One foot was sent to Llywelyn ap Gruffyd, and the other ended up at the Premonstratensian Abbey of Alnwick in Northumberland. After the mutilation, the trunk was taken on an old broken ladder, covered by a tunic, to Evesham Abbey, and with the body [of] his eldest son, Henry, and that of Hugh le Despenser, was buried, with the King's permission, in the Abbey Church. Historians' opinions seem to differ as to what happened next. Some assert that Simon became so venerated by the common people that many pilgrims came to his burial place and miracles occurred. The Royalists, wishing to stop this cult of veneration and talk of miracles, had his remains removed. It is perhaps surprising that the Chronicle of Evesham Abbey makes no reference to any of this though, purportedly a Monk of Evesham compiled a list of over 200 miraculous cures effected by Simon's remains[38]. Article 8 of the Dictum of Kenilworth (October 1266) forbade anyone to regard Simon as a saint; and the Annals of Osney state that his remains were `....exhumed, and thrown down in some remote spot ..... known to a very few people'[39]. The Annals of Waverley (a Cistercian Abbey near Simon's castle of Odiham and known to be favourably disposed to the de Montforts) speak of the king giving permission for the bodies of the Earl and his son to lie at the lower step before the high altar of the abbey church at Evesham[40]. This, after the intervention of the Pope on behalf of Amaury de Montfort in 1267. On the assumption the head was returned from Dame Maud, its whereabouts are not accounted for, nor those of the arms and legs.

---

[37] Cox, D.C., The Battle of Evesham, a New Account, The Vale of Evesham Historical Society, 1988
[38] Cox, D.C., The Battle of Evesham, a New Account, The Vale of Evesham Historical Society, 1988
[39] Cox, D.C., The Battle of Evesham, a New Account, The Vale of Evesham Historical Society, 1988
[40] Margaret Wade Labarge, Simon de Montfort, Eyre & Spottiswood, 1962

A Discovery at Kenilworth Abbey

Jumping now 655 years to 1920 and to the ruins of Kenilworth Abbey, we have an interesting newspaper report[41] that referred to a tomb that still lies in the centre of the nave of the abbey Church, although now under grass. The report stated:

'an interesting discovery was made when in the course of repairing what was always assumed to be the tomb of Thomas Warmington [1313-38], it was found that the grave was only about four feet deep and it contained less than two feet of soil This was carefully removed and at four feet two inches deep a slab covering the entire grave was disclosed. At the head was found a carved stone pillow, upon which rested the remains of a skull with about two inches of vertebrae attached. Immediately below were two leg bones crossed. No other bones or remains were found. At the head, foot and on the sides were four bas-relieved foliated crosses. The tomb itself was of ashlar stonework. The carved pillow or head-rest was mortared into the bed-stone; a portion of it was removed and a hole about two feet deep sunk, but the gravel underneath has never been disturbed. The fragments of skull and the leg bones were, in the presence of the vicar; re-interred under the slab, which was put back in its original position, and the tomb thoroughly cleaned out and recovered'

The nave of the church is now a Garden of Rest, and the said tomb is no doubt under a foot or so of deposited soil.

Were these the remains of the body of Simon de Montfort? Robert Hyde Greg (1795-1875 economist and antiquary) stated that Eleanor de Montfort, Simon's widow, said to be still residing at Kenilworth Castle after the Battle of Evesham, secured the remains and had them buried at the Abbey. For some reason, not explained, the newspaper report suggests that they might be those of Henry de Montfort, Simon's eldest son, who was also killed at Evesham. Because they are incomplete, they are most unlikely to be those of Abbot Thomas de Warmington. It must be admitted that there is some evidence in favour of the bones being Simon's. When I spoke to the de Montfort Society on the 'Great Siege of Kenilworth' in May 2005, there was interest in this account. Because of the buried remains of cremations overlying this tomb, it will be many years before this might be re-investigated, and of course, this still does not account for the whereabouts of Simon de Montfort's arms.

---

[41] Kenilworth Advertiser of October 2nd 1920. This was first published in *Kenilworth Abbey: The Tombs in the Nave of the Church,* Harry Sunley, Kenilworth History 200302004, pages 30-32

One of the surprising features of this newspaper article is that Carey-Hill, who reported on the 1922 excavation of Kenilworth Abbey failed to mention the discovery of human remains. He merely reports that two tombs were found by Whitley (the 1890 excavator of the Abbey). The one of our concern, the eastern one, is mentioned by Whitley as having six carved crosses on the sides, but he made no mention of bones.

During the nineteenth century excavations at Evesham Abbey[42] a skeleton was found in the nave which had been laid to rest on a wooden slab, without any coffin, and upon examination appeared to suggest that it was the remains of someone killed in the battle. An incorrect statement in the catalogue of the Rudge collection of finds from the Abbey, which said that the skeleton was found in the quire, led to the unlikely suggestion that it might be Henry de Montfort.

I will add just two notes. The first picks up on the possibility that the skeleton that the Rudges excavated might be that of Henry de Montfort. The skull is on display in the Abbey Room of the Almonry Museum in Evesham. The back of the skull bears a deep 'L'-shaped wound from an edged weapon delivered with such force that it has burst the sutures of the skull. It has been examined by a radiographer, who is also a medieval re-enactor, who concluded that the wound was consistent with a heavy single-edged blade, possibly an axe or a falchion (a short but fearsome single-edged sword not unlike a modern machete), the shorter arm of the wound being made as the weapon was levered out of the skull. There are also signs of damage at the base of the skull, suggesting a deliberate beheading. Suggestions that the wound was caused by a spade during the excavation are unlikely to be true. The wound was not exposed until the skeleton, which had been lying on its back, was removed from the grave, and it was lifted out not dug out.

At present two local societies are seeking funds to have a modern forensic examination of the skull. That should confirm or disprove the nature of the wound(s), provide an idea of the age at death, a rough estimate of the date of death, an indication of the skeleton's class or rank, possibly at least a rough idea of his place of origin and it might even tell us

---

[42] Cox, D.C., The Battle of Evesham, a New Account, The Vale of Evesham Historical Society, 1988, page 15

what position he was in (standing, kneeling, lying) when he was killed. Until that can be carried out, we can only speculate.

My second note concerns the report in the Kenilworth Advertiser, which describes the (supposed de Montfort) burial as ...

... At the head was found a carved stone pillow, upon which rested the remains of a skull with about two inches of vertebrae attached. Immediately below were two leg bones crossed, No other bones or remains were found ...

... which is also a fine description of a typical Templar burial.

A challenge to the 'Kenilworth view' was published last year. Dr David Cox's article: *The Tomb of Simon de Montfort* (Transactions of the Worcestershire Archaeological Society, 3rd Series, Vol. 26 (2018)) goes into greater detail on the death of Simon de Montfort and the disposal of his remains in Evesham Abbey where Dr Cox believes they remain. With sufficient local support it should be feasible to test Dr Cox's hypothesis. The Simon de Montfort Society has republished this article, with the kind consent of the Worcestershire Archaeological Society, as a Lion Occasional Paper: *The Tomb of Simon de Montfort* (2019).

Annex F. 'St George, he is for England'

The national symbol of England, the cross of St George, might first have been advanced in battle at Evesham. St George's Day celebrates this 'most invincible athlete... whose name and protection the English nation invoke as that of their patron', as Edward III of England once described him.

By the time of the Norman Conquest in 1066, St George had become known as a Christian martyr, making him a highly popular figure among the Anglo-Norman knights of the day. Legend told how he appeared as an apparition to those taking part in the first Crusade towards the end of the eleventh century, and particularly during the siege of Antioch in 1098, to encourage the attackers.

Richard the Lionheart also claimed to have beheld a vision of St George during a different siege, this time at Acre, in 1189, and he subsequently adopted the saint's emblem of the red cross on a white background as England's distinguishing mark, although this provenance is disputed by some historians.

Ironically, in 1263, de Montfort and his devotees believed that the righteousness of their cause constituted a crusade. When the papacy later got behind the royalists and conferred crusader status on their campaign to suppress the baronial revolt, Lord Edward selected a red crusader cross for his men to wear to distinguish themselves from the Montfortians.

Certain of the nobility of their cause, it seems that both sides rode into battle at Evesham with invisible crusader crosses sewn onto their surcoats. Just possibly, they may have worn tangible and visible crusader crosses, in Edward's case a red cross on a white background.

That is the story and some historians maintain that this is the earliest recorded use of the St George's Cross anywhere in England. This is what we have been led to believe by accounts dating back to the thirteenth century and I think it is plausible. Edward had adopted St George, although not as a national symbol, and it is not unlikely that he would fight under the banner of his personal saint and use his symbol to distinguish his own troops from the enemy. By contrast, Simon de Montfort's troops would have had white crosses, as the cross was used by every knight who had gone on a crusade. Both sides would therefore have carried the cross and regarded themselves as crusading against the other. This would have confused many observers, including the monks at Evesham Abbey, as it complicated how people viewed the battle, as two crusades colliding.

Bibliography

Royal Writs

Close Rolls 1261-1264 (HMSO 1936) and *Close Rolls 1264-68* (HMSO 1937): letters addressed by the king to specific individuals

Calendar of Patent Rolls 1258-66 (HMSO 1910): letters patent

Calendar of Liberate Rolls 1260-67 (HMSO 1961): letters about payments and allowances

Original Sources and Commentaries

HAMILTON, H.C. (ed.) (1848) *The Chronicle of Walter of Hemingburgh (or Hemingford)*, (s.l.) English Historical Society

ROTHWELL, H. (ed.) (1957) *The Chronicle of Walter of Guisborough*, 3rd Series, Camden: Royal Historical Society

STUBBS, W. (ed.) (1880) *The Historical Works of Gervase of Canterbury*, ii, Canterbury/Dover: Rolls Series

LUARD, H.R. (ed.) (1855) *Annales Monastici, iii*, Dunstable: Rolls Series

Bodleain Library, *MS Laud Misc. 529*, ff. 70-71, Evesham

LUARD, H.R. (ed.) (1884) *Matthaei Parisiensis, monachi Sancti Albani, Chronica majora, Chronicles and memorials of Great Britain and Ireland during the Middle Ages*, London: Longman & Co.

MARIX EVANS, MARTIN (1998) *The Military Heritage of Britain & Ireland* (s.l.: s.n.)

POWICKE, F.M., *Henry III and the Lord Edward*, Oxford: Clarendon Press

Biographies of Simon de Montfort

MADDICOTT, J. R. (1994) *Simon de Montfort*, Cambridge: Cambridge University Press

AMBLER, S.T. (2019) *The Song of Simon de Montfort: The Life and Death of a Medieval Revolutionary*, Oxford: Oxford University Press

BLAAUW, W.H. and CHARLES, H.P. (1871) *The Barons' War: Including the Battles of Lewes and Evesham*, London: Bell and Daldy

BÉMONT, C. (1884) *Simon de Montfort*, Paris (s.n.)

TREHARNE, R.F., *Simon de Montfort and Baronial Reform*, (s.l.) Hambledon Press

PROTHERO, G. W. (1877) *The life of Simon de Montfort, Earl of Leicester: with special reference to the parliamentary history of his time*, London: Longmans Green and Co.
BAKER, D. (2018) *Simon de Montfort and the Rise of the English Nation*, Stroud: Amberley Publishing

Context of the Battle

The broad political context within which the de Montfort rebellion should be viewed is discussed in numerous books, but one of the best assessments is:

CARPENTER, DAVID (2004) *The Struggle for Mastery: Britain 1066-1284*, (s.l.) Penguin pp.369-391

Then consider reading:

CARPENTER, DAVID (1996) *The Reign of Henry III*, London: Hambledon Press
POWICKE, F. M. (1953) *The Thirteenth Century: 1216-1307*, Oxford: Clarendon Press
PRESTWICH, MICHAEL (1988) *Edward I*, London: Methuen
PRESTWICH, MICHAEL (2005) *Plantagenet England: 1225-1360*, Oxford: Oxford University Press
DAVIES, H. W. C. (1924) *England Under the Normans and Angevins 1066-1272*, (s.l.) Methuen & Co. Ltd

Accounts of the Battle of Evesham

There are a number of original accounts that give details of the action. The book by David Carpenter (1987) uses the evidence from most, but does not provide a complete transcription and translation of them.

COX, D. C. (1989) *The Battle of Evesham in the Evesham chronicle*, Historical Research, no. 62 : 337-45.
The Simon de Montfort Society. The *Last Hours of Simon de Montfort: A New Account*, A Lion Occasional Paper. Evesham, undated.
COX, D.C. (1988) *The Battle of Evesham: a New Account*, The Vale of Evesham Historical Society, Evesham.

LABORDERIE, OLIVIER, MADDICOTT, JOHN and CARPENTER, DAVID (2000) *The last hours of Simon de Montfort : a new account*, English Historical Review, no. 115, pp. 378-412. Provides a translation of the newly discovered account. Also: A Lion Occasional Paper (2000) *The Last Hours of Simon de Montfort: A New Account*, Evesham: The Simon de Montfort Society. Provides a copy of the text of the newly discovered account from the Laborderie translation.

LEAMON, ROSEMARY and SPICER, TONY (eds.) (2012) *William de Nangis, an Account of the Battle of Evesham*, Evesham: The Simon de Montfort Society

SPICER, TONY (ed.) (2015) *Walter of Guisborough, an Account of the Battle of Evesham*, Evesham: The Simon de Montfort Society

LEAMON, ROSEMARY and SPICER, TONY (eds.) (2015) *Four Accounts of the Battle of Evesham*, Evesham: The Simon de Montfort Society

(Includes accounts by Osney, Wykes, Trivet and the Evesham Chronicle)

COX, D.C. (1989) *The Battle of Evesham in the Evesham chronicle*, Historical Research, no. 62 pp. 337-45

COX, D.C. (1988) *The Battle of Evesham: a New Account*, Evesham: The Vale of Evesham Historical Society

The detail of the military campaign is also reviewed in many studies, although the publication in 2000 by Laborderie et al means that all earlier discussions are out of date to some degree. The most useful include:

CARPENTER, DAVID (1987) *The Battles of Lewes and Evesham 1264/65*, (s.l.) Mercia Publications Ltd

English Heritage (1995). '*Battlefield Report: Evesham, 1265*'

(Provides extracts from Matthew Paris)

Town of Evesham

RUDGE, E. J. (1820) *A short account of the history and antiquities of Evesham*, Evesham: Printed and sold by J. Agg

TINDAL, WILLIAM (1794) *The History and Antiquities of the Abbey and Borough of Evesham* (s.l.:s.n.)

MAY, GEORGE (1845) *A descriptive history of the town of Evesham, from the foundation of its Saxon monastery: with notices respecting the ancient deanery of its Vale*, Evesham: George May

NEW, HERBERT (1873) *A day at Evesham : the visitors' guide to its antiquities and other objects of interest*, Evesham: W. & H. Smith (no, not that one, this was a local printer)

Battlefield Guides and Atlases

BURNE, A. H. (1950, reprint 2002) *The Battlefields of England,* London: Penguin

BARRETT, CHARLES RAYMOND BOOTH (1896) *Battles and Battlefields in England,* London: Innes & Co.

BROOKE, RICHARD (1857) *Visits to Fields of Battle in England of the Fifteenth Century*, London: John Russell Smith

CHANDLER, DAVID (1989) *A Guide to the Battlefields of Europe* (s.l.) Wordsworth Editions

CLARK, DAVID (1993) *Battlefield Walks: Midlands* (s.l.) Alan Sutton

GETMAPPING (2002) *British Battles: Amazing Views* (s.l.) Collins

DANIELL, DAVID SCOTT (1961) *Battles and Battlefields* (s.l.) B.T. Batsford

DODDS, GLEN LYNDON (1996) *Battles in Britain 1066-1746* (s.l.) Weidenfeld Military

GREEN, HOWARD (1973) *Guide to the Battlefields of Britain and Ireland,* Constable: London

GUEST, KEN & DENISE (1996) *British Battles* (s.l.) Harper Collins

KINROSS, JOHN (1988) *Walking and Exploring The Battlefields of Britain*, Newton Abbot: David & Charles

RAYNER, MICHAEL (2004) *English Battlefields,* Stroud: Tempus

SEYMOUR, WILLIAM (1979) *Battles in Britain 1066-1746* (s.l.) Sidgwick and Jackson

SMURTHWAITE, DAVID (1993) *The Complete Guide to the Battlefields of Britain*, London: Michael Joseph

WARNER, PHILIP (2002) *British Battlefields: The Definitive Guide to Warfare in England and Scotland* (s.l.) Barnes & Noble Books

YOUNG, PETER and ADAIR, JOHN (1979) *From Hastings to Culloden,* Kineton: The Roundwood Press

Medieval Warfare

NORMAN, VESEY (2010) *The Medieval Soldier* (s.l.) Pen & Sword

SHOWALTER, DENNIS E. *'Caste, Skill, and Training: The Evolution of Cohesion in European Armies from the Middle Ages to the Sixteenth Century'*, The Journal of Military History, July 1993 (Vol. 57, No. 3), pp. 407-430

AYTON, A. and PRICE, J. (eds.) (1995) *The Medieval Military Revolution: State, Society, and Military Change in Medieval and Early Modern Europe.* London: I.B. Tauris

CONTAMINE. PHILLIPPE; translated from the French by Michael Jones. *War In The Middle Ages.* Oxford: Basil Blackwell, 1984

DAVID, R. H. C. (1989) *The Medieval Warhorse: Origin, Development and Redevelopment.* London: Thames and Hudson

DeVRIES, KELLY (1992) *Medieval Military Technology.* Lewiston: Broadview

FRANCE, JOHN (1999) *Western Warfare in the Age of the Crusades, 1000-1300.* Ithaca: Cornell University Press

HYLAND, ANN (1994) *The Medieval Warhorse from Byzantium to the Crusades.* Stroud: Alan Sutton

KEEN, MAURICE, ed. *Medieval Warfare. A History.* Oxford: Oxford University Press, 1999

OMAN, SIR CHARLES W. C. (1953) *The Art of War in the Middle Ages: A.D. 378-1515.* 2 volumes. Revised and edited by John H. Beeler. Ithaca: Cornell University Press

VERBRUGGEN, J.F. (1997) *The Art of Warfare in Western Europe During the Middle Ages from the Eighth Century to 1340.* Second edition, revised and enlarged. Trans. Col. S. Willard and Mrs. R.W. Southern. New York: Boydell Press, (first published 1954)

PRYOR, JOHN H., (ed.) *Logistics of Warfare in the Age of the Crusades.* Proceedings of a Workshop held at the Centre for Medieval Studies, University of Sydney, Australia, 30 September to 4 October 2002. Burlington, VT: Ashgate Publishing, 2006

PRESTWICH, MICHAEL (1996) *Armies and Warfare in the Middle Ages: The English Experience.* New Haven, CT: Yale University Press

PRESTWICH, MICHAEL (1980) *The Three Edwards: War and State in England 1272-1377,* London: Wiedenfeld and Nicolson

SUPPE, FREDERICK C. (1994) *Military Institutions on the Welsh Marches. Shropshire, AD 1066-1300,* Woodbridge: Boydell Press

McPEAK, WILLIAM J. *Falchion: The Short Sword that Made Good.* Command, Issue 41 (January 1997), pp. 62-64

OAKESHOTT, EWART (1997) *A Knight and His Weapons.* 2nd ed. Chester Springs: Dufour Editions

OAKESHOTT, EWART (1998) *A Knight and His Horse.* 2nd ed. Chester Springs, PA: Dufour Editions, (first published 1962)

FOLEY, VERNARD, GEORGE PALMER and WERNER SOEDEL, *The Crossbow*, Scientific American, Vol. 252, No. 1 (January 1985), pp. 104-110
BRADBURY, JIM (1985) *The Medieval Archer*. New York: St. Martin's.
HARDY, ROBERT (1993) *Longbow: A Social and Military History,* New York: Lyons & Burford
PAYNE-GALLWEY, SIR RALPH (1958) *The Crossbow: Mediaeval and Modern, Military and Sporting, Its Construction, History, and Management, With a Treatise on the Balista and Catapult of the Ancients and an Appendix on the Catapult, Balista, & the Turkish Bow*, New York: Bramhall House
(originally published 1903)
STIRICKLAND, MATTHEW and HARDY, ROBERT (2005) *The Great Warbow; From Hastings to the Mary Rose,* Stroud: Sutton Publishing

De Re Militari

There is almost an industry in commentaries on Vegetius, some of which are listed in this section.

ALLMAND, CHRISTOPHER (2004) *The De Re Militari of Vegetius: A Classical Text in the Middle Ages*, History Today, Vol. 54, No. 6 (June 2004), pp. 20-25
ALLMAND, CHRISTOPHER, *The De re militari of Vegetius in the Middle Ages and the Renaissance, in Writing War. Medieval Literary Responses to Warfare*, eds. Corinne Saunders, Françoise Le Saux and Neil Thomas, Cambridge, 2004, pp. 15-28
GOFFART, WALTER (1997) *The Date and Purpose of Vegetius' De Re Militari,'* Tradition 33 (1977), pp. 65-100
CHARLES, MICHAEL B. (2007) *Vegetius in Context. Establishing the Date of the Epitoma Rei Militaris* (Historia. Einzelschriften; Heft 194), Stuttgart: Franz Steiner Verlag
MILNER, N.P., trans. (1996) *Vegetius: Epitome of Military Science*, Liverpool: Liverpool University Press
REEVE, M.D., ed. (2004) *Vegetius, Epitoma rei militaris. Scriptorum classicorum bibliotheca oxoniensis,* Oxford: Clarendon
REEVE, MICHAEL D. (2000) *The Transmission of Vegetius's Epitoma rei militaris*, Aevum 74, pp. 479-499
SHRADER, CHARLES R. (1979) *A Handlist of Extant Manuscripts Containing the De re militari of Flavius Vegetius Renatus*, Scriptorium 33, no. 2, pp. 280-305

SHRADER, CHARLES R. (1981), *The Influence of Vegetius' 'De re militari'*, Military Affairs 45, pp. 167-172

Dramatis Personae

The Cast of Our Drama

Potted biographies of some of the people you might meet in this book.

Abergavenny, 10th Lord	A powerful Marcher lord, William de Braose, 10th Lord Abergavenny, married Eva Marshal. Both held estates in the Welsh Marches and Ireland.
Adrian V, Pope	Born between 1210 and 1220 as Ottobuono de' Fieschi, Adrian V (La. *Adrianus V*), was Pope from July 11th 1276 until his death on August 18th 1276.
Almain, Henry of	Born in 1235, Henry of Almain was the son of Richard, 1st Earl of Cornwall. His surname was derived from his father's status as the elected German King of the Romans. He was murdered by his cousins Guy and Simon (the younger) de Montfort in 1271.
Alice de Lusignan of Angoulême	Born in 1236 Alice de Lusignan was the first wife of Marcher baron Gilbert de Clare, 7th Earl of Gloucester, and half-niece of King Henry III of England. It was rumoured that she became the mistress of her half first cousin, Lord Edward. She died in 1290.
Isabella of Angoulême	Born around 1186/1188 Isabella of Angoulême was queen consort of England as the second wife of King John from 1200 until John's death in 1216. She was also Countess of Angoulême in her own right from 1202 until 1246. Isabella had five children by the king, including his heir, later Henry III. In 1220, Isabella married Hugh X of Lusignan, Count of La Marche, by whom she had another nine children.

Thomas II d'Arderne	Born in 1236, Thomas II d'Arderne fought on the Montfortian side at the Battle of Evesham. He survived the battle, dying in 1287 at the ripe old age of 51.
Earl of Arundel	Thomas Howard, 2nd Earl of Arundel, amassed what stands as the first major British art collection, which included painting, sculpture and manuscripts. In 1666 his grandson, Henry Howard, divided the collection between the Royal Society and the College of Arms.
Thomas de Astley	Born in 1215, Son of Walter (William) de Astley and Isabel de Astley, Sir Thomas de Astley died at the Battle of Evesham, fighting alongside Simon de Montfort.
Baldwin IV	Baldwin IV, Count of Flanders, was a grandfather of Simon VI de Montfort, who was killed at the Battle of Evesham.
Guy de Balliol	Guy de Balliol, Simon de Montfort's standard bearer at the Battle of Evesham, was the son of Sir Henry de Baliol of Cavers, Chamberlain of Scotland, and Lora de Valognes, daughter of William de Valognes, lord of Panmure. Guy de Balliol died at the Battle of Evesham.
William of Barres	Born in the Ile De France, on 1135 to Guillaume Ier DesBarres and Guillaumees Barres. Married Helissente De Chaumont and had 3 children. He died in 1234.
Ralph Bassett of Sapcote	Born at Sapcote, Leicestershire, in 1215, Sir Ralph Basset of Sapcote was the 1st Baron of Sapcote. He died in 1282.
Warin of Bassingbourne	Born between January 8th 1224 and January 7th 1227 at Royston, Hertfordshire, Warin of Bassingbourne was the son of Warin de Bassingbourn and Eve de Bassingbourne. He died in 1266, a year after fighting on the Marcher side at Evesham.
Jean de Beauchamp	Jean or John de Beauchamp of Holt was the son of Sir William de Beauchamp, who was Earl of Warwick, 5th Baron Beauchamp and Sheriff of Worcester & Worcestershire, and Isabel Mauduit. Jean de Beauchamp was born c. 1238 at Elmley & Salwarpe, Worcestershire.

He died in June 1298 at the family's castle of Elmley, Worcestershire and was buried at Friars Minor, Worcester.

Amicia de Beaumont Born in 1160 in Leicester, Amicia was Comtesse of Leicester and Dame de Breteui. She died in 1215 at Haute Bruyere, Rouen.

Henry de Berham Born c.1225 in Barham, Henry de Berham or Bereham died at Cranbrook in Kent in 1276.

Richard de Berham *Other than the fact that he fought at Evesham on the baronial side, fate unknown, I have little information about John Recard. Has anyone more information?*

William of Berton *The records of his trial for the murder of 'John the Deacon' are sparse so I have no further details about William of Berton. If anybody can provide any biographical information I will be glad to include it in a future edition with a suitable acknowledgement.*

Roger Bigod Born c. 1209, Roger Bigod was 4th Earl of Norfolk and Marshal of England. He was the eldest son and heir of Hugh Bigod, 3rd Earl of Norfolk (1182-1225) by his wife Maud, a daughter of William Marshal, 1st Earl of Pembroke (1147-1219). Together with his younger brother Hugh Bigod (1211-1266), Justiciar, he was prominent among the barons who opposed Henry III. He died in 1270.

Gilbert de Birteley *I am afraid that Gilbert has escaped me. I have only a brief mention of his participation in the Battle of Evesham. Any further information will be gratefully received.*

William Blount, 4th Baron Mountjoy William Blount, 4th Baron Mountjoy (c. 1478–1534) of Barton Blount, Derbyshire, was an influential English courtier, a respected scholar and patron of learning. He was one of the most influential and wealthiest English noble courtiers of his time.

Humphrey IV de Bohun Humphrey (IV) de Bohun (1204–September 1275) was 2nd Earl of Hereford and 1st Earl of Essex, as well as Constable of England. He was the son of Henry de Bohun, 1st Earl of Hereford, and Maud

	FitzGeoffrey. He was one of the nine godfathers of Lord Edward. In 1258, Humphrey defected to the baronial cause but returned to his royal allegiance.
Humphrey V de Bohun	Unlike his father (see above), Humphrey V de Bohun, remained loyal to the baronial side throughout the Barons' War, and was captured at Evesham. In October that year he died in captivity at Beeston Castle in Cheshire from injuries he had sustained in the battle.
Humphrey de Bolesdon	*Humphrey was a Montfortian who fought at Evesham. I have been unable to identify him sufficiently to discern his fate after Evesham.*
John de Boseville	Born c. 1201, John de Bosville was the son of John de Bosville and Alice (de Darfield). His date and place of death are unknown. John is mentioned in his mother's charters as well as Agnes his wife, but little else is available about him.
William de Boyton	*Is this the William de Boynton born c. 1220 in Sadbury, Yorkshire, son of Sir Ingraham de Boynton, Lord of Acklam & Roxey and Joan Aklam?*
Eleanor de Braose	Eleanor de Braose, was the youngest daughter of a powerful Marcher lord, William de Braose, 10th Lord Abergavenny, and Eva Marshal, both of whom held estates in the Welsh Marches and Ireland.
William de Braose	Father of Eleanor de Braose and 10th Lord Abergavenny.
Guillaume le Breton	William the Breton (c. 1165–c. 1225) was a French chronicler and poet who served on diplomatic missions for Phillipe Augustus of France.
Matthew Breton	*Other than the facts that he was a Montfortian who fought at Evesham and his fate is unknown, I know very little about Matthew. Anybody know anything more?*
John de Burg	Born at Barnstead, Surrey in 1185, John de Burg was the son of Hubert de Burgh, 1st Earl of Kent and Beatrix Bardolph, Lady Wormgay. He died in 1275.

1265 - The Murder of Evesham

William de Burmugham [Birmingham] — William supported Simon de Montford and was said to have died at the Battle of Evesham. The manor of Birmingham was confiscated by the King and given to Roger de Clifford. William was married to the daughter of Thomas de Astley.

Thomas de Caleye — I believe that this was the Sir Thomas de Caleye (or Cayly or Cailly) who was related to Hugh de Cayly (who, in the reign of Henry III, held a quarter of a fee of the honour of Richmond) and who witnessed land deeds for his relative.

King Canute — Born in 990, Cnut the Great, also known as Canute, whose father was Sweyn Forkbeard, was King of Denmark, England and Norway; together often referred to as the North Sea Empire. He died in 1035 in England.

Blanche of Castile — Blanche of Castile was Queen of France by marriage to Louis VIII. She acted as regent twice during the reign of her son, Louis IX: during his minority from 1226 until 1234, and during his absence from 1248 until 1252.

Eleanor of Castile — Born in 1161, Eleanor was Queen of Castile and Toledo as wife of Alfonso VIII of Castile. She was the sixth child and second daughter of Henry II, King of England, and Eleanor of Aquitaine.

Charles the Simple — Charles III, called the 'Simple' or the 'Straightforward', was the King of West Francia from 898 until 922 and the King of Lotharingia from 911 until 919–23. He was a member of the Carolingian dynasty.

Gilbert de Clare — Gilbert de Clare, 6th Earl of Hertford, 7th Earl of Gloucester, 3rd Lord of Glamorgan, 9th Lord of Clare (1243 - 1295) was a powerful English noble. Known as 'Gilbert the Red' or 'The Red Earl', he held Glamorgan, a powerful and wealthy Marcher lordship as well as over 200 English manors (172 in the Honour of Clare).

Roger Clifford — Born in 1243, Roger Clifford was Lord of Kingsbury, Warwickshire, Justice of the Forest South of Trent in August 1265 and Baron Clifford.

	He died in 1282, drowning in the Menai Straits, Anglesey.
Geoffrey de Clinton	Geoffrey de Clinton (died c. 1134) was an Anglo-Norman noble, chamberlain and treasurer to King Henry I of England. He was foremost amongst the men king Henry 'raised from the dust'. Kenilworth Castle was his creation.
Richard Grey of Codnor	Born in 1202, Richard de Grey of Codnor, Derbyshire, was Warden of the Isles (Channel Islands) and later both Constable of Dover Castle and Warden of the Cinque Ports. Captured at the Battle of Evesham, he died in 1271.
Richard de Coleworth	*This might be the Richard de Coleworth who was second husband of Erneburga de Assartis, widow of Ralph de Arderne.*
Richard of Cornwall	Richard, second son of John, King of England, was the nominal Count of Poitou, Earl of Cornwall and King of Germany. Born in 1209, in the Great Hall, Winchester, Richard of Cornwall died in 1272 in Berkhamsted Castle.
Henry de Crammarvill	A vassal of Henry III, de Crammarvill supported the Barons in their dispute with the king.
Thomas de Cranesly	Sir Thomas de Cransley was reported as killed at Evesham. This Thomas had married Maud de Hardwick, the widow of Sir Bartholomew de Rakelinton, and had no land except from her dower.
Walter de Crespigny	A leading Montfortian who was killed at the Battle of Evesham.
Robert de Crevequer	Sir Robert de Crevequer was born in 1239 in the manor of Leeds Castle in Kent, possibly the son of Hamon de Crevequer and Maud de Avranche.
Urse d'Abitot	Urse d'Abitot was a Norman who followed Duke William to England, and became High Sheriff of Worcestershire under him, and under Kings William II and Henry I.

Giles d'Argentin	Born c. 1218, Giles d'Argentin survived Evesham to die c. 1282, aged about 64 years old. His parents were Richard d'Argentin, Vicomte de Cantebrigge, and Cassandra de Insula. He was married to Margaret d'Aguillon.
King David of Scotland	David I or Dauíd mac Maíl Choluim was a twelfth-century ruler who was Prince of the Cumbrians from 1113 to 1124 and later King of the Scots from 1124 to 1153. The youngest son of Malcolm III and Margaret of Wessex, David spent most of his childhood in Scotland, but was exiled to England temporarily in 1093.
Ottobuono de' Fieschi	Ottobuono belonged to a feudal family of Liguria, the Fieschi, Counts of Lavagna. Fieschi was distantly related to Henry III. His sister had married Thomas II of Savoy, a cousin of Henry's wife, Eleanor of Provence. He was sent to England in 1265 by Pope Clement IV to mediate between King Henry III of England and his barons, and to preach the Crusades.
John de la Haye	This may be the Sir John de la Haye who was born about 1215 in Burwell, Lincolnshire, and who died in 1274 in Austria or Hungary.
Maud de Lusignan	Maud de Lusignan was the daughter of Raoul de Lusignan, 7th Comte d'Eu and Alice d'Eu, Comtesse d'Eu. She married Humphrey de Bohun, 2nd Earl of Hereford, son of Henry de Bohun. She died in 1241.
Nicholas de Segrave	Nicholas de Segrave, 1st Baron Segrave, was grandson of Stephen de Segrave. Segrave was one of the most prominent baronial leaders during the reign of King Henry III. In 1295 he was summoned to Parliament as Baron Segrave.
Fulk de Den	*I am afraid that I have little information about Fulk de Den, only a brief mention of his participation in the Battle of Evesham. Any further information will be gratefully received.*

Hugh le Despenser	Born in 1223, Hugh le Despencer, 1st Baron le Despencer, was an important ally of Simon de Montfort. He served briefly as Justiciar of England. Despencer was present at the Battle of Lewes and died fighting on de Montfort's side at the Battle of Evesham. He was interred in Evesham Abbey.
William Devereux	William Devereux (1219-1265), was an important Marcher Lord, who held Lyonshall Castle controlling a strategically vital approach to the border of Wales. He was killed at Evesham.
Sir John D'Eiville	Sir John D'Eiville (correctly *de Daiville*), of Egmanton, Nottinghamshire, son and heir of Sir Robert de Daiville of Egmanton and Dionis or Denise, daughter of Sir Thomas Fitz William of Sprotborough, Yorkshire. He was not present at the battle of Evesham but after the battle he became one of the most active leaders of the disinherited barons.
John Dive	*Included in the available lists of Montfortians who fought at Evesham, fate unknown.*
Robert Doye	*Included in the available lists of Montfortians who fought at Evesham, fate unknown.*
Simeon of Durham	Simeon entered the Benedictine abbey at Jarrow, in the county of Durham, in about 1071. This abbey was moved (1083) to the town of Durham, and there he made his religious vows in 1085/86 and later became choirmaster.
William Robert Earl	Born in 1806 in Chichester, Sussex, William Robert Earl was a landscape painter who achieved some acclaim while he was alive. He exhibited nineteen paintings at the Royal Academy of Arts between 1823 and 1854, fifty-two at the British Institute, and over forty at the Society of British Artists. He died in 1880 in Plumstead at seventy-three years of age.

1265 - The Murder of Evesham

Saint Ecgwine Egwin (Ecqwin, Egwine or Ecgwine) of Evesham was a Benedictine monk and, later, the third Bishop of Worcester. Born in Worcester he died in 717, at his own foundation, Evesham Abbey.

Edward I Edward I (1239 – 1307), also known as Edward Longshanks and the Hammer of the Scots (La. *Malleus Scotorum*), was King of England from 1272 to 1307. Before his accession to the throne, he was commonly referred to as The Lord Edward. The first son of Henry III, Edward was involved from an early age in the political intrigues of his father's reign. In 1259, he briefly sided with a baronial reform movement, supporting the Provisions of Oxford. After reconciliation with his father, however, he remained loyal throughout the subsequent armed conflict, known as the Second Barons' War. After the Battle of Lewes, Edward was hostage to the rebellious barons, but escaped after a few months and defeated the baronial leader Simon de Montfort at the Battle of Evesham in 1265. Within two years the rebellion was extinguished and, with England pacified, Edward joined the Ninth Crusade to the Holy Land. The crusade accomplished little, and Edward was on his way home in 1272 when he was informed that his father had died. Making a slow return, he reached England in 1274 and was crowned at Westminster Abbey on August 19th.

Edward II Born in 1284, Edward II was King of England until he was deposed. The fourth son of Edward I, Edward became the heir apparent to the throne following the death of his elder brother Alphonso. Beginning in 1300, Edward accompanied his father on campaigns to pacify Scotland, and in 1306 was knighted in a grand ceremony at Westminster Abbey. Following his father's death, Edward succeeded to the throne in 1307. He married Isabella, the daughter of the powerful King Philip IV of France, in 1308, as part of a long-running effort to resolve tensions between the English and French crowns. After an unsuccessful reign, the king was forced to relinquish his crown in January 1327 in favour of his 14-year-old son, Edward III, and he died in Berkeley Castle, probably murdered on the orders of the new regime.

Edward III	Edward III (1312–1377) was King of England and Lord of Ireland from January 1327 until his death; he is noted for his military success and for restoring royal authority after the disastrous and unorthodox reign of his father, Edward II. Edward III transformed the Kingdom of England into one of the most formidable military powers in Europe.
Edward the Confessor	Edward the Confessor was among the last Anglo-Saxon kings of England. The last king of the House of Wessex, he ruled from 1042 to 1066. Edward was the son of Æthelred the Unready and Emma of Normandy. He succeeded Cnut the Great's son – and his own half-brother – Harthacnut. Edward died in 1066 and was succeeded by Harold Godwinson.
Lord Edward	The future Edward I of England was commonly known as 'Lord Edward' before his father's death elevated him to the throne.
Gilbert Einesfield	*Included in the available lists of Montfortians who fought at Evesham, Gilbert Einesfield was killed in the battle.*
Robert fitz Neil	Robert fitz Neil held the manor of Iffley and many lands in Bedfordshire and Buckinghamshire. A member of Hugh le Despencer's household it is possible that he survived the defeat at Evesham, dying sometime in 1266, possibly of injuries received at the battle.
John Fitzjohn	Fitzjohn was the eldest son of John Fitzgeoffrey and Isabel Bigod. He married Margery, daughter of Philip Basset and Hawise de Lovaine. He led a battle of the baronial army at the Battle of Lewes, and was appointed, Sheriff of Westmorland and governor of Windsor Castle. He was captured at Evesham and imprisoned. Having recovered his lands under the Dictum of Kenilworth he died in 1275 without issue.
Hubert Fitz-Matthew	A member of Henry III's household affinity, he was with the king during the 1242 Gascony campaign and was one of those who won fame in the heroic rearguard action at the Battle of Saintonge.

Ralph Fitz-Nicholas	A Steward of the Household to Henry III, he accompanied the king on the disastrous Gascony campaign of 1242, acquitting himself heroically during the rearguard action at the Battle of Saintonge.
Frederick II, Holy Roman Emperor	Born in 1194, Frederick II was King of Sicily from 1198, King of Germany from 1212, King of Italy and Holy Roman Emperor from 1220 and King of Jerusalem from 1225. He was the son of emperor Henry VI of the Hohenstaufen dynasty and of Constance, heiress to the Norman kings of Sicily.
John Giffard	John Giffard, 1st Baron Giffard of Brimsfield (1232–1299), was an English nobleman prominent in the Second Barons' War and, under Edward I, in Wales. From 1263 he was a leading member of the baronial cause; however, he defected to the royalist side after the Battle of Lewes.
William Giffard	Son of Walter Giffard, Lord of Longueville, and Ermengarde, daughter of Gerard Flaitel, William Giffard was the Lord Chancellor of England under William II and Henry I, from 1093 to 1101, and Bishop of Winchester from 1100–1129. He died in January 1129.
Gilbert the Red	Nickname of Gilbert de Clare, supposedly a reference to his red hair.
Robert of Gloucester	Robert of Gloucester (c. 1260–c. 1300) wrote a chronicle of British, English and Norman history sometime in the later thirteenth century. Roughly contemporary with the Battle of Evesham, he may have been a witness to the circumstances surrounding Evesham and the eclipse of the baronial cause.
Godgifu Leofric (Lady Godiva)	Godiva, Countess of Mercia (in oe. *Godgifu*), was an English noblewoman who, according to a legend dating at least to the thirteenth century, rode naked through the streets of Coventry to gain a remission of the oppressive taxation that her husband, Leofric, Earl of Mercia, imposed on his tenants.

Robert Grosseteste	Robert Grosseteste (c. 1175-1253) was an English statesman, scholastic philosopher, theologian, scientist and Bishop of Lincoln. He was born of humble parents at Stradbroke in Suffolk. He was a leading spiritual influence on Simon de Montfort.
Llewellyn ap Gruffydd	Born in 1223, Llywelyn ap Gruffydd (sometimes *Llywelyn ap Gruffudd*), also known as Llywelyn the Last or *Llywelyn Yr Ail*, was Prince of Wales from 1258 until his death at Cilmeri in 1282.
Walter of Guisborough	Walter of Guisborough was a canon regular of the Augustinian Guisborough Priory, Yorkshire and English chronicler of the fourteenth century.
Princess Gwladys Ddu	Gwladus Ddu, (Gwladus ferch Llywelyn) was a Welsh noblewoman, a daughter of Llywelyn the Great of Gwynedd, mother of Roger Mortimer, 1st Baron Mortimer. She married Reginald de Braose, Lord of Brecon and Abergavenny in c. 1215 and Ralph de Mortimer of Wigmore c. 1230.
Saer de Harcourt	Born in 1239, Saer de Harcourt, of Kibworth Harcourt, Leicestershire, was the son of Sir Richard de Harcourt and Orabilis de Quincy. A member of Simon de Montfort's familia, He died in 1278.
Robert de Hardredishull	Born in 1240, Robert was the son of William and Maud de Hardreshull. He died at the battle of Evesham, fighting on the side of Simon de Montfort.
Henry de Hastings	Born in 1235, son of Henry Hastings and Ada de Huntingdon, Henry de Hastings was created Baron in 1264 by Simon de Montfort. He led the Londoners at the Battle of Lewes, where he was taken prisoner and was captured again at the Battle of Evesham.
Richard de Havering	A member of Simon de Montfort's affinity, Earl's steward, Financial Agent and general right-hand man, largely in charge of the family's finances. By the time that Havering died in 1267 he and his family had been reconciled to the royalists.

1265 - The Murder of Evesham

Thomas Hearne Thomas Hearne or Hearn (1678–1735) was an English diarist and antiquary, remembered for his published editions of many medieval English chronicles and other important historical texts.

Walter of Hemingburgh Walter of Guisborough's chronicle was previously edited as the *Chronicle of Walter of Hemingford* or *Hemingburgh*.

Henry I Henry I (c. 1068–December 1135), was King of England from 1100 to his death. He was the fourth son of William the Conqueror. He allied himself with one brother, William Rufus against another brother, Robert. When William died in a hunting accident in 1100, Henry seized the English throne, which he defended against Robert until he invaded Normandy, finally defeating Robert at the Battle of Tinchebray. Henry kept Robert imprisoned for the rest of his life.

Henry III Henry III (October 1207–November 1272), was King of England, Lord of Ireland and Duke of Aquitaine from 1216 until his death. The son of King John and Isabella of Angoulême, Henry assumed the throne when he was only nine in the middle of the First Barons' War. By 1258, Henry's rule was increasingly unpopular, the result of the failure of his expensive foreign policies and the notoriety of his Poitevin half-brothers, the Lusignans, as well as the role of his local officials in collecting taxes and debts. A coalition of his barons, initially possibly backed by Eleanor, seized power in a *coup d'etat*; the baronial regime collapsed but Henry was unable to reform a stable government. The Second Barons' War included the Battle of Lewes in 1264, where Henry was defeated and taken prisoner. Henry's eldest son, Edward, escaped from captivity to defeat de Montfort at the Battle of Evesham the following year and freed his father. Henry initially enacted a harsh revenge on the remaining rebels, but was persuaded by the ferocious resistance from the 'disinherited' to modify his policies. Nevertheless, reconstruction was slow and not entirely complete when Henry died.

Henry Knighton	Henry Knighton, Augustinian canon at the abbey of St Mary of the Meadows, Leicester, wrote a four-volume chronicle, first published in 1652, giving the history of England from 959 to 1366.
Henry the Forester	*Included in the available lists of Montfortians who fought at Evesham, the fate of Henry the Forester (or 'le Forester') is unclear.*
Thomas de Hestelel	*Included in the available lists of Montfortians who fought at Evesham, the fate of Thomas de Hedstelel (or 'Estley') is unclear.*
Stephen de Holwell	One of the few Montfortians who died during Edward I's raid on Kenilworth, shortly before the Battle of Evesham, was Stephen de Holwell, Montfort's clerk, who was forcibly taken from the abbey church and beheaded on de Clare's orders.
Hugh de Hopville	*Included in the available lists of Montfortians who fought at Evesham, Hugh de Hopville's fate is unclear.*
Robert de Hoveden	Roger of Howden or Hoveden (c. 1174–1201) was a twelfth-century chronicler. He is believed to have been a native of Howden in the East Riding of Yorkshire. Nothing is known of him before the year 1174. He was used as a negotiator between the king and a number of English religious houses. In 1189, he acted as a justice of the forests in Yorkshire, Cumberland and Northumberland.
Henry of Huntingdon	Henry of Huntingdon, the son of a canon in the diocese of Lincoln, was a twelfth-century English historian, the author of a history of England, the *Historia Anglorum*, 'the most important Anglo-Norman historian to emerge from the secular clergy'.
John de Inde	*Included in the available lists of Montfortians who fought at Evesham, John de Inde was killed in the battle.*
Llywelyn ap Iorwerth	Llywelyn the Great (We. *Llywelyn Fawr*) full name *Llywelyn ap Iorwerth*, (c. 1173–1240) was a prince of Gwynedd in north Wales and temporarily ruler of all Wales. By a combination of war and diplomacy he dominated Wales for forty-five years.

John the Deacon of Littleton	Known from his killer's endictment: 'for murdering John the Deacon of Littleton at the 'bridge of Twyford' in August 1285'.
King John	Born in 1166, John, also known as John Lackland, was King of England from 1199 until his death in 1216. The baronial revolt at the end of John's reign led to the sealing of Magna Carta, and laid the foundations for a second baronial revolt against his son, Henry III.
John de Lacy	John de Lacy (c. 1192–1240) was the 2nd Earl of Lincoln, of the fourth creation. He was the eldest son and heir of Roger de Lacy and his wife, Maud or Matilda de Clere (not of the de Clare family).
Earl Leofric	Leofric (died August 31st or September 30th 1057) was an earl of Mercia and King Canute's chief enforcer in the Midlands. He founded monasteries at Coventry and Much Wenlock. Leofric is best remembered as the husband of Lady Godiva.
Roger de Leybourne	Roger de Leybourne (1215–1271) was the younger son of another Sir Roger de Leybourne, by his first wife, Eleanor, the daughter and heir of Stephen of Thornham. De Leybourne fought at the Battle of Northampton and as a defender at the siege of Rochester Castle, was captured at the Battle of Lewes, took part in the escape of Lord Edward and fought at Evesham, reportedly saving the king's life.
Louis IX	Born in 1214, Louis IX, commonly known as Saint Louis, was King of France from 1226 to 1270, the ninth from the House of Capet. He is a canonised Catholic and Anglican saint.
Louis VIII	Born in 1187, Louis VIII (nicknamed 'The Lion'), was King of France from 1223 to 1226, the eighth from the House of Capet.
Lusignans	After King John's death in 1216 his widow, Isabella of Angouleme, married Hugh X of Lusignan. They had five children together, half-brothers to Henry III of England.

William of Malmesbury	Born in 1095 or 1096, William of Malmesbury was the foremost English historian of the twelfth century. His father was Norman and his mother English. He spent his whole life in England and his adult life as a monk at Malmesbury Abbey in Wiltshire.
William Malteyn	*Included in the available lists of Montfortians who fought at Evesham, the fate of William Malteyn (or 'Malteyne') is unclear.*
William Maltravers	Coming from a family that had profited from the confiscation of lands from the de Lacy family, William Maltravers has the distinction of being named the man who dismembered Simon de Montfort's corpse after the Battle of Evesham. *Has anybody got more information about him?*
William de Mandeville	*Included in the available lists of Montfortians who fought at Evesham, William de Mandeville (or 'Amundeville'?) was killed in the battle.*
William de Manners	*Included in the available lists of Montfortians who fought at Evesham, the fate of William de Manners is unclear.*
Margaret, Countess of Winchester	Simon de Montfort's great aunt, Lady Margaret de Beaumont Countess of Winchester was born in Leicester in 1154 and died at the age of 80 in Brackley, Northamptonshire in 1235.
Margoth	A female spy, accompanying the army of the younger Simon de Monfort and reporting to Lord Edward. From her recorded exploits, an early incarnation of Wonder Woman.
William Marmion	*Is this the Sir William Marmion who was born c. 1223 in Withringham, Lincolnshire, son of Robert Marmion and Avice Tanfield? This Sir William died some time before 1277, in Horncastle, Lincolnshire.*
William Marshal	William Marshal, 1st Earl of Pembroke (1146 or 1147–1219), also called William the Marshal, was an Anglo-Norman soldier and statesman. He served five English kings: Henry II, his sons the 'Young King' Henry, Richard I, John and his grandson, Henry III.

1265 - The Murder of Evesham

Anketin de Martival	Steward on Earl Simon's estate, son of Anketin De Martival and Agnes de Martival.
Thomas Menill	See Maddicott.
Geoffrey of Monmouth	Geoffrey of Monmouth (L. *Galfridus Monemutensis, Galfridus Arturus*, W. *Gruffudd ap Arthur, Sieffre o Fynwy*), c. 1095–c. 1155, was a British cleric and one of the major figures in the development of British historiography and the popularity of tales of King Arthur. He is best known for his chronicle: *The History of the Kings of Britain*.
Henry de Monmouth	*I have been unable to identify this Henry de Monmouth (Henry V was also known as 'Henry of Monmouth'). Has anybody got any information?*
Warren de Montchesnil	Another of the nobles who accompanied Henry III on the disastrous Gascony campaign of 1242, and acquitted himself heroically during the rearguard action at the Battle of Saintonge.
Amaury de Montfort	Amaury de Montfort (1242 or 1243–1301) was the third son of Simon de Montfort and Eleanor of England. Amaury entered the priesthood as a young man and held the positions of Treasurer of York Minster, canon of Rouen, Évreux, London and Lincoln. He also served as a papal chaplain.
Eleanor de Montfort	Eleanor of England (also called Eleanor Plantagenet and Eleanor of Leicester), 1215– 1275, was the youngest child of John, King of England and Isabella of Angoulême. Eleanor bore seven children by her husband, Simon de Montfort: 1. Henry de Montfort (1238 – 1265) 2. Simon de Montfort the Younger (1240 – 1271) 3. Amaury de Montfort (1242/1243–1300) 4. Guy de Montfort, Count of Nola (1244–1288)[4] 5. Joanna, born and died in Bordeaux between 1248 and 1251 6. Richard de Montfort (1252–1281) 7. Eleanor de Montfort Princess of Wales (1258–1282)

1265 - The Murder of Evesham

Guy de Montfort
Guy de Montfort, Count of Nola (1244–1291) was the fourth son of Simon de Montfort and Eleanor of England. He was seriously wounded and captured at Evesham. Escaping to France from Windsor Castle he joined his brother, Simon the Younger, in his wanderings across Europe. In 1271 Simon and Guy murdered their cousin, Henry of Almain in revenge for the deaths of their father and brother at Evesham.

Henry de Montfort
Sir Henry de Montfort (1238 – 1265) was the eldest son of Simon de Montfort and Eleanor of England. Henry was killed in the aftermath of the Battle of Evesham although the East End of London legend of the 'Blind Beggar' suggests that he escaped the battlefield and lived in obscurity for the rest of his life.

Peter de Montfort
Peter de Montfort or Piers de Montfort (c. 1205–1265) of Beaudesert Castle was an English magnate, soldier and diplomat. He is the first person recorded as having presided over Parliament as a *parlour* or *prolocutor*, an office now known as Speaker of the House of Commons. He was killed at Evesham.

Peter de Montfort, junior
Peter or Piers de Montfort married Alice Audley, daughter of Henry Audley, by whom he had two sons, Peter and Robert. His eldest son, Peter de Montfort, succeeded him. He was pardoned by Henry III for 'all trespasses at the time of the disturbance in the kingdom', and eventually recovered part of his father's lands. He died some time before March 1287.

Robert de Montfort
Son of Peter (or Piers) de Montfort. He fought alongside his father at Evesham where he was wounded and captured.

Simon de Montfort, elder
Born c. 1208, Simon de Montfort, 6th Earl of Leicester, was a French nobleman who married Henry III's sister, became a member of the English peerage and led the baronial opposition to his brother-in-law's rule culminating in the Second Barons' War. Following his victory at the Battle of Lewes he became de facto ruler of the country and played a major role in the constitutional development of

England. After a rule of just over a year, Simon de Montfort was killed by forces loyal to the king in the Battle of Evesham.

Simon de Montort, younger Born in 1240, Simon de Montfort the Younger was the second son of Simon de Montfort, Leicester and Eleanor of England. After Evesham the younger Simon tried to raise a rebellion in Lincolnshire, but this failed. With his younger brother Guy he escaped to France and Italy where, in 1271, they discovered and murdered their cousin Henry of Almain at the church in Viterbo. Young Simon died later that year.

Simon de Montfort (the other one) Father of 'our' Simon de Montfort, Simon de Montfort, 5th Earl of Leicester, was a French nobleman and soldier who took part in the Fourth Crusade and was a prominent leader of the Albigensian Crusade, in which he gained a reputation for greed and brutality. He died at the Siege of Toulouse in 1218.

Alix de Montmorency Daughter of Bouchard IV de Montmorency and Laurette, daughter of Baldwin IV, Count of Hainaut. 'Our' Simon de Montfort's mother.

Bouchard V de Montmorency Born at Montmorency, Seine-Et-Oise, France in 1129, Bouchard V de Montmorency was a crusader who died at the age of 60 in 1189 in Jerusalem. He was the half-brother of Alix de Montmorency.

Ralph de Mortimer Ralph (or Ranulph) de Mortimer was the second son of Roger de Mortimer and Isabel de Ferrers of Wigmore Castle in Herefordshire. He succeeded his elder brother in 1227 and built Cefnllys and Knucklas castles in 1240. He died in 1246.

Roger de Mortimer Roger Mortimer, 1st Baron Mortimer (1231–1282), of Wigmore Castle in Herefordshire, was a marcher lord who was a loyal ally of Henry III of England and at times an enemy, at times an ally, of Llywelyn ap Gruffudd, Prince of Wales. Roger was the son of Ralph de Mortimer and his Welsh wife, Gwladys Ddu, daughter of Llywelyn ap Iorwerth, and Joan Plantagenet, daughter of John, King of England. Mortimer almost lost his life in 1264 at the Battle of Lewes but in

1265 Mortimer's wife, Maud de Braose helped to rescue Lord Edward and Mortimer led a battle of the Marcher army at Evesham.

Robert Motun de Peyclinton

Robert de Motun (or Moton) was killed at the Battle of Evesham, fighting on the side of Simon de Montfort, his overlord, and his estates were consequently forfeited.

Adam de Mohaut

Born sometime between 1167 and 1227, Adam de Mohaut has been named as the knight who recognised Henry III and removed him to safety with the assistance of Lord Edward in at the Battle of Evesham.

William of Newburgh

William of Newburgh or Newbury (La. *Guilelmus Neubrigensis*, *Willelmus Neubrigensis*, *Wilhelmus Neubrigensis*, or *Willelmus de Novoburgo*), 1136-1198, also known as William Parvus, was a twelfth-century English historian and Augustinian canon of Anglo-Saxon descent from Bridlington, Yorkshire.

Adam of Newmarket

Born in or before 1226, Adam de Newmarket sided with the baronial party, and in December 1263 was one of their representatives at Amiens. He was taken prisoner at Northampton and his lands seized. He regained his lands and his freedom after the Battle of Lewes. He was captured again during the Kenilworth raid but made his peace with the king under the Dictum de Kenilworth.

Robert de Newton

This may be Robert de Newton (or Neuton or Neweton), born about 1199 in Weston under Lizard, Staffordshire, son of John de Weston and an unknown mother. This de Newton took cross with Edward I for Crusade and died some time after 1271.

Ralph de Normanville

A Ralph de Normaville was born around 1259 at Empingham, Rutland, which would have made him around six years old at the time of the battle. His father, of the same name, died in 1259 so I would welcome any information about the Ralph de Normanville who fought at Evesham, fate unknown.

Charles William Chadwick Oman	Born in 1860, Sir Charles William Chadwick Oman was a British military historian whose reconstructions of medieval battles, and theories around military organisation and operations through the ages, were pioneering. He died in 1946 after a long and distinguished career.
Ralph de Otterden	I am guessing that this is the 'Ralph de Ottringden' who held the manor of Ottringden of William de Leyborne, as one knight's see, in the reign of Henry III.
Archbishop Parker	Matthew Parker was the Archbishop of Canterbury in the Church of England from 1559 until his death in 1575. He was an influential theologian and co-founder of a distinctive tradition of Anglican theological thought.
John Passelow	*Possibly John Passelow, tenant, in the Hundred of Sonning.*
William Perons	*Included in the available lists of Montfortians who fought at Evesham, fate unknown.*
Phillip III	Philip III (ironically nicknamed 'Philip the Bold', Fr. 'Philippe le Hardi'), 1245-1285, was king of France from 1270 to 1285. During his reign the power of the monarchy was enlarged and the royal domain extended, although his foreign policy and military adventures were largely unsuccessful owing to his indecisiveness and timidity.
Eleanor of Provence	Born in 1223 at Aix-en-Provence, Eleanor of Provence was Queen consort to Henry III of England from 1236 until his death in 1272. She served as regent of England during Henry's absence in 1253. She died in 1291 at Amesbury and was buried in Amesbury Priory.
Abbot Ranulph	Ranulph (sometimes given as Randulf or Reginald) was Abbot of Evesham from 1130-1149. He was responsible for a building campaign that included erecting a twelve-foot-high wall round the abbey precinct and installing a gateway from the churchyard to the market square.
Raymond-Berengar IV	Otherwise known as Ramon Berenguer IV (F. Raimond-Bérenger), 1198–1245, was a member of the House of Barcelona who ruled

as count of Provence and Forcalquier. He was the son of Alfonso II, Count of Provence, and Garsenda, Countess of Forcalquier. In 1219 he married Beatrice of Savoy, daughter of Thomas, Count of Savoy. One of their four daughters, Eleanor of Provence (1223–1291), became the wife of Henry III, King of England.

John Recard	*Other than the fact that he fought at Evesham on the baronial side, fate unknown, I have little information about John Recard. Any offers?*
Richard the Lionhearted	Born in 1157, Richard I was King of England from 1189 until his death at the Siege of Chalons in 1199. He also ruled as Duke of Normandy, Aquitaine and Gascony, Lord of Cyprus, Count of Poitiers, Anjou, Maine, and Nantes, and was overlord of Brittany at various times during the same period. He was an uncle of Henry III.
William of Rishanger	William Rishanger (born 1250), nicknamed '*Chronigraphus*', was an English annalist and Benedictine monk of St. Albans. He is credited with writing the *Opus Chronicorum*, a continuation from 1259 of Matthew Paris's Chronicle (a history of his own times from 1259 to 1307) and a work on the Barons' War. He was broadly sympathetic to the reformers' cause.
Robert de Rowley	*Included in the available lists of Montfortians who fought at Evesham, fate unknown.*
Beatrice of Savoy	Beatrice of Savoy (c. 1198–c. 1267) was the daughter of Thomas I of Savoy and Margaret of Geneva. She was Countess consort of Provence by her marriage to Ramon Berenguer IV, Count of Provence.
Peter of Savoy	Peter of Savoy, Earl of Richmond (d. 1268), 9th Count of Savoy, and marquis in Italy, was seventh son of Thomas I of Savoy by Margaret de Faucigny. He was born at the castle of Susa in Italy, possibly in 1203, but the true date may be as much as ten years later.
Thomas II of Savoy	Thomas II (c. 1199-February 1259) was the Lord of Piedmont from 1233 to his death, Count of Flanders *jure uxoris* from 1237 to 1244,

and regent of the County of Savoy from 1253 to his death, while his nephew Boniface was fighting abroad. He was the son of Thomas I of Savoy and Margaret of Geneva.

Robert de Sepinges	*Included in the available lists of Montfortians who fought at Evesham, fate unknown.*
Stephen Soundan	*Included in the available lists of Montfortians who fought at Evesham, fate unknown.*
Richard de Spetchesley	*Included in the available lists of Montfortians who fought at Evesham, fate unknown.*
King Stephen	Born c. 1097, Stephen of Blois, was King of England from 1135 to his death in 1154, as well as Count of Boulogne from 1125 until 1147 and Duke of Normandy from 1135 until 1144. Stephen's reign was marked by The Anarchy, a civil war with his cousin and rival, the Empress Matilda.
Robert de Tregoz	Born in 1190 Robert de Tregoz, Lord of Ewyas Harold, was the son of Robert Tregoz, Sheriff of Wiltshire, and Sibil d'Ewyas. He was killed at the Battle of Evesham and buried at Little Dunmow, Essex.
William Tressell	Born c. 1226 at Billesley, Warwickshire, Sir William Trussell, was the son of Richard Trussell, Lord of Billesley Manor, and Isabel de Malesours.
Thomas Trevet	It is unclear whether Sir Thomas Trevet (d. 1283), was a member of a Norfolk family or of a Somerset family. Thomas Trevet was a justice in eyre (an itinerant judge) for Dorset and the neighbouring counties from 1268 to 1271. However, when Norwich Cathedral was burnt by rioters in August 1272, Trevet was sent to try the malefactors.
Nicholas Trivet	Trivet (or Trevet) was born in Somerset and was the son of Sir Thomas Trevet, a judge who came of a Norfolk or Somerset family. Nicholas became a Dominican friar in London, and studied first at Oxford and later in Paris, where he first took an interest in English and French chronicles.

Richard Trussel	A member of an ancient Warwickshire family, possessing the Lordship of Billesley in that county from the time of Henry I, Richard Trussell was killed at Evesham.
Urban IV	Born in 1195, Pope Urban IV, born Jacques Pantaléon, was the head of the Catholic Church and ruler of the Papal States from August 1261 to his death in 1264. He received a request from Henry III to intercede on his behalf against the reformers.
William de Valence	William de Valence (died 1296), born Guillaume de Lusignan, was a French nobleman and knight who became important in English politics due to his relationship to Henry III of England. He took the name de Valence after his birthplace, Valence, near Lusignan.
John de Vescy	John de Vescy was born in 1244. He supported de Montfort during the Baron's war, being wounded and captured at Evesham. Early in 1267 he led a rising in the north, but was besieged at Alnwick and forced to submit by Prince Edward, whose devoted friend he afterwards became.
Baldwin Wake	Baldwin Wake, Lord of Bourne was born between 1238 and 1258. He married his second wife, Hawise de Quincy, daughter of Robert de Quincy, Lord of Ware and Helen ap Llywelyn, circa 1268 and died 1281/2.
Abbot Walter	Walter, Abbot of Evesham or 'Walter de Cerisy' was an eleventh-century abbot and church leader of England, following the Norman conquest. He is known from the Domesday Book and several legal documents surrounding property disputes. He died in 1104.
John de Warenne	John de Warenne, 6th Earl of Surrey (1231–c. 1304) was a prominent English nobleman and military commander during the reigns of Henry III of England and Edward I of England. During the Second Barons' War he switched sides twice, ending up in support of the king. Warenne was later appointed a Guardian of Scotland and featured prominently in Edward I's wars in Scotland.

Matthew of Westminster	Long regarded as the author of the *Flores Historiarum*, Matthew of Westminster is now known never to have existed.
Richard Whitford	Richard Whitford (or Whytford) was an English (or Welsh) Catholic priest known as an author of devotional works. He studied at Oxford, but was elected a fellow of Queens' College, Cambridge, from 1495 to 1504. He was given leave of absence by his college for five years in 1496-7 that he might attend William Blount, 4th Baron Mountjoy, as chaplain and confessor, on the continent.
Thomas Wykes	Born in 1222, Thomas Wykes was an canon regular of Osney Abbey, near Oxford and the author of a chronicle extending from 1066 to 1289. He gives an account of the Second Barons' War from a royalist standpoint, and is a severe critic of Montfort's policy. He died between 1291 and 1293.
William de York	Possibly the knight better known as 'William de Ebor', the son of Nicholas de Ebor and Ellena de Hebden. Born in 1240 he was killed fighting for Earl Simon at Evesham.

Glossary

In a book full of technical terms, some of them shrouded in the mists of time, a glossary defining those terms, and other concepts, might be useful especially for newcomers to the field of medieval military history. What follows is a small working vocabulary and definitions for important terms or terms frequently encountered elsewhere in this book. I hope that it helps.

Akheton	(Arabic *al-qutun* – 'cotton') a type of fabric armour comprising a short-sleeved or sleeveless coat, usually padded or quilted vertically, a.k.a. *wambais*, *pourpoint*.
Arbalest	See 'Crossbow'.
Arbalester	A crossbowman.
Archer	Used a stave bow to shoot arrows, a.k.a. *bowman*.
Arming Cap	A padded or quilted cap to wear under armour, some of which incorporated a thick ring of material around the top to provide a snug fit and some support for the flat-topped great helm.
Arrowsmith	A craftsman who made arrows.
Axes	A popular weapon, from the Danish axe carried by infantrymen to a long-handled single-handed axe favoured by horsemen.
Banner (1)	A standard or battle flag.
Banner (2)	A subdivision of the medieval *battle* or *bataille* formation, each *battle* containing several subsidiary tactical units called *banners* that were grouped around a battle flag of their leader
Bard	See 'Trapper'.
Bataille	See 'Battle'.
Battle	A division in a medieval army, which were typically organised into three battles that, on the march, formed a vanguard (leading), main body (middle) and rearguard, a.k.a. *bataille*.
Bevor	See 'Gorget'.
Bill	Derived from an agricultural implement, the bill consisted of a chopping blade, curving forward to form a hook, which may have several pointed projections, mounted on a staff, a.k.a. *billhook*.

Billhook	See 'Bill'.
Boar spear	Derived from hunting weapons, a boar spear had a short thick shaft with two 'lugs' or 'wings' jutting out from the spearhead's socket behind the blade.
Boiled leather	See 'Cuir bouilli'.
Bow (1)	The front support of a war saddle, a.k.a. *Pommel*.
Bow (2)	The 'self' or 'stave' bow made of a single piece of wood, such as the English longbow.
Bow (3)	'Longbow': the modern name for the ordinary 'stave' or 'self' bow.
Bowknocker	A craftsman who added the 'knocks' or notches, to hold the ends of the bow string at the tips of a bowstaff.
Bowman	See 'Archer'.
Bowyer	A craftsman who made bow staves.
Braies	The medieval equivalent of Y-fronts.
Brases	Carrying straps rivetted to a shield, a.k.a. *enarmes*.
Broadsword	The most common type was a flat cut-and-thrust weapon with a light-blade that, until the latter part of the century, tapered to a relatively acute point with a fuller (a groove to lighten the blade without weakening it) on each side running at least three-quarters of the way down the blade.
Buckler	A small circular wooden parrying shield with a central metal boss riveted or nailed over a single central hand grip.
Cantle	The back support of a war saddle.
Caparison	See 'Trapper'.
Cervellière	A small brimless close-fitting skull of iron that covered the ears but left the face free.
Champrin	See 'Shaffron'.
Chapel-de-fer	A shallow broad-brimmed open-faced helmet, a.k.a. *kettle hat*.
Chausses	A pair of complete mail stockings fitted with leather soles for grip and braced up at the waist to a belt or girdle and worn over cloth stockings.
Chevauchée	A mounted raid intended to destroy an enemy's resources and enrich the raiding army.
Chivalry (1)	(After *chevallerie*, meaning 'skill on horseback' in French) a fusion of Germanic and Christian cultural elements into a new code of honour. From the eleventh century onward, chivalry was reinforced by the religious ceremony of dubbing to knighthood, the adoption of distinguishing emblems and

	blazons (and the science of heraldry to develop and interpret these symbols of station), and the emergence in the twelfth century of court poets known as troubadours to sing the praises of knights living, past and legendary.
Chivalry (2)	A generic term for noble heavy cavalry from any period.
Club	From chance-gathered broken branches to heavy wooden staves studded with large nails.
Coat of Plates	Body armour worn like a Second World War flak jacket, pulled over the head with side panels that wrapped over the back flap where they were tied or buckled in place.
Coif	The neck of a hauberk was often extended up to form a mail hood or *coif*.
Coif-de-mailles	A mail hood made separate from the *hauberk*, that spread out across the wearer's shoulders to provide extra protection from overhand blows.
Conical helm	An open-faced helmet favoured by many armies in western Europe, characterised by the way it tapered up to a point.
Constables	In most medieval nations, the constable was the highest-ranking officer of the army and was responsible for the overseeing of martial law.
Corrida	Spanish-style bullfighting is called *corrida de toros*, literally 'coursing of bulls'.
Courser	A knight's second-best warhorse.
Croc	A medieval polearm.
Crossbow	A short stave bow set at right angles across a grooved stock and equipped with a trigger, a.k.a. *arbalest*.
Cuir bouilli	A type of light armour made by boiling leather in wax, moulding the softened leather to fit and then leaving it to harden, a.k.a. boiled leather.
Cuirie	Leather body armour worn with or without metal reinforcements, laced down one side.
Curb bit	A type of bit used for riding horses that uses lever action to act on several parts of the horse's head.
Dagger	Single-handed weapon with a double-edged tapering blade.
Destrier	A knight's larger and heavier warhorse or 'great horse'.
Dirk	Welsh stabbing dirks could have blades up to 60 centimetres (2 feet) long, almost a short sword.
Enarmes	See 'Brases'.

Falchion	A heavy-bladed single-edged sword similar to a large modern machete.
Faus or Faussa	A medieval polearm.
Flail	An early agricultural implement used to thresh grain which was modified for war. Essentially a spiked ball (sometimes multiple balls) and chain attached to a haft, the flail became a contusion weapon of choice for both infantry and cavalry during the medieval period.
Fletcher	A craftsman who attaches flights or *fletchings* to the shaft of arrows.
Foraging	Living off the land which, for non-soldiers in the area, included losing their food stores, animals, harvests etc.
Gaesa	A medieval polearm.
Gambeson	Similar padded fabric armour to and *akheton* but with long sleeves.
Gamboised cuisse	This was a quilted or padded tube probably tied to the same belt as the *chausses,* designed to protect the thigh and knee.
Genouilliers	See 'Poleyns'.
Godendac	A combination of club and spear with a wooden staff roughly 92 centimetres to 150 centimetres (3 to 5 feet) long with a diameter of roughly 5 centimetres to 10 centimetres (2 to 4 inches) as a body. It was wider at one end, and at this end a sharp metal spike was inserted by a tang.
Gorget	Armour to protect the throat and chin.
Great Helm	A fully enclosed helmet that protected the back and sides of the head as well as the face.
Greaves	See 'Schynbalds'.
Guige strap	A strap to hang a shield from the man-at-arms' neck when he needed his hands free.
Guisarme	A pruning hook or scythe blade mounted vertically on a spear shaft to form a type of crescent-shaped double socketed axe, used like a two-handed battle axe.
Hack	See 'Hackney'.
Hackney	A cheaper mount for more lowly servants and thought suitable for mounted infantry, a.k.a. *Hack*.
Haubergeon	A short mail shirt with sleeves only to the elbow or forearm.
Hauberk	Élite cavalry were protected by *hauberks*, knee-length coats, usually of mail, split to the crotch at the front and back to ease riding astride.

Heavy spear	Some long thrusting spears had weighted heads.
Host	An army pulled together on a temporary basis.
Housing	See 'Trapper'.
Javelin	A light spear primarily intended for throwing.
Javelineer	A light infantryman who wielded a javelin.
Kettle hat	See 'Chapel-de-fer'.
Knife	Knives were single-edged single-handed weapons.
Lamellar armour	A type of composite armour consisting of a shirt of laminated layers of leather sown or glued together, then fitted with iron plates. It was popular with Saracens and eastern European fighting men.
Lance (1)	A spear used from horseback as a shock weapon, usually in conjunction with a built-up saddle and stirrups.
Lance (2)	Collective term for a small unit of knights who usually fought within a *banner*.
Long thrusting spear	Purely hand-to-hand weapons for use by the infantry, although similar in design to the cavalryman's lance.
Mace	A long-handled implement with a spiked or flanged ball at the tip. The flanged type of mace became the most common in the west, although the earlier studded wooden variety would have been in use at Evesham.
Magnus equus	*A destrier* or 'great horse' of the late Middle Ages was a sturdy steed of up to 17 hands and 1,200 to 1,300 pounds, capable of supporting its own barding and a knight in full armour.
Mail	Often referred to, incorrectly, as 'chain mail(le)' was a type of armour, usually consisting of small metal rings linked together in a pattern to form a mesh, a.k.a. *maille*.
Maille	See 'Mail'.
Marshals	As a military leader, the Marshal was originally subordinate to the constable in the various states of western Europe. By the thirteenth century, the marshal had come to prominence as a commander of the royal forces and a great officer of state.
Materiel	Stores, supplies, equipment, weapons and ammunition in military supply chain management.
Military orders	Monastic orders sanctioned by the medieval papacy to protect pilgrims on their way to the Holy Land or to fight against pagans in eastern Europe.
Milites	A medieval Latin term for knights, soldiers or 'men-at-arms'.

Palfrey	A knight's or man-at-arms' travelling horse.
Picadores	One of the pair of horsemen in a Spanish bullfight that jab the bull with a lance.
Pilote	A medieval polearm.
Polearm	A long-hafted heavy infantry weapon designed to be used with two hands against infantry and cavalry formations.
Poleyns	Small cup-shaped pieces of plate armour occasionally worn over the knees a.k.a. *genouilliers*.
Pommel	See 'Bow' (saddle).
Pourpoint	See 'Akheton'.
Provost	An officer whose duty it was to ensure that the army of the king did no harm to the citizenry.
Ronson	See 'Rouncey'.
Rouncey	A travelling horse appropriate for superior servants, a.k.a. *ronson*.
Scale Armour	An armoured coat constructed from small scales of iron, bronze or, occasionally, boiled hardened leather or whalebone, sewn to a textile backing with the scales overlapping downwards like those of a fish.
Schynbalds	Gutter-shaped plates of metal strapped around the lower leg over the mail to protect the shins, a.k.a. *greaves*.
Shepherd's Sling	See 'sling'.
Shields	Shields gradually diminished in size from the Norman 'kite' shields to the smaller and thicker 'heater' shield.
Short spear	Light enough to be thrown at close range but was essentially a hand-to-hand weapon.
Sling	A projectile weapon used to throw a blunt projectile such as a stone, clay or lead 'sling-stone' from a *pouch* in the middle of two lengths of cord, a.k.a. *shepherd's sling*.
Snaffle bit	A bit mouthpiece for riding a horse, with a ring on either side, that acts with direct pressure.
Spearman	A spearman can be a heavy infantryman if he uses his spear as a shock weapon or a light infantryman if he throws his weapon as a missile.
Spears	Medieval polearms designed for stabbing or, if fitted with a broad head, for cutting and thrusting.
Squire	A knight in training.

Staff Sling	The staff sling, also known as the 'stave sling', consisted of a staff with a short sling at one end, operated with both hands, a.k.a. *stave sling*.
Stave Sling	See 'staff sling'.
Stringer	A maker of rope or strings, particularly for bows.
Sumpters	Pack ponies.
Surcoat	A garment, usually of linen, worn over the hauberk, often close-fitting across the chest but falling more loosely from the waist down.
Trapper	This was a cover or housing that came down to a horse's hocks and sometimes covered the tail, sometimes made in one piece but more often divided at the saddle, a.k.a. *caparison, bard, housing*.
Ventail	A protective flap of armour that could be drawn up over the chin and mouth when going into action.
Voulge	A polearm with a single-edged blade optimised for slicing.
Wambais	See 'Akheton'.

Index

Abbey House, 114
Abbey Manor, 10, 96, 97, 114, 175, 176, 178, 186, 194, 195, 204, 207, 208, 212
Abbey Manor House, 96, 204, 208, 212
Abbey of St Mary and St Ecgwine, 100, 167
Abbot Walter, 101, 252
Abergavenny, Lord, 32, 229, 232
Act of Settlement (1701), 5
Adrian V, Pope, 23, 229
Akheton, 52, 53, 54, 55, 56, 60, 61, 69
Albigensian Crusade, 10, 25, 247
Alcester, 90, 92, 97, 115, 119, 122, 135, 139, 154, 155, 185, 186, 189, 194, 196, 202, 203, 204, 206, 211, 213
All Saints Church, 101, 104, 127, 168
Almonry Museum, 10, 1, 32, 110, 111, 112, 167, 168, 173, 210, 211, 213, 219
Alnwick Castle, 216
Alnwick Priory, 216
Alphonso, 29, 237
Amiens, 15, 18, 29, 32, 248
Angouleme, Alice of, 30
Anjou, 8, 179, 182, 250
Archer, 61, 66, 152, 227
Arderne, Ralph de, 87, 234
Armour, 50, 52, 53, 54, 55, 61, 111
Arrow, Warwickshire, 97
Arrows, 53, 57, 71, 131, 152
Arrowsmith, 66

Arsouf, 53
Avon, River, 9, 1, 40, 41, 90, 91, 92, 93, 96, 97, 100, 101, 104, 105, 106, 107, 109, 115, 133, 141, 142, 150, 154, 155, 156, 157, 158, 159, 160, 161, 162, 163, 164, 167, 168, 186, 187, 189, 190, 193, 195, 203, 204, 207, 208, 210, 211, 212, 213
Axholme, Isle of, 165, 179
Baldwin IV, Count of Hainaut, 25, 247
Banneret, 82
Barres, William of, 52, 230
Battle Abbey, 19
Battlefields Trust, The, 3, 8, 9, 11, 1, 4, 20, 22, 45, 46, 98, 113, 117, 149, 171, 175, 177, 178, 199, 209, 211, 271, 272, 273
Battlewell, 9, 3, 98, 110, 112, 113, 114, 115, 116, 119, 122, 125, 150, 167, 171, 173, 174, 186, 193, 194, 195, 198, 204, 205, 206, 208, 211, 212, 213, 214, 271
Battlewell Conservation Area, 167, 213
Battlewell Field, 171
Battlewell Pool, 173
Bayeux Tapestry, 51, 58, 62
Beauchamp, de, 1, 105, 230
Beaumont, Amicia de, 25, 231
Beckett, Thomas á, 36
Beeston Castle, 32, 232

Bengeworth, 1, 41, 90, 91, 96, 101, 104, 105, 107, 115, 120, 124, 133, 142, 156, 157, 159, 170, 171, 186, 189, 195, 204
Bengeworth Castle, 105
Berton, William of, 108, 231
Bevor, 56
Bill, 65
Bill of Rights (1689), 5
Black Prince, 11
Blanche of Castile, 26, 28, 233
Blayney's Lane, 91, 97, 98, 189, 193, 204, 212
Blount, William, 38, 231, 253
Boar spears, 65
Boat Lane, Evesham, 109, 127
Bohun, de, 18, 32, 133, 161, 201, 202, 231, 232, 235
Boulogne, 14, 15, 18, 251
Bow, 65, 66, 68, 152
Braies, 55
Braose, Eleanor de, 32, 232
Braose, William de, 32, 229, 232
Brases, 57
Breton, Guillaume le, 52, 55, 232
Bridge Street, Evesham, 102, 132, 142, 170
Bristol, 13, 79, 105, 149, 191
Broadsword, 61, 62, 66
Bromsgrove, 101
Brooke, Richard (1857), 206
Brut, 38
Burg, John de, 10, 232
Burgundy, 13
Burne, Lt.Col. Alfred Higgins, 13, 88, 115, 119, 133, 151, 185, 188, 189, 204, 205
Bury St Edmunds Abbey, 91
Caerleon, 30
Cantilupe, Bishop Walter de, 124, 143, 186
Canute, King, 105, 171, 233, 243
Caparison, 68
Carpenter, Dr David, 11, 3, 20, 67, 115, 119, 139, 154, 223
Castelnaudary, Siege of, 25
Castile, Eleanor of, 29, 183, 233
Castle Baynard, 40
Catesby, 15
Cathar heretics, 25
Catharism, 10
Cervellière, 59
Champron, 69
Chancellor, Office of, 8, 33
Chape, 62
Chapel-de-fer, 59
Charles I, 12
Charles the Simple, 27, 233
Chausses, 55
Chichester, Bishop of, 23, 30
Chinewrde, 84, 88
Chivalry, 7, 145, 147
Chronica majora, 42, 222
Chronicon Walteri de Hemingburgh, vulgo Hemingford nuncupati, de gestis regum Angliae, 43
Church Street, Bengeworth, 105, 171
Cinque Ports, 19, 32, 234

Clare, Gilbert de, 19, 23, 30, 40, 41, 45, 46, 74, 78, 79, 89, 91, 92, 93, 95, 115, 119, 120, 122, 127, 135, 136, 137, 139, 143, 148, 158, 163, 165, 166, 186, 187, 189, 190, 191, 197, 201, 202, 204, 212, 229, 233, 239, 242, 243
Cleeve Hill, 41
Cleeve Prior, 40, 92, 115, 156, 158, 186, 189, 196, 204
Clevelode, 41, 157
Clifford, Roger, 12, 233
Clinton, Geoffrey de, 84, 234
Coif, 52, 53, 59, 60
College of Arms, 43, 44, 138, 139, 230
Combwell, 19
Conrois (troops), 118
Cornwall, Earl of, 26, 229, 234
Cornwall, Richard of, 11, 12, 22, 47, 148, 234
Council of Fifteen, 28
Councils of Three and Nine, 23
County Sites and Monuments Record, 100
Cowl Street, Evesham, 9, 102, 104, 170
Cox, Dr David, 11, 3, 41, 91, 96, 115, 119, 215, 220
Craycombe, 41, 93, 157, 158
Crécy, Battle of, 11, 43
Croc, 65
Cromwell, Oliver, 1
Cropthorne, 92
Crossbow, 65, 66, 67, 71, 112, 134, 227
Crossbowman, 61
Croydon, 20
Cuir bouilli, 55, 56

Cwmaron, 30
Daggers, 63
David, King of Scotland, 47, 235
De Montfort, Amaury, 10, 25, 45, 148, 179, 217, 245
De Montfort, Guy, 10, 11, 25, 32, 45, 129, 132, 139, 148, 157, 159, 179, 197, 229, 230, 245, 246, 247
De Montfort, Simon, younger, 1, 19, 80, 82, 83, 84, 85, 88, 89, 90, 105, 188, 244, 247
De Nangis, William, 10, 45, 46, 224
De Re Militari, 182, 227
Dead Man's Ait, 97, 122, 134, 141, 190
Denning, Lord, 5
Despenser, Hugh le, 131, 144, 186, 187, 197, 215, 217, 236
Destrier, 67, 68
Deyville, Sir John de, 165, 166
Dictum of Kenilworth, 165, 215, 217, 238, 248
Disinherited, The, 165, 166
Domesday Book, 101, 104, 252
Dover, 15, 18, 19, 32, 179, 222, 234
Droitwich, 108, 152
Dunnington, 90, 97
Dunstable Chronicle, 48
Dunstable Priory, 48
Durham Cathedral, 216
Durham, Richard of, 138, 142
Ecgwine, Bishop of Worcester, 101, 108, 124, 237
Echelles (squadrons), 118
Edmund, 14, 28, 179

Edward I, 7, 8, 27, 29, 39, 40, 44, 48, 64, 66, 73, 98, 152, 166, 180, 183, 199, 201, 203, 223, 237, 238, 239, 242, 248, 252
Edward III, 11, 42, 50, 91, 221, 237, 238
Edward the Confessor, 29, 238
Eleanor, Queen, 19, 27
Empress Matilda, 1, 251
Enarmes, 57
English Heritage, 8, 3, 4, 120, 191, 198, 201, 202, 205, 224
Epitoma Rei Militaris, 182, 227
Espaulier, 57
Evesham Abbey, 10, 44, 100, 101, 102, 105, 108, 120, 124, 125, 128, 132, 139, 169, 173, 179, 194, 201, 215, 217, 219, 220, 221, 236, 237
Evesham Chronicle, 41, 43, 44, 46, 75, 83, 115, 134, 153, 155, 224
Falchion, 62, 219
Falkirk Campaign, 73
Father of Parliament, 166
Faus, 65
Faussa, 65
Feckenham Forest, 101
Fieschi, Ottobuono de, 23, 229, 235
First Baronial War, 5
Fitz-Matthew, Hubert, 10, 238
Fitz-Nicholas, Ralph, 10, 239
Fladbury, 90, 92
Flanders, 13, 26, 199, 230, 250
Flemish Campaign, 73
Fletching, 20
Flimwell, 19
Flores Historiarum, 39, 41, 42, 253

Flyford Flavell, 90
Frederick II, 28, 239
Gaesa, 65
Gale, Thomas, 43
Gambeson, 53, 54, 57, 61
Hamboised cuisse, 55
Gascony, 8, 10, 27, 28, 29, 31, 238, 239, 245, 250
Genouilliers, 55
Gerald of Wales, 65
Giffard, Bishop William, 49
Giffard, John, 79, 239
Gifford, John, 152
Glamorgan, 30, 233
Glasbury, 79
Gloucester, 1, 18, 24, 30, 32, 33, 38, 39, 79, 80, 88, 122, 127, 150, 153, 155, 191, 196, 199, 215, 216, 239
Gloucester castle, 18, 79
Gloucester, Earl of, 19, 23, 28, 40, 45, 46, 93, 150, 155, 157, 158, 163, 201, 229, 233
Gloucester, Robert of, 38
Glover's Roll of Arms, 174
Godendac, 65
Gorget, 56
Great Helm, 58
Great horse, 67
Great Mere, Kenilworth, 85, 165
Greaves, 55
Greenhill, 9, 2, 41, 91, 96, 97, 98, 100, 110, 111, 114, 115, 116, 117, 118, 119, 120, 122, 124, 125, 128, 131, 133, 134, 138, 141, 142, 150, 155, 156, 157, 159, 161, 162, 163, 164, 167,

169, 171, 174, 181, 186, 189, 190, 198, 200, 202, 204, 205, 208, 211, 212, 213, 214, 271
Grey, Richard de, 89, 234
Grosseteste, Robert, Bishop of Lincoln, 28, 240
Guige strap, 58
Guisarme, 65
Guisborough, Walter of, 42, 43, 91, 155, 222, 224, 240, 241
Gwladys Ddu, Princess, 30, 240, 247
Gwrtheyrnion, 31
Habeas Corpus Act (1679), 5
Hack, 64, 68
Hackney, 68
Hamilton, H. C., 43
Haubergeon, 51
Hauberk, 50, 51, 52, 53, 54, 55, 57
Hearne, Thomas, 43, 241
Heavy spears, 65
Helmet, 58, 59, 60, 61
Hemingburgh, Walter of, 42, 222, 241
Henry III, 9, 2, 5, 6, 7, 8, 9, 10, 11, 12, 13, 14, 15, 18, 19, 20, 21, 22, 23, 24, 26, 27, 28, 29, 30, 31, 32, 40, 41, 43, 45, 46, 48, 49, 66, 85, 105, 131, 136, 138, 139, 140, 143, 148, 150, 154, 165, 166, 179, 180, 182, 186, 187, 191, 197, 199, 200, 202, 203, 206, 215, 216, 217, 218, 219, 222, 223, 229, 230, 231, 233, 234, 235, 237, 238, 239, 240, 241, 242, 243, 244, 245, 246, 247, 248, 249, 250, 252
Henry I, 5, 48, 84, 234, 239, 241, 252
Henry III, 9, 2, 6, 7, 8, 9, 10, 11, 26, 27, 29, 30, 31, 40, 66, 85, 150, 154, 179, 180, 191, 199, 200, 202, 203, 206, 222, 223, 229, 231, 233, 234, 235, 237, 238, 239, 241, 243, 244, 245, 246, 247, 248, 249, 250, 252
Hereford, 18, 24, 30, 31, 32, 77, 80, 81, 90, 100, 127, 133, 150, 151, 154, 191, 193, 200, 201, 231, 235
Hertford, Earl of, 30
High Street, Evesham, 10, 84, 102, 124, 131, 150, 169, 170, 172, 173, 174, 211, 213
Historiae Anglicanae scriptores quinque, 43
Hog, Thomas, 40
Holwell, Stephen de, 89, 242
Holy Land, 11, 20, 27, 53, 72, 179, 180, 183, 237
House of Commons, 166, 168, 173, 210, 246
Hoveden, Roger of, 43, 48
Huntingdon, Henry of, 43, 49, 242
Innocent III, Pope, 10
Iron Cross, 97
Isabella of Angoulême, 26, 229, 241, 245
Javelin, 64
Jews, 14, 19, 26, 165
John the Deacon of Littleton, 108, 243
Just War, 145
Justiciar, Office of, 8
Kempsey, 47, 90, 92, 124, 151, 154, 160, 185, 189
Kenilworth, 7, 9, 4, 15, 18, 23, 32, 40, 45, 47, 78, 80, 81, 82, 83, 84, 85, 86,

87, 88, 89, 90, 97, 125, 139, 151, 152, 153, 154, 155, 156, 159, 160, 164, 165, 179, 185, 187, 188, 193, 195, 196, 200, 201, 203, 215, 216, 217, 218, 219, 220, 234, 238, 242, 248

Kettle hat, 59

King John, 5, 6, 8, 25, 26, 30, 84, 170, 229, 241, 243

King Stephen, 1, 40, 105, 251

Knighton, Henry, 82, 242

Knives, 63

Labordiere, 44, 45, 92, 137, 148

Lacy, John de, 30, 243

Lances, 62

Laurette, 25, 247

Leg armour, 54

Leicester, 9, 10, 17, 23, 24, 25, 26, 27, 33, 82, 95, 133, 155, 176, 177, 179, 196, 199, 201, 206, 208, 211, 212, 223, 231, 242, 244, 245, 246, 247

Lenchwick parish, 96, 204

Leofric, Earl, 101, 239, 243

Leominster, 78, 80

Lewes, 7, 9, 18, 20, 21, 22, 23, 30, 31, 32, 39, 43, 67, 117, 118, 120, 139, 150, 153, 154, 163, 191, 198, 199, 222, 224

Lewes, Battle of, 20, 29, 31, 32, 79, 119, 236, 237, 238, 239, 240, 241, 243, 246, 247, 248

Leybourne, Roger, 12, 15

Lincoln, Earl of, 30, 243

Llanbleddian, 30

Llywelyn ap Gruffydd, 12, 31, 196, 240

Llywelyn ap Iorwerth, 30, 215, 217, 242, 247

Logistics, 70, 226

London, 13, 15, 18, 19, 20, 21, 23, 24, 27, 29, 30, 40, 42, 55, 80, 82, 88, 91, 100, 119, 120, 127, 133, 149, 150, 159, 166, 188, 191, 205, 206, 207, 222, 223, 225, 226, 245, 246, 251

Long thrusting spear, 64

Longbow, 65, 66

Lord Edward, 2, 8, 12, 13, 21, 23, 24, 28, 29, 30, 31, 67, 81, 82, 86, 90, 95, 111, 131, 137, 148, 150, 179, 180, 181, 183, 191, 194, 195, 197, 221, 222, 229, 232, 237, 238, 243, 244, 248

Lorica hamata, 51

Louis IX, 27, 29, 45, 233, 243

Louis VIII, 6, 45, 233, 243

Ludlow, 30, 31, 78

Lusignans, 8, 13, 14, 27, 32, 229, 235, 241, 243, 252

Maciejowski Bible, 50, 51, 54, 56, 60, 61, 63, 64, 65, 71

Mad Parliament, 28

Maddicott, Dr John, 3

Magna Carta, 7, 5, 6, 7, 43, 85, 166, 243

Main Street, Evesham, 102

Malmesbury, William of, 49, 244

Maltravers, William, 139, 215, 217, 244

Marcher, 12, 15, 25, 29, 31, 32, 73, 74, 75, 76, 80, 81, 97, 114, 118, 119, 120, 123, 125, 129, 133, 135, 137, 141, 160, 186, 189, 193, 194, 217, 229, 230, 232, 233, 236, 248

Marchers, 13, 31, 32, 73, 76, 79, 96, 98, 122, 131, 133, 135, 139, 164, 186, 188, 189, 193
Margoth, 87, 91, 244
Market Square, Evesham, 170
Marshal, Eva, 32, 229, 232
Marshal, William, 7, 26, 231, 244
Massey, Colonel, 1
Maurice's Strategicon, 183
Melrose Abbey, 47, 48
Melrose Chronicle, 47
Mere, The, 83
Merstow Green, 101, 124, 169
Monmouth, 79, 191, 245
Monmouth, Geoffrey of, 49, 245
Montchesnil, Warren de, 10, 245
Montfort, Amaury de, 10, 25, 45, 148, 179, 217, 245
Montfort, Guy de, 10, 11, 25, 32, 45, 129, 132, 139, 148, 157, 159, 179, 197, 229, 230, 245, 246, 247
Montfort, Simon de, 1, 2, 3, 4, 6, 8, 9, 10, 11, 14, 15, 18, 19, 20, 21, 23, 24, 25, 27, 28, 29, 30, 31, 32, 33, 34, 36, 37, 39, 40, 41, 42, 43, 44, 45, 46, 47, 48, 58, 70, 74, 76, 78, 79, 80, 81, 82, 83, 85, 89, 90, 91, 93, 95, 97, 98, 101, 105, 110, 112, 113, 120, 122, 124, 125, 126, 127, 128, 129, 131, 132, 133, 134, 136, 137, 138, 139, 140, 142, 145, 148, 149, 150, 157, 158, 159, 163, 165, 166, 167, 168, 171, 172, 173, 174, 175, 179, 181, 183, 185, 186, 187, 188, 190, 191, 194, 199, 200, 201, 206, 208, 210, 211, 213, 214, 215, 216, 217, 218, 220, 221, 222, 223, 224, 230, 236, 237, 240, 244, 245, 246, 247, 248, 253, 271
Montfort, Simon de, Younger, 1, 19, 45, 80, 81, 82, 83, 84, 85, 88, 89, 90, 105, 151, 153, 154, 155, 179, 188, 244, 247
Montmorency, Alix de, 25, 247
Montmorency, Bouchard IV de, 25, 247
Mortimer, Roger de, 12, 18, 24, 29, 30, 31, 41, 46, 74, 78, 85, 90, 91, 92, 115, 119, 120, 122, 133, 135, 136, 137, 139, 141, 142, 143, 148, 150, 152, 153, 154, 155, 156, 157, 158, 159, 160, 161, 164, 186, 187, 189, 193, 194, 196, 201, 202, 204, 212, 215, 217, 240, 247, 248
Mosham Meadow, 7, 9, 4, 41, 44, 92, 93, 94, 95, 137, 163, 212
Mowhaut, Adam de, 138, 139
Natural England, 98, 113, 171, 172
Neck Defences, 56
New Temple, 13
Newburgh, William of, 43, 248
Newmarket, Adam of, 89, 248
Newport, 79, 80
Nicholas the Barber, 39, 40, 89, 125, 128, 155, 162, 235, 251, 253, 271
Norfolk, Earl of, 7, 10, 39, 231, 251
Norman Conquest, 47, 221
Normandy, 8, 49, 238, 241, 250, 251
Northampton, 19, 31, 80, 179, 193, 243, 248
Norton, 92, 93, 97, 191, 195

Oakeshott, Ewart, 61
Oat Street, Evesham, 102
Odiham Castle, 217
Offenham, 40, 91, 92, 96, 97, 109, 115, 156, 158, 161, 163, 186, 189, 190, 195, 204, 205, 207, 210, 212
Oman, Sir Charles William Chadwick, 3, 90, 155, 185, 186, 187, 188, 249
Optone, 84, 88
Osney Abbey, 46, 47, 253
Osney Annals, 46
Outremer, 27
Oxford, 12, 18, 19, 28, 40, 46, 80, 100, 127, 133, 193, 222, 223, 226, 227, 251, 253
Palfrey, 68
Paris, Matthew, 10, 11, 39, 42, 51, 65, 148, 174, 202, 224, 250
Paris, Treaty of, 8
Pembroke, 78, 199
Pembroke, Earl of, 7, 26, 231, 244
Pershore, 55, 90, 115, 154, 160, 204
Petition of Right (1628), 5
Petition of the Barons, 7
Pilote, 65
Pipton, 79
Plantagenet, Joan, 30, 247
Poitou, 8, 27, 234
Poleyns, 55
Pourpoint, 53
Priory Pool, 83
Provence, Eleanor of, 13, 29, 235, 249, 250
Provisions of Oxford, 7, 12, 14, 15, 18, 22, 28, 29, 47, 197, 237

Quarrels, 57, 67, 71, 131
Ramsay, Sir James, 114, 185
Ramsay, Sir James Henry, 3, 114, 115, 156, 185, 186, 204
Ranulf, Earl of Chester, 25
Redditch, 101
Reformers, 15, 18, 19
Rhayader, 31
Rhuthin, 30
Richard the Lionhearted, 52, 250
Richards Luard, 41, 49
Rishanger, William of, 39, 250
Rishangles, 39
Riveaulx Abbey, 47
Rochester, 19, 20, 243
Roger Bigod, 7, 10, 231
Ronsons, 68
Rounceys, 68
Rudge, Family, 10, 100, 113, 114, 171, 177, 194, 198, 207, 208, 219
Runnymede Meadow, 5
Saintonge, Battle of, 10, 11, 27, 238, 239, 245
Salisbury, Earl of, 10
Salt Street, 97, 195, 204, 212
Savoy, 13, 26, 27, 28, 235, 250, 251
Savoyards, 13, 14
Scale armour, 52
Schynbalds, 55Sscurriers, 80
Second Baronial Revolt, 6
Second Baronial war, 47
Second Baronial War, The, 2
Severn, River, 41, 79, 80, 82, 90, 105, 150, 151, 154, 157, 161, 185, 187, 188, 189, 191, 193, 199, 200

Shaffron, 69
Shields, 57, 58
Short spear, 64
Shrewsbury, 84, 153, 154, 193
Siflaed's stone, 91, 115, 204
Simeon of Durham, 48, 236
Slings, 65
Southwark, 15
Spears, 64
Spicer, Tony, 7, 9, 11, 3, 45, 46, 117, 148, 149, 209
St Cuthbert, 47
St Denis, Abbey of, 45
St Lawrence Church, 9, 10, 101, 104, 124, 126, 128, 168, 175, 211
St Mary, Priory of, Kenilworth, 84
St Peter's, Church, 48, 105, 171
St. Alban's Abbey, 39
Sumpters, 68
Surcoats, 54
Swine Street, Evesham, 124, 129
Sword, 1, 10, 32, 52, 57, 61, 63, 78, 146, 219
Talyfan, 30
Tewkesbury, Battle of, 1
The Lickeys, 101
The Squires, 95, 97, 119, 122, 194, 198, 204, 205, 208, 211, 212
Thomas de Cantilupe, Thomas de, 18
Thomas Wykes, Chronicle of, 46
Tindal, William, 82, 87, 89, 112, 115, 119, 193, 198, 205
Tippet, 59
Tonbridge, 19
Toulouse, Siege of, 25

Transport, 70
Trevet, Thomas, 39, 251
Trivet, Nicholas, 39, 40, 251
Twyford, 9, 40, 41, 97, 106, 107, 108, 109, 110, 119, 133, 141, 142, 163, 243
Twyford-Offenham, 40, 41
Urse d'Abitot, 105, 234
Usk, 30, 79, 80
Vale of Evesham Civic Society, 167, 208
Vale of Evesham Historical Society, 100, 173, 198, 214, 217, 219, 223, 224
Valence, William de, 78, 191, 252
Vegetius, 70, 82, 181, 182, 183, 227, 228
Vescy, John de, 144, 215, 216, 252
Vine Street, Evesham, 124, 131, 169
Viterbo, 140, 148, 179, 247
Voulge, 65
Wake, Baldwin, 89, 252
Wambais, 53
Warenne, John de, 20, 78, 191, 252
Warhorses, 67
Warwick, 84, 88, 152, 206, 230
Warwick Castle, 152
Waverley Abbey, 49
Waverley Annals, 38
Waverley Chronicle, 49
Westminster, 7, 12, 23, 29, 41, 42, 120, 154, 197, 237, 253
Westminster Abbey, 7, 42, 237
Westminster, Matthew of, 42
Whitford, Richard, 38, 253
Wigmore Castle, 24, 30, 31, 78, 139, 150, 215, 217, 240, 247
William Aldis Wright, 38
Winchelsea, 19, 179

Windsor, 13, 14, 15, 238, 246
Windsor castle, 13
Wood Norton, 93
Woodstock, Edward of, 11
Woolf, Lord, 5
Worcester, 7, 1, 5, 6, 32, 40, 47, 77, 79, 80, 81, 82, 83, 84, 87, 90, 92, 93, 97, 98, 100, 101, 105, 122, 149, 151, 153, 154, 155, 156, 157, 158, 160, 176, 185, 188, 189, 191, 193, 194, 195, 198, 199, 202, 204, 207, 230, 237
Worcester Cathedral, 5, 6
Wykes, Thomas, 47, 253
Wyre, 90

The Simon de Montfort Society

The object of the Society shall be to advance the education of the public in the life and times of Simon de Montfort and particularly, but not exclusively, his connection with Evesham and his part in reforming the government of England ...

The Simon de Montfort Society is a heritage and educational charity, founded in 1987, registered in the UK (**Charity Number 1092319**) affiliated to the Battlefields Trust and a member of the Three Battles Consortium. The Society's programme includes regular monthly lecture meetings with an historical theme, visits to sites of particular historical interest, social events, an annual day-school and a traditional wreath-laying ceremony, service and battlefield walk on the weekend nearest to the anniversary of Earl Simon's death at the Battle of Evesham. The Society publishes *The Lion* magazine, its newsletter, three times a year. It also publishes books and leaflets, including Dr Patrick Rooke's biography of Simon de Montfort.

The Simon de Montfort Society seeks to protect and preserve the site of the Battle of Evesham and other places connected with Simon de Montfort. It expands education resources, making them available to students of all ages and to encourage further research into the twelfth century and arranges visits to places with medieval connections. In December each year the society holds a St Nicholas Supper.

Please visit: www.simondemontfort.org

Battlewell on Greenhill, Evesham, is the traditional place where Simon de Montfort was killed on 4th August 1265

The Battlefields Trust

The Battlefields Trust aims to:

- Save battlefields from destruction by motorways, housing developments etc.
- Provide a range of battlefield-related activities and information, including the quarterly journal *Battlefield*, battlefield walks and conferences
- Liaise with local and national organisations to preserve battlefields for posterity
- Improve the interpretation and presentation of battlefields

Nearly everyone in the UK lives within half an hour's drive of a battlefield. Some, like Hastings, Bosworth and Culloden, are familiar to most of us. Others are relatively unknown. Yet the battles fought on them all played their part in shaping the way that we live today. The Battlefields Trust works to ensure that these priceless historical sites are preserved for everyone to understand and enjoy, both now and in the future.

The Trust campaigns both locally and nationally to defend Britain's battlefields from inappropriate development or even destruction. Its members work hard to make the most of their educational and recreational potential. Members have helped set up information boards at sites across the country and also prepared battlefield trails for you to follow. The resource centre on The Trust's website is a superb source of information if you are studying or visiting a battlefield.

Joining The Trust is a great way of learning more about Britain's battles and battlefields. Many of the Trust's members are experts in their field and are happy to share their knowledge. There are regular talks and study days and there is a full programme of battlefield walks, sometimes in areas not normally accessible to the public. Members can also join a local group, dedicated to the care and interpretation of an individual battlefield. Many people have commented on how they have made new friends and learned new skills as a result of their membership.

Members enjoy:

- *Battlefield*, The Trust's quarterly Magazine
    - Keep informed about the latest fights to preserve battlefields
    - Keep informed about forthcoming battlefield walks, study days and conferences

- - Provides a wide range of articles on battlefields and battlefield-related themes
  - Feeds stimulating debate on many battlefield issues
- An extensive programme of battlefield walks and talks
- An active regional network, providing opportunities to become more involved locally.
- An annual residential conference
- Other battlefield-related events
- Discounts with affiliated organisations
- A dedicated members' section on the Battlefields Trust website with articles and notice board

Please visit: www.battlefieldstrust.com

www.ingramcontent.com/pod-product-compliance
Lightning Source LLC
Chambersburg PA
CBHW080240170426
43192CB00014BA/2503